WSH and ADSI Administrative Scripting

Gerry O'Brien

SAMS

201 West 103rd St., Indianapolis, Indiana 46290 USA

Trademarks

Warning and Disclaimer

ASSOCIATE PUBLISHER
Jeff Koch

ACQUISITIONS EDITOR
Neil Rowe

DEVELOPMENT EDITOR
Steve Rowe

MANAGING EDITOR
Matt Purcell

PROJECT EDITOR
Andy Beaster

PRODUCTION EDITORS
Emylie Morgan
Matt Wynalda

INDEXER
Tom Dinse

PROOFREADER
Harvey Stanbrough

TECHNICAL EDITOR
John Purdum

TEAM COORDINATOR
Vicki Harding

INTERIOR DESIGNER
Anne Jones

COVER DESIGNER
Aren Howell

PAGE LAYOUT
Rebecca Harmon
Lizbeth Patterson

Overview

Contents

About the Author

Gerry O'Brien has been working with computers for over 14 years. He has over 5 years of experience in network administration using Windows NT 4.0 and Windows 2000. He has worked with multiple domains using both NT 4.0 and Windows 2000 Active Directory in a WAN environment using PPTP connections.

His programming experience started when he got hooked on programming with GW Basic and Quick Basic from the DOS days. He started Windows programming with Visual Basic 3 and has used VB for most of his programming tasks since then. Of course, the natural extension of VB was Visual Basic for Applications and VBScript, where he customized office applications and created Active Server Pages for various companies.

Gerry presently works full-time as a facilitator with the Information Technology Institute (ITI), where he teaches HTML, project management, FrontPage, RDBMS theory, Microsoft Access, VBA, VBScript, and distributed application design with Visual Basic. He holds an MCP in Windows NT 4.0 and Visual Basic.

He also has a part-time consulting company and serves as a beta tester for Microsoft Operating Systems and Visual Studio .NET.

Dedication

*To my wife Dianne. She always backs me 110% in whatever I do, even if
it means taking time from her. She understands and offers her support
wherever it is needed.*

Also to my son Brandon for his understanding and patience.

Everything I do is for the two of you. My love to you both.

Acknowledgments

First and foremost, I would like to thank Neil Rowe for putting his faith in me and for offering me the opportunity to write for Sams Publishing again. Neil is great to work with and a professional in every sense of the word (even when my deadline slipped).

Thanks to Steve Rowe as well for keeping me on track and offering some excellent insight and direction during the writing and reviewing process. Steve has some excellent ideas and is easy to work with.

I'd also like to thank the technical reviewers and editorial staff. You help to make sure the product is what customers want and need and that their best interests are at heart always. To that end, you do a lot of work ensuring that my examples function as indicated and that as much relevant material as possible is covered.

There are so many others behind the scenes as well, including the indexing staff and the layout staff, who have to put up with my quirky way of writing and placing things.

The whole process of creating a book is a lot more complicated than I originally thought. It takes a great team to coordinate and put the finishing touches on a quality product. Sams has that team in place. I hope my writing lives up to that standard as well.

Tell Us What You Think!

As the reader of this book, *you* are our most important critic and commentator. We value your opinion and want to know what we're doing right, what we could do better, what areas you'd like to see us publish in, and any other words of wisdom you're willing to pass our way.

As an associate publisher for Sams, I welcome your comments. You can fax, e-mail, or write me directly to let me know what you did or didn't like about this book—as well as what we can do to make our books stronger.

Please note that I cannot help you with technical problems related to the topic of this book, and that due to the high volume of mail I receive, I might not be able to reply to every message.

When you write, please be sure to include this book's title and author as well as your name and phone or fax number. I will carefully review your comments and share them with the author and the editors who worked on the book.

Fax: 317-581-4770
E-mail: feedback@samspublishing.com
Mail: Jeff Koch, Associate Publisher
          Sams Publishing
          201 West 103rd Street
          Indianapolis, IN 46290 USA

Introduction

This book is intended to help you, the network administrator, make your job somewhat easier by teaching you to script and automate many of your administrative tasks. As you are well aware, mundane chores such as adding user, group, and computer accounts take more time than they should. The tasks of mapping network shares and creating login scripts can't be left to end users. The best solution follows the saying, "If you want something done right, you have to do it yourself." The concepts you will learn in this book will aid you in ensuring that the job is done right and will also free some of your valuable time by allowing you to automate some of these tasks.

Microsoft incorporated a set of interfaces known as ADSI, or Active Directory Service Interfaces, into Windows NT, Windows 2000, and the upcoming Windows XP/2002 product. These interfaces allow access to the networking structure of these operating systems as well as other LDAP-compliant network operating systems such as Novell NetWare.

Using ADSI, you have high-level access to network resources and file systems using COM-compliant scripting and programming languages. This means that you don't need to understand the implications of COM to implement it with the scripting languages available today.

In concert with the information that you will find on ADSI, this book shows you how to use the interfaces with an easy-to-learn scripting language known as VBScript. A few examples use the JScript scripting language as well. The reason for using VBScript and JScript is quite simply that Windows Script Host (WSH), the scripting host environment used in Windows, offers built-in support for both languages. Learning either scripting language will offer you the ability to use WSH and ADSI effectively.

You will find all you need in this book to get started using WSH and ADSI to automate your administrative tasks and perform other functions as well. You will learn how to incorporate multiple jobs into one script and execute the correct job based on input parameters.

There are also two sections on security. The first deals with security of your scripts in terms of what they are permitted to do on a system. This section also discusses the process of digitally signing your scripts to ensure their validity. The second security section deals with the security of ADSI objects. Everything in ADSI is considered to be an object that exists on the system and network. These objects are the printers, drives, users, and computers that make up the network. ADSI security deals with Access Control Entries (ACEs) and Access Control Lists (ACLs), which make up the security access mechanisms for your network resources.

This book was somewhat difficult to write due to the nature of the content that it contains. There were some questions I needed to answer concerning the target audience and skill level expected. Should the book target administrators with no experience in programming? Should it target programmers who want to write applications to perform administrative tasks or to access network resources using ADSI? The possibilities for using WSH are almost endless in terms of what you can do for programming tasks, and that made it a bit harder to nail down an exact purpose.

I finally decided to write the book primarily for experienced network administrators who need or want to learn scripting in order to simplify administrative tasks in their daily work with Windows networks and LDAP-compliant directory service networks. This includes heterogeneous networks that consist of NOS (network operating system) software that is LDAP compliant.

To this end, I hope you will find that this book is informative and that its examples stimulate your thought process while giving you enough knowledge to enable you to pursue more advanced functions and features afterward. I think you'll find that by using WSH with the scripting language of your choice and taking advantage of the access provided by ADSI, you can make your job much easier and more enjoyable. Scripting allows your creativity to come out, giving you the opportunity to explore areas you didn't think possible before.
Enjoy the book!

—Gerry O'Brien, MCP

Introduction to Scripting

IN THIS CHAPTER

In this chapter, you will take a look at scripting in general to get an idea what it is, where it comes from, and why you might want to use it. You will also take a look at some scripting languages, and you will explore the Windows hosting environment for the scripts you write.

This chapter is provided to help bring any users new to scripting up to speed on the technology. If you are familiar with scripting and have been using VBScript or JScript already, feel free to skip this chapter and carry on with the rest of the book.

Of course, you can always use it as a refresher if you like. The material will not be highly technical in nature, as it is intended as an introduction to scripting. The more technical aspects will be discussed and shown in later chapters.

What Is Scripting?

For those new to scripting, it may seem like something that a Web developer might do. Although this is true, scripting has been used for far more complex tasks than Web development in the world of Windows administration. Essentially, a script is a small program written in a scripting language, and often network administrators build scripts that complete administrative tasks automatically.

Scripting for administrative automation is similar to creating batch files for automating tasks. If you have been administering a Windows NT or Windows 2000 network, you have no doubt run across many tasks that are time-consuming and could be or have been automated using batch files. A prime example is adding multiple user accounts. This task is not difficult, and most administrators have created template accounts with group assignments already made for the purpose of speeding up the creation of new accounts. Others use batch files that resemble the old DOS batch files, such as the autoexec.bat file, to help automate the task of adding users.

You may also be familiar with logon scripts. Novell NetWare environments use login scripts regularly to map and connect users to network shares when they first log in to the system. Windows NT/2000 administrators use logon scripts for the same purpose.

The smaller batch and script files just described are executed in much the same way. They start at the beginning of the file and step through one line at a time, executing each command in turn. These are fine for simple tasks such as logon scripts and adding users, but if you need more control over the execution of your scripts or batch files, they can leave you short. Thus, you may need something stronger to script out automated tasks. The use of more powerful scripting languages such as VBScript and JScript plus a hosting environment such as Windows Script Host helps you rectify that problem. These tools give you better control over the execution of your script through the use of decisions, structures, and loops. As a result, you can create powerful, long-lasting scripts that can help automate many things in your daily administration routine. Another added feature of using scripting languages is that you have the capability to perform error handling. This helps you out in a couple of ways. First, you can catch errors in your code that might otherwise go unnoticed in a batch file. Second, you can handle user created errors such as a disk not inserted into a removable drive such as a floppy, and rectify the error or inform the user that an action is needed.

Types of Scripting Languages

Scripting languages, such as VBScript and JScript, are interpreted languages. This means that they must have a scripting engine available to translate their instructions into an executable piece of code. This executable code piece is something that the computer will understand and act upon.

> **NOTE**
>
> Authors of scripting languages normally provide scripting engines. Scripting engines are necessary in order for script host environments, such as WSH 5.6, to understand the syntax of the language and work with it using the necessary objects that will be exposed.

There are other scripting languages besides VBScript and JScript available. Some of them have been used for many years, such as Perl (Practical Extraction and Reporting Language) and REXX.

Perl is quite common in the Unix and Linux communities, and has been ported to the Win32 platform as well. REXX is perhaps most familiar to users of IBM's OS/2 operating system, although it has been used elsewhere as well. We won't be covering Perl or REXX in this book, but will concentrate on VBScript and JScript. The reason is quite simple; Windows Script Host 5.6, referred to as WSH from this point forward, includes built-in support for both VBScript and JScript.

VBScript is a subset of the Visual Basic programming language, while JScript is Microsoft's interpretation of the ECMA(European association for standardizing information and communication systems) script standard that is derived mostly from JavaScript. JavaScript was created by Netscape and Sun Microsystems. You will see examples of both VBScript and JScript in this book.

From this introduction to scripting, we can see that it is another method of automating tasks and administrating your Windows NT/2000 systems. You can do other things with scripting, but this book concentrates on the administrative tasks of the operating system (OS). Once you have a firm grasp of the way these scripting languages work in administrative environments, you can implement them in other environments as well, such as Internet Explorer and DHTML (Dynamic HTML) pages.

Why Learn a Scripting Language at All?

Some may ask, "Why should we learn a new language when we are already familiar with creating and using batch files?" The short answer is, flexibility. To expand on this, the use of scripting allows you much more control over your administrative tasks and even offers access to some areas that batch files cannot go. You can use scripting to run programs automatically based on an event that occurs. For example, you can ask the user for input to a script and provide some dynamic capabilities based on that input. Batch files don't always offer this capability to the administrator, as they are hard-coded to perform the task at hand.

NOTE

The term *hard-coded* is used by programmers to indicate when a piece of data that might change is written in the code as the literal. The best method is to use a variable to hold the data.

You would need multiple batch files for different jobs. WSH allows you to create a script file that contains multiple jobs. You specify which job to run by using a specific command when you start the script. This allows you to perform multiple tasks with one script file.

Let's take a look at an example with the Active Directory Service Interfaces (ADSI) that shows the flexibility of scripting over batch files. Windows 2000 and XP use ADSI for dealing with the administrative tasks associated with the operating system and Active Directory (Windows NT uses some ADSI as well). ADSI is the *object model* that is used to gain access to the various administrative and security regions of Windows. Scripting allows you to access this object model where batch files do not, thus opening more doors to automate tasks that previously would not have been possible with batch files.

What Is an Object Model?

Almost all software is developed today through the use of *object-oriented programming* or *OOP*. This design methodology allows the programmer to model the software after real-world objects (hence the name *object-oriented* programming). What this means is that the software is created using components. These components are much the same as parts for an automobile. Cars have starters, tires, seats, and so on. These are all objects or components. You can assemble a car from these components in the same way that you can assemble a software program from software components modeled after real-world objects.

An object model is made up of a variety of components, beginning with a top-level object known as the root object and extending down through the hierarchy to the various child objects in the model. Each object is made up of what are known as properties and methods. Properties are the physical characteristics of the object such as a color, size or shape. Methods are used to represent the actions that an object can perform such as accelerate or stop for a car. Figure 1.1 shows an example.

As you can see from this partial object model for Internet Explorer 5.0, there is a root object known as the Window object. The Document object is a child object of the Window object. The remaining objects in the figure are all child objects of Document.

This means that you can gain access to each of the objects in this hierarchy quite easily. All you have to do is traverse the hierarchy in the order that you see it here. That is, you must access the Window object first in order to get to the Document object.

We access these objects using the dot notation. That is, we separate each object using a dot (for example, window.document). From this point forward, we can gain access to the properties and methods of the object to manipulate it however we wish.

As mentioned earlier, the administrative tasks of Windows 2000 and XP can be accomplished using ADSI. The ADSI services are accessed in a similar way. We will look at ADSI in Chapter 6, "Introduction to ADSI."

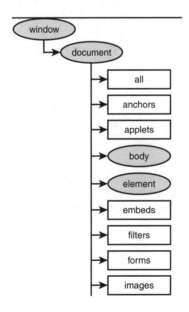

FIGURE 1.1

An example of the Internet Explorer object model showing the root object and some child objects.

Besides the ability to access objects and services of ADSI, what are some other reasons for using scripting? As we mentioned before, scripting gives you greater flexibility than batch files do. Scripting languages such as VBScript and JScript allow you to make decisions within the code and perform different actions based on the results. You can solicit feedback from users via input boxes and display graphical messages to users with the pop-up message boxes that Windows uses. Batch files lack these capabilities.

Script files also allow you to repeat operations a number of times based on certain criteria. This is useful for iterating arrays of items, such as a list of database fields that contain user-names to be added as user accounts.

NOTE

VBScript and JScript are easy languages to learn and if you have Visual Basic or Java developers in your organization, they already know the syntax and can write scripts for you with minimal effort.

Scripting engines allow you access to the file system of the computer, which makes it easier to map network drives, copy files, create folders, and install and map network printers. The list goes on. Once you learn how to use WSH, I am sure you will find many more advantages to using it, regardless of which language you choose.

Scripting Languages in Depth

Scripting languages have been around for some time now and are gaining more and more popularity with computer users, network administrators, and even software developers. One of the biggest reasons is the power, flexibility, and ease of development that they bring to the table.

VBScript

First and foremost, VBScript is a scripting language. This in itself tells you that you cannot use it to create standalone binary executable applications. As you saw in the preceding section, with a script engine, this is not a cause for concern because the script engine interprets and executes your scripts.

As mentioned earlier in the chapter, VBScript is a subset of the Visual Basic programming language. This means that it inherits most, but not all, of the capabilities of Visual Basic. In the days of DOS, every computer had a programming language included with it as a part of the operating system. This language was called Quick Basic, Q Basic, and then GW Basic. Essentially, each of these variations was based on the BASIC language.

BASIC is actually an acronym that stands for Beginners All-purpose Symbolic Instruction Code. For the most part, the language is easy to learn, especially when compared to today's modern object-oriented development languages such as C++ and Java.

The "Visual" portion was added when Microsoft created Visual Basic version 1.0 for developing Windows-based applications. Microsoft added an Integrated Development Environment (IDE) to use for writing and compiling the programs. The IDE, shown in Figure 1.2, gives programmers a visual interface to work with that includes some nice add-ins. Examples of these add-ins are color-coding of keywords and comments, syntax checking, and IntelliSense, which can offer a list of choices or complete a line of code based on what you are doing at the moment.

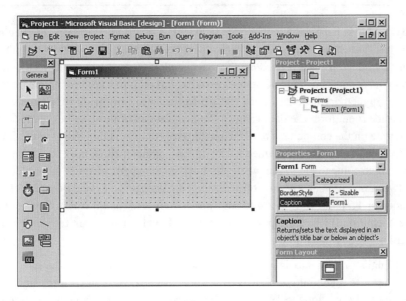

FIGURE 1.2
A screen shot of the Visual Basic IDE that VB developers use to create applications.

VBScript is as easy to learn as BASIC was because it uses a very English-like syntax. An example of a simple code routine in VBScript follows in Listing 1.1. As you will see, the code is fairly easy to read, especially when you begin to understand the syntax.

LISTING 1.1   A simple VBScript Routine That Checks the Time and Displays an Appropriate Output

```
Public Sub Greeting()
  Dim dtTime
  Dim strResponse
```

LISTING 1.1   Continued

```
dtTime = Time(Now)

If dtTime > #12:00:00 AM # And dtTime < #12:00:00 PM # Then
   strResponse = "Good Morning!"
ElseIf dtTime > #12:00:00 PM # And dtTime < #5:00:00 PM # Then
   strResponse  = "Good Afternoon!"
Else
   strResponse = "Good Evening!"
End If
End Sub
```

Let's analyze what is happening in this code listing. The first thing you see is the beginning of a subprocedure, which is where code executes, with the line `Public Sub Greeting()`. The name `Greeting` identifies this procedure so you can call it from elsewhere in your code by simply using its name. The next two statements that start with `Dim` are used to create temporary holding areas in memory for data values that we will need to work with. (`Dim` means to dimension or set aside room for these data values.) We then set one of those values, `dtTime`, equal to the current time on the computer. That is what the `Time(Now)` function does for us. Once the time has been determined, it is assigned to the `dtTime` variable. Next, the `If...Then...Else` clause does some comparison to see where the time lies in regard to the 24-hour clock. If the time is between midnight and noon, you want the computer to say "good morning," if it is between noon and 5 p.m., you want it to say "good afternoon," and if it is not one of those conditions, then it must be after 5 p.m. and before midnight, so you want the computer to say "good evening." Pretty much like English.

VBScript's English-like syntax is what makes it so easy to learn. Don't let the ease with which you can master it fool you into thinking that it isn't powerful. You can perform any function with VBScript that you can with JScript or other scripting languages. You can do more with and maintain better control of your programs with VBScript than you could ever hope to do with batch files.

NOTE

Another important point to note in regards to learning VBScript is that it has the same code syntax as Visual Basic and Visual Basic for Applications (VBA). This translates into a lower learning curve for programming Windows applications with Visual Basic or customizing Microsoft Office and other applications that include VBA.

Throughout this book, I will demonstrate most of the examples using VBScript and JScript. There are a great many changes for the scripting world coming with the .NET framework, and we will look at some of those later in the book as well.

JScript

JScript is Microsoft's implementation of the ECMA script standard, much the same as JavaScript is Netscape's implementation of the same ECMA standard.

Originally, JScript targeted the Internet and Web browsers for creating dynamic and interactive Web content by targeting the client browser. The advantage that JScript has over VBScript in this arena is the ability to be recognized by more browsers. This is due to the ECMA standard. If a browser supports the ECMA standard, it should have no trouble recognizing the script embedded in HTML pages.

Of course, when it comes to Windows Script Host JScript is native anyway, so there really is no issue when it comes to using either VBScript or JScript.

JScript follows the same syntax as C++ and Java. Everything in JScript is a function. You start and end functions with braces ({}), and each line of code within the function must end with a semicolon. Listing 1.2 demonstrates a simple JScript code sample.

LISTING 1.2   The Familiar "Hello World" Example in JScript

```
<SCRIPT LANGUAGE="JScript">
<!--
    function sayhello ()
    {
        alert("Hello, world!");
    }
//-->
</SCRIPT>
```

If you were to type this into the HTML code for a Web page and call the function, you would receive a message box window displaying the text "Hello, world!"

You may notice that the language is specified in the SCRIPT tag as JScript. This tag is used to tell the browser which script engine to use to interpret the code. The keyword alert is used to tell the browser to display the text in the brackets in a message box window.

Other Scripting Languages

As mentioned earlier in the chapter, there are other scripting languages available besides VBScript and JScript. One of the more popular is Perl. Created by Larry Well because he needed a Usenet-like file system and awk wasn't up to the task, Perl has grown tremendously, mostly as a result of feedback from the Internet community.

Perl's beginnings were on the Unix operating system. It has been ported to the Windows platform for use on 32bit Windows systems since and many network administrators, power users, programmers, and Webmasters rely on Perl to perform repetitive tasks or other administrative duties as needed.

Perl is not a difficult language to learn and has been used for many different tasks as a result. Some of the more common uses are listed here:

- *CGI Scripting*—On Web servers, Perl can be used as a scripting language that can process forms and other submissions sent from clients' Web browsers.
- *E-mail and Usenet Filtering*—Perl can be used to retrieve and sort your e-mail or Usenet articles.
- *ActiveX Scripting*—Perl can also be used as an ActiveX scripting language providing OLE automation capabilities for working with applications that are OLE aware.

Although Perl is a powerful language and can be used with WSH, it won't be used for examples in this book.

Other scripting languages on the market include REXX and Python. REXX is a procedural programming/scripting language that has its roots in IBM. It has been used on the IBM mainframe computer systems and I first came into contact with it when I was using OS/2 2.1 and 3.0. REXX looks similar to VBScript in terms of language syntax. As an example, Listing 1.3 shows a quick example of a REXX script that will count to ten and display each number as it does so.

LISTING 1.3   A REXX Script Used to Count to Ten and Display the Numbers as Each Is Counted

```
/* Counting to 10 */

        say "Counting numbers..."
        do i = 1 to 10
            say "Number" i
        end
```

As you can see, the syntax here is very simple. The keyword say is used to display information to the screen and this snippet uses a do loop to perform the counting.

Although included here as a scripting language, Python is actually a high-level programming language used by Unix and Linux gurus as an alternative to C for the purpose of creating scripts and programs. Python is somewhat similar to C and C++ in that it contains existing modules of functionality that you can reuse and it enables you to create your own reusable modules as well.

With the proper scripting engine, these languages can be incorporated into Windows Script Host and used as your scripting language of choice. However, I am quite sure that you will find that VBScript and JScript will provide all the features and functionality that you require for use in WSH.

Various Types of Script Files

With the scripting languages you create the script files that are used to automate administrative tasks. Some script files, such as batch files, don't use the powerful scripting languages. There are various types of files that are considered script files. Examples are batch files, Active Server Pages script files, HTML/DHTML files, JScript files, and VBScript files. We will take a look at each file type in turn.

Batch Files

Batch files have been used since the days of DOS, and can be a powerful tool for the network administrator. Batch files still use the .bat extension and are essentially ASCII text files.

A typical example of this type of file in the days of DOS was the autoexec.bat file. This was a file that was executed each time the computer was rebooted, and in many current systems is still executed. A typical DOS autoexec.bat file is shown here in Listing 1.4.

LISTING 1.4 DOS autoexec.bat Batch File Used to Configure Settings for a Computer at Bootup

```
echo off
prompt $p$g
path = C:\;C:\Windows;C:\PCTools;
```

Although not a very long file, this demonstrates some of the simplest concepts of batch files. The file is created using an ASCII text editor. (We use ASCII text editors to avoid any formatting codes that may be inserted by word processing software for fonts or style.)

When the computer starts, DOS sees this file and executes it one line at a time. The first line turns off the echoing of the file to the screen as it is executed. The second line sets the prompt style, which in this case provides the popular style that is still used today in the Windows command prompt, C:\>. Finally, the last line sets up some path variables for the environment, which causes DOS to search through these directories when it needs to find an executable program.

As you can see, the batch file is relatively simple and easy to create. It takes mundane tasks away from the user and performs them automatically. Isn't that what computers are best at, repetitive tasks that drive us crazy?

The Active Server Pages Script File

The next type of script file we will look at is the .asp, or Active Server Pages script file. ASP is actually a great technology for use with Microsoft's Internet Information Server (IIS). ASP pages enable the Web developer to create interactive Web sites using feedback forms, cookies for session state, and other dynamic content such as database access while still providing browser independence. ASP accomplishes this by sending raw HTML to the browser and keeping all processing on the server. Unlike client-side scripting, where different browsers implement the functionality differently, server-side scripting using ASP only requires that a browser be at least version 3.0 or higher.

> **NOTE**
>
> For some reason the computing industry uses the acronym ASP to refer to two different terms: Active Server Pages and application service provider. Throughout this book I will be referring to Active Server Pages when I use the ASP acronym.

A simple example of using a script file in ASP is shown in Listing 1.5.

LISTING 1.5 An ASP Page Using VBScript to Access a Database and Generate a Table Dynamically Based on the Contents of That Database

```
<%@ language=vbscript %>
<html>
<head>
<title>Microprocessors</title>
<body>
<%
Set dbGK = Server.CreateObject("ADODB.Connection")
dbGK.Open "Components"
SQLCPU = "SELECT * FROM CPU_Query"
Set rsCPU = dbGK.Execute(SQLCPU)
%>
<table BORDER="1" WIDTH="75%" bordercolordark="#330099" bordercolorlight=
➥"#FFCC00">
  <tr>
    <td bgcolor="#C0C0C0"><!--mstheme--><font face="times new roman, times">
➥<p align="center"><b><font color="#FF0000">CPU</font></b><!--mstheme-->
➥</font></td>
```

LISTING 1.5   Continued

```
    <td bgcolor="#C0C0C0"><!--mstheme--><font face="times new roman, times">
➥<p align="center"><b><font color="#FF0000">Price</font></b>
➥<!--mstheme--></font></td>
  </tr>
<%    Do While Not rsCPU.EOF %>
  <tr>
    <td align="center"><!--mstheme--><font face="times new roman, times">
➥<% =rsCPU("CPU") %>
<!--mstheme--></font></td>
    <td align="center" style="text-decoration: blink" width="4"><!--mstheme-->
➥<font face="times new roman, times">$<% =rsCPU("Price") %>
➥<!--mstheme--></font></td>
  </tr>
<%
rsCPU.MoveNext
Loop
dbGK.Close
%>
</table>
</body>
</html>
```

This ASP page, when requested by the browser, will create a connection to a database on the
server, run an SQL SELECT statement based on a query in the database, and create a table based
on the number of records available in that query. Note that the table and the HTML page do
not contain any content until the ASP script file is executed on the server.

HTML and DHTML

Some consider HTML to be a script file. I suppose that this classification is based on the idea
that the file itself causes the Web browser to render the contents a certain way, meaning that
the HTML code is actually a set of instructions.

For the most part, I don't buy into the theory that HTML is static and is not interactive.
Dynamic HTML or DHTML is another story, due to the fact that it contains scripting code to
make its pages dynamic. Each DHTML tag can have an ID assigned to it. You can use this tag
ID to programmatically affect the way the element is displayed. An example follows in Listing
1.6. Type this code into Notepad and save it as an HTML file on your computer, then open it
with Internet Explorer 4.0 or later.

LISTING 1.6 An Example of a DHTML Page That Uses Tag IDs as a Way of Making an HTML Page Dynamic

```
<html>
<head><title>DHTML Example</title></head>
<body>
<center><h1 id="H1">DHTML Sample</h1></center>

<script language="vbscript">

Public Sub H1_onMouseOver()
  H1.style.color = "Red"
End Sub

Public Sub H1_onMouseOut()
  H1.style.color = "Black"
End Sub

</script>

</body>
</html>
```

As you can see after opening this page in IE 4 or later, when you move the mouse over the title on the page, the words change to a red color and then back to black when you move the mouse off the title. This is, of course, a very simple example of DHTML, but it demonstrates that the ability to add scripts to HTML offers you more ways to create dynamic effects in your HTML pages.

In case JScript is your language of choice, let's take a look at the same DHTML functionality using JScript in the file. Listing 1.7 shows the same effect using JScript.

LISTING 1.7 The Same Color Change Effect Using JScript in Place of VBScript

```
<html>
<head><title>DHTML Example</title>
<script language="JScript">
function Red()

    { // Set all headings to red
      var coll = document.all.tags("H1");

      for (i=0; i<coll.length; i++)
      coll.item(i).style.color = "red";
    }
```

LISTING 1.7 Continued

```
function Black()
   { // Set all headings to black
        var coll = document.all.tags("H1");

        for (i=0; i<coll.length; i++)
        coll.item(i).style.color = "black";
    }

</script>

</head>
<body onmousedown="Red()" onmouseup="Black()">
<center><h1 onmouseover="Red()" onmouseout="Black()">DHTML Sample</h1></center>

</body>
</html>
```

You can see here that the use of scripting provides you with the ability to perform actions based on events happening within the browser window, such as a mouseover event. This is the same kind of control you can get by using scripting with your administrative tasks in Windows 2000 and Windows XP.

By using script files for administrative tasks such as adding users or mapping to network shares, you can poll the user or other administrators for specific information to customize the script each time it is executed. As an example, say you are the head of an IT department working with a network that extends over multiple geographic locations and contains multiple servers and network resources. You can write a script to map printers or add users and groups with generic information that applies to all of your servers, but prompt the network administrators for the specifics regarding the network at their location.

JScript Files

The next type of script file that we will look at is the JScript file, which has the extension .js. These files are written in ECMA-compliant JScript. I say ECMA-compliant because Microsoft ensured that JScript would be compliant with ECMA 262, which is actually ECMAScript Edition 3. You can check out the latest information on ECMA at their Web site, http://www.ecma.ch.

There are actually two scripting languages that conform to the ECMA script standard: JScript, as mentioned here, and Netscape's JavaScript. ECMA 262 is the standard that JScript and JavaScript follow. We will only cover JScript in this section.

One advantage that JScript has over VBScript is that it is an object-oriented scripting language. Microsoft classes it, to a certain degree anyway, as object-based, which means that it can work with objects but is not a fully object-oriented development environment. What this means to you is that you cannot create standalone executable programs with it as you can with Java, and it doesn't offer built-in support for reading and writing files. This is mostly for security purposes, as it was originally intended for use in Web browsers, where you don't want the capability to write or read files on the user's computer.

Listing 1.7 showed you an example of a JScript file used to create a DHTML document. JScript can also be used with WSH, and, as mentioned earlier, is actually one of the two default languages supplied with WSH. You will see many more examples of using JScript throughout this book.

VBScript Files

As you learned earlier in the chapter, VBScript is a subset of the Visual Basic programming language and uses the same syntax and coding style. One of the main differences between VB and VBScript is that VBScript is a typeless language, meaning that all data types used for variable names are of type variant. You cannot declare variables to hold data values with specific data types such as integer, double, or string. For more information about data types, see the "VBScript" subsection of the "Scripting Languages in Depth" section earlier in the chapter.

VBScript is also able to talk to host applications using ActiveX Scripting. What this means is that any ActiveX Scripting–compliant host can execute your VBScript code without needing special integration code.

VBScript is used as a scripting language in Internet Explorer, Internet Information Server (IIS), and now in WSH. If you are a software developer, Microsoft also makes the binary implementation available to you at no charge to integrate into your own applications.

Listing 1.6, which appears in the "HTML and DHTML" section, showed an example of a VBScript file used to create DHTML effects on a Web page. This is an example of client-side scripting. The same language can be used to create server-side scripts in IIS.

WSH also includes some other files known as container files that give you the ability to mix script languages in one file. The first of these is the .wsf file, which is a container, or project file, and is only supported in versions 2.0 and later of WSH.

The .wsf file is actually a text document that contains Extensible Markup Language (XML) code. The file is not script engine–specific and therefore can contain script from any of the Windows-compatible script engines. As mentioned previously, they are used as containers for script files and instructions. An example of a .wsf file is shown in Listing 1.8.

LISTING 1.8 An Example .wsf File Showing Some VBScript Code and a Reference to a
JScript File That Contains a Function That Is Being Called

```
<job id="JScriptFunctionCall">
    <script language="JScript" src="FileSysObj.JS"/>
    <script language="VBScript">
      ' use this function call to obtain the free space for drive C.
      s = GetFreeSpace("c:")
      WScript.Echo s
    <sScript>
</job>
```

As you can see, this file contains some actual VBScript code along with an instruction to
include the JScript file called FileSysObj.js that contains the GetFreeSpace function.

The last type of file is the Windows Script Host Files type, which uses .wsh for an extension.
This file is used as a property file for the script file. It is supported in versions 1.0 and later.

As you can see, there is quite a range of choices available for scripting files and the one to
choose is based on your own needs and preferences. This book focuses on those scripting files
that can be used with WSH; therefore, we will only work with VBScript, JScript, and .wsf
files.

Script Host Environments

In order for a script to execute, it has to be run from within a host environment. The reason for
this, as stated earlier, is that script files are interpreted and are not standalone binary executable
programs.

To give you an example of hosting environments, VBScript, JScript, or JavaScript code can be
executed in Web pages because the Web browser provides the hosting environment. Internet
Explorer and Netscape Navigator can host script files and provide the necessary interpretation
for the script to execute correctly. This is done by a *scripting engine* built into the browser
itself.

> **NOTE**
>
> At the time of this writing, VBScript cannot be executed from within Netscape
> Navigator.

Another example of a hosting environment is Internet Information Server (IIS). IIS can host VBScript and JScript on the server side. The scripts that you write for IIS execute on the server. When you create scripts and execute them under IIS, you are creating Active Server Pages.

These ASP pages can place a cookie on a user's computer and then extract information from that cookie for use as a means of maintaining session state.

> **NOTE**
>
> The computing population in general is still reluctant to allow the use of cookies on their computers. Many people see them as an invasion of their privacy and believe that companies use them to keep track of the Internet sites they have visited.

Also, as mentioned earlier in the chapter, ASP pages allow you to add functionality to your Web pages in a language you are familiar with but still only present raw HTML code to the browser. This is a great time saver in that you don't have to worry about coding for multiple browsers.

For our purposes in this book, we are concerned with the scripting environment known as Windows Script Host 5.6. WSH is now a part of Windows XP and Server 2002 and Microsoft makes update releases available for free download from their Web site. To see the latest versions available visit that site at `http://msdn.microsoft.com/scripting`.

What Is Windows Script Host?

In short, WSH is an administration tool that makes your life as a network administrator or power user much easier. It provides a hosting environment for scripting languages. This simply means that WSH allows your script files to exist as ASCII text files and uses file association to determine what language the file is written in. For example, VBScript files use the extension .vbs. WSH recognizes this as a VBScript file and will invoke the correct interpreter when you attempt to execute a script written in VBScript. JScript files use a .js extension. WSH will invoke the JScript interpreter to execute these script files.

As mentioned, these are the two default scripting languages that are supplied with WSH and for the most part, you shouldn't have to worry about using or learning any other scripting languages. If you are already familiar with other script languages such as Perl, REXX, or Python, you can obtain and use scripting engines for these script files as well. We will concentrate on the VBScript and JScript languages in this book. If you would like to learn any of the scripting languages mentioned here, check out the Sams Publishing Web site at `http://www.samspublishing.com` for available titles related to those scripting languages.

Titles such as *Sams Teach Yourself Perl in 21 Days* (ISBN 0-672-31305-7) or *Sams Teach Yourself Python in 24 Hours* (ISBN 0-672-31735-4) will help you get a foothold on some scripting languages other than VBScript or JScript.

In terms of scripting engines for VBScript and JScript, WSH uses two available methods for executing your scripts; you can use the command-line script engine CScript.exe or the Windows version WScript.exe. We will look at these two methods in Chapter 4, "How to Use Your Scripts."

WSH provides the necessary objects to your scripts so that you can work with an object model in terms of creating robust scripts that can access operating system services, user and group accounts, and network services and devices. The objects that you will be working with will include the network resources that you manipulate, such as users, groups, printers, and files.

WSH places these objects into an object model that is diagrammed using a tree-style approach. This diagrammed approach lays out the various objects, showing their relationships with each other and providing the necessary information on what properties and methods the various objects expose for you to work with. You will see examples of these object models in later chapters.

WSH is also responsible for providing security to the operating system when your scripts are running. It acts like a referee in that it only allows safe and legal actions to take place in the scripts that you write. This is to ensure that a malicious script doesn't step out of line.

WSH also allows you to create your scripts in your favorite scripting language, provided there is a compatible script engine for that language. You can then execute your scripts from the command line or from within Windows itself. WSH will provide the necessary objects so that your scripts can print messages to the screen in command-line mode or as message boxes in Windows mode.

You can also work with network resources, such as mapping drives and printers, or you can create and work with environment variables within WSH. These environment variables are the various paths and user-specific settings that set up the environment for the user in the operating system. WSH even allows you access to the Windows Registry.

As a script hosting environment, WSH provides the features necessary to make your life a lot easier. The flexibility that you have and the ease with which you can learn the scripting languages will provide you with a very powerful tool for automating your daily administrative tasks. For example, many administrators really hate it when they need to add multiple users. Most have a user template set up that makes the process somewhat easier, but WSH enables you to write a script that can read the user information from an Excel spreadsheet file or a text file and enter hundreds of users at a time. All you have to do is provide some simple information and the script does all the repetitive work for you.

WSH can also make life easier when you need to map multiple network printers. One script can map as many printers as you have on the network much more easily than you can do it manually. As you probably now realize, learning to script in WSH 5.6 is going to provide you with the tools to make your administrative load a little easier to carry!

Summary

This chapter has given you an understanding of what scripting is as well as offering some insight into how you might use scripting for your administrative tasks with Windows 2000 or Windows XP.

You have covered what Windows Script Host actually is and have learned about some of the scripting environments in which scripting languages can execute. The addition of WSH to the Windows environment means a great tool is now available for administrators and power users to aid in automating mundane and repetitive tasks.

I also introduced you to some of the available scripting languages that are in use today, with a couple of examples of scripts created in the languages. You are free to choose the scripting language of your choice provided it has a compatible scripting engine for Windows Script Host.

What's New in WSH 5.6?

IN THIS CHAPTER

In this chapter we take a look at the new features that have been added to Windows Script Host version 5.6. Likely by the time you read this book the version will have changed, but the core of WSH remains the same. These new features will likely be present in any new version as well. Although some areas may not be new, you will find that some existing functionality has been enhanced or renewed.

Some of the new features that you will be introduced to are listed here:

- *Script switches*—allow you to use `named` or `unnamed` switches in your code when executing from the command line
- *Self-documenting code*—makes it easier to use the scripts by providing the ability to add example and usage style help to your scripts
- *Accessing and manipulating environment variables*—allows you to work with the environment variables and determine what each user has set
- *Remote scripting*—gives you the ability to execute scripts remotely on another computer from your workstation

These are not all of the new or enhanced features you will find in version 5.6, but you will be introduced to each of them in this chapter. You can also download the latest version from Microsoft's scripting Web page at `http://msdn.microsoft.com/scripting`.

Each new or enhanced feature will be discussed in turn as we go through the chapter, with a discussion and example usage of each. Let's start with the first new feature you will discover, grouping script switches.

Grouping Script Switches

Switches for scripts are not a new concept in 5.6, but they have been taken a step further by allowing them to be used in script files and selectively applied. WSH allows you to use files that can contain multiple script files or jobs. This is done through the use of script switches and grouping those switches together. They are used to group together a set of run-time arguments for a script. These run-time arguments are found in the .wsf files and are used to pass the necessary information to the executing script as needed. They form the basis for running one specific job within the .wsf file. The switches can be `named` or `unnamed` arguments along with an example element and/or a description element. This is all written in XML format and the `<runtime>` element will exist within a `<job>` element. An example is shown in Listing 2.1.

LISTING 2.1 An Example of a `<runtime>` Element Within a `<job>` Element Displaying Some `named` Attributes

```
<job>
    <runtime>
```

LISTING 2.1 Continued

```
        <named>
            name="server"
            helpstring="job will run on the specified server"
            type="string"
            required="true"
        </named>
    </runtime>
</job>
```

Because the <runtime> element is used within a set of <job> tags, it will only be used for that particular job. Also, if you have more than one named or unnamed element, each must appear in its own separate set of named or unnamed elements. Don't be too concerned about the syntax just yet as we will see more on these features throughout the book.

named Switches

This section and the next, "unnamed Switches," deal with a new concept in WSH 5.6. As you saw in the first section dealing with <runtime> elements, there are named arguments available. Each <named></named> element provides a specific named argument to the script. These arguments will be used at the command line when you issue the script command.

There are four available arguments and they are listed here:

- name—This is a string value that is used to represent the name of the argument that you are passing in. This is defined as the argument at the command line and in the script as well.

- helpstring—This is a string value as well. The helpstring is used to provide a help description for the argument. The ShowUsage method is used to provide the description in the WSH runtime.

- type—This is an optional argument used to determine the type of argument used. The value you provide here will be used to determine how the argument will be parsed at the command line. There are three possible values, simple, boolean, and string. If you don't specify a value, simple is used by default.

- required—This is an optional boolean value. This value is used as a flag and indicates if the argument is required by the script in order for it to run.

Using the example in Listing 2.1, I will show you how the arguments translate into the command-line usage.

When you want to execute the script at the command line with the named argument, you have to specify it in the command line as shown in the following code snippet:

```
cscript %scriptname% /server:"DCHeadQuarters
```

This command line would run the script provided in the `%scriptname%` by using the command-line script interpreter `cscript`. It will use a `named` argument of `server` to specify that the script should run on the `DCHeadQuarters` server.

unnamed Switches

As with the `named` switch, you can use `unnamed` switches as well. `Unnamed` switches work in the same manner as the `named` switches do with the exception that you don't specify a name in the command line before you use the switch. There are four arguments used in the `unnamed` switch example. They are listed here:

- `helpstring`—A `string` value that displays a description when a user executes the `ShowUsage` method.

- `type`—An optional argument used to indicate the type of the `unnamed` argument and how it is passed at the command line. The possible values are the same as for the `named` argument with `simple` being the default.

- `many`—This is an optional argument as well. It is used to indicate whether there will be multiple occurrences of the `unnamed` argument. If set to `True`, there can be any number of occurrences of the `unnamed` argument.

- `required`—An optional `boolean` argument that determines whether the `unnamed` argument is required or not.

For an example, Listing 2.2 displays the same code as Listing 2.1 but uses unnamed switches instead.

LISTING 2.2   A Job Showing the Use of unnamed Switches (These Are the Same as named Switches with the Exception That They Don't Use a named Element)

```
<job>
    <runtime>
        <named>
            helpstring="job will run on the specified server"
            type="string"
            required="true"
        </named>
    </runtime>
</job>
```

This little code snippet sets up a `helpstring` that will be displayed to users of the script when they execute the `ShowUsage` method. Note that the extra entry `named=` is not present in this example. This shows that switches can be used without being named.

Script Self-Documenting

As another new addition to version 5.6, you can make your scripts self-documenting with the use of <example> and <description> elements. You make your scripts self-documenting so that users can see the syntax or description of your script by issuing the ShowUsage method or by asking for help from the command line with the /? Switch.

The use of these elements is of course optional, and if you are the only one using your scripts, they may not be necessary. Most scenarios will involve a network administrator using the scripts while a programmer has created them, or, you may have an administrator who is well versed in writing scripts and who creates them for others to use. In any case, using these elements can be a great aid for the users of your script. These two elements are the <example> and <description> tags and they are discussed next.

<example>

The <example> element is used, as mentioned, for making your script self-documenting. It gives you the ability to present an example of the usage to the user. Listing 2.3 shows a sample file with an <example> element.

LISTING 2.3   A Script File Showing the Use of the <example> Element

```
<job>
    <runtime>
        <named
            name = "Server"
            helpstring = "Name of the server that this script will run on"
            type = "string"
            required = "true"
        />
        <example>Example: createuser.wsf /Server:scripting</example>
    </runtime>
</job>
```

This sample listing shows the usage of the script command at the command prompt with the <example>Example: createuser.wsf /Server:scripting</example> line seen above. Users can view this information in the script file itself or they can run the ShowUsage method, which will output information similar to that shown here:

```
Usage: createuser.wsf /server:value
Options:
server :Name of the server that this script will run on
Example:
createuser.wsf /server:scripting
```

As you can see, the ShowUsage method provides the user with information as to the syntax to use for the script as well as an example of how the user would issue the command.

<description>

The other element that can be used to make your scripts self-documenting is the <description> element. The <description> element provides a means for you to give users a quick description of what the script file will do when they use the help command-line switch /?. Listing 2.4 shows a script file with the <description> element used. When you execute the script with the /? switch at the command line, you will see the text string This script creates new users on the specified server.

LISTING 2.4   The <description> Element That Provides a Text String to the User When the Help Switch is Used

```
<runtime>
    <description>
        This script creates new users on the specified server
    </description>
    other elements would go here
</runtime>
```

Sharing the Environment

The sharing of the environment with other processes is done through the use of the Exec method. This method is used to run an application in a child command shell. This also provides access to the StdIn, StdOut, and StdErr streams with the use of the WshScriptExec object.

The Exec method can be used only with command-line applications and cannot be used with remote scripts. Remember this point when you are using the Exec method or the Execute method. The Execute method is used to execute a remote script; the Exec method is used only locally at the command line.

The syntax for the Exec command is shown here:

```
object.Exec(command)
```

The object portion is a WshShell object. The Exec portion is the Exec method and the command is the command line used to run the script. The usage of the command parameter is the same as if you were running the script from the command line.

An example of this is seen with this JScript snippet:

```
//Jscript
var argJob = WshShell.Exec("%comspec% /c scriptname.js");

' Vscript
Dim argJob
Set argJob = WshShell.Exec("%comspec% /c scriptname.vbs")
```

Accessing Standard Streams Programmatically

As mentioned in the previous section, you can access the status information of running scripts by using the Exec method, which returns information in the WshScriptExec object. You covered the Exec method in the previous section so it will not be covered here again. Instead, let's examine the WshScriptExec object more fully.

WshScriptExec Object

This object is part of the WshShell object, which is used to provide access to the Windows Shell for executing applications and accessing environment variables, and is used to return status information about running scripts. This is another of the new features added to 5.6.

It also provides access to the StdIn, StdOut, and StdErr streams so that you can determine errors and other information regarding the scripts that are running. Table 2.1 offers an explanation of these three streams so you can better understand their use.

This object will return the information at one of two possible times, before the script has executed or after it has completed executing.

The WshScriptExec object contains the following properties. They are briefly described in Table 2.1; for a more thorough reference, please see Appendix A.

TABLE 2.1　Properties of the WshScriptExec Object

Name	Description
Status	Returns a value from an enumerated type, 0 for running and 1 for completed.
StdOut	Contains a copy of the information sent to the standard output by the script. It is read-only.
StdIn	Use this property to pass information between processes.
StdErr	Used to gain access to any error information that was sent by a process.

The WshScriptExec object also has one method, Terminate. This method does not return a value but rather is reserved for ending a script's execution. It should only be used as a last resort, such as when a script doesn't end correctly and clean up after itself (for example, when setting objects to Nothing to free memory resources).

Programmatically Accessing Environment Variables

WSH 5.6 offers you the ability to access environment variables on your system. This functionality is made possible with the use of the WshEnvironment object, which was also available in earlier versions of WSH but has been enhanced in 5.6 allowing you more access and control over the environment variables. This object returns a collection of environment variables with the use of the Environment property.

The WshEnvironment Object returns the entire collection of environment variables, which you can access using the name of the environment variable. The environment variables belong to one of four categories. We will only be working with three of these four so they are listed here. The reason is that the Volatile category is not required for our purposes in this book and pertains more to software developers writing applications than someone wanting to simply do scripting, not to mention the fact that the remaining three contain all the functionality we need.

- *System*—This provides variables from the hardware- and OS-specific areas.
- *User*—This accesses variables related to user-specific items, such as Path and temporary directory information.
- *Process*—This is the only category available on Windows 9x and ME machines and provides most of the same variables as the Process area does but adds a few others, such as HomeDrive, Prompt, and SystemDrive variables.

Within each of these categories reside the various environment variables that you can access. Table 2.2 contains the available variables and what they are used for along with the category in which they are available.

TABLE 2.2 A Comparison of the Environment Variables You Can Work with and Which Category They Fall Under

Name	Description	Category
NUMBER_OF_PROCESSORS	Number of CPUs on Computer	System, Process
PROCESSOR_ARCHITECTURE	Type of CPU on the Computer	System, Process
PROCESSOR_IDENTIFIER	Processor ID	System, Process
PROCESSOR_LEVEL	Processor level	System, Process
PROCESSOR_REVISION	Version of the CPU	System, Process

TABLE 2.2   Continued

Name	Description	Category
OS	Operating system	System, Process
COMSPEC	File used for the command prompt (this is usually cmd.exe)	System, Process
HOMEDRIVE	Primary drive on the local computer	Process
HOMEPATH	User's default home directory	Process
PATH	Path used on computer	System, Process, User
PATHEXT	Extension used in path to indicate executable files	System, Process
PROMPT	Format used for command prompt (for example, pg)	Process
SYSTEMDRIVE	Local directory that contains the system files	Process
SYSTEMROOT	System directory such as C:\WINNT	Process
TEMP	Location of the directory used for storing temporary files	Process, User
TMP	Same as TEMP	Process, User
WINDIR	Same as SYSTEMROOT	System, Process

NOTE

You can see an example of using the environment variables in the code snippet in Listing 3.14 in Chapter 3, "Creating Scripts."

WSH also gives you the ability to remove environment variables as well. These variables are not deleted permanently, only removed for the current session. They will be restored for the next session. An example of removing an environment variable follows in Listing 2.5.

LISTING 2.5   An Example of Removing an Environment Variable for the Current Session

```vbscript
' ************************************************************************
' removeEnv.vbs
' This script demonstrates creating an environment variable
' and then removing that variable.
'
' Author: Gerry O'Brien
' Date:    April 7, 2001
' Platform: Windows 2000/XP
' Language: VBScript
' ************************************************************************

Dim objShell
Dim objEnv
Set objShell = WScript.CreateObject("WScript.Shell")
Set objEnv = objShell.Environment("PROCESS")
WScript.Echo objShell.ExpandEnvironmentStrings
➥("About to create an _ environment variable")
objEnv("TempVariable") = "New Temp Variable"
WScript.Echo objShell.ExpandEnvironmentStrings
➥("The new environment _ variable '%TempVariable%' added")
WScript.Echo objShell.ExpandEnvironmentStrings
➥("About to remove: _ '%TempVariable%'")
objEnv.Remove "TempVariable"
WScript.Echo objShell.ExpandEnvironmentStrings
➥("Environment variable has been removed successfully")
```

```jscript
//************************************************************************
// removeEnv.js
// This script demonstrates creating an environment variable
// and then removing that variable.
//
// Author: Gerry O'Brien
// Date:    April 7, 2001
// Platform: Windows 2000/XP
// Language: JScript
//************************************************************************

var objShell = WScript.CreateObject("WScript.Shell");
var objEnv = objShell.Environment("PROCESS");
WScript.Echo(objShell.ExpandEnvironmentStrings
➥("About to create an _ environment variable"));
objEnv("TempVariable") = "New Temp Variable";
WScript.Echo(objShell.ExpandEnvironmentStrings
➥("The new environment _ variable '%TempVariable%' added"));
```

LISTING 2.5   Continued

```
WScript.Echo(objShell.ExpandEnvironmentStrings
➥("About to remove: _ '%TempVariable%'"));
objEnv.Remove("TempVariable");
WScript.Echo(objShell.ExpandEnvironmentStrings
➥("Environment variable _ has been removed successfully"));
```

Spawned Processes in WSH 5.6

What exactly is a *spawned process*? As you may already be aware, a process is an instance of an executable or script that is running on the computer. A spawned process is simply a script that has been executed using the WshScriptExec method and is still in the process of running.

While the process is running, you have access to some information concerning that process. Specifically there are four areas that you can use to determine what is taking place with your script. You can determine if the script is still running for one thing. WSH uses two constants for this purpose, WshRunning and WshFinished.

The next two bits of information are actually retrieved from what are known as streams. Processes have two streams that you can read, an input stream and an output stream. These streams can be accessed by using the StdIn and StdOut properties, respectively, of the WshScript object. Each is explained in the appropriate sections that follow.

The final piece of information that you can obtain from a spawned process is error information. For scripts that have been executed using the WshScriptExec method, a property known as StdErr holds the error messages generated, if any, during the execution of a script. Examples follow on how each are used to obtain information from the spawned processes which help you in determining the status of your scripts.

Checking for Spawned Script Processes

When you execute a script using the Exec method asynchronously, you have the ability to check the status of that script and determine whether it is still executing or not. You do this through the use of the status property of the WshScriptExec object.

WSH provides two constants for the status:

WshRunning = 0

WshFinished = 1

You can check for the numerical value if you wish to determine the status of the script. Listing 2.6 shows an example of checking the status.

> **NOTE**
>
> This code is not intended to be executed. It merely serves as an example.

LISTING 2.6   An Example Code Snippet That Shows How to Check the Status of a Script Running Asynchronously

```
Dim objExec
Set objExec = WScript.Exec("myScript.vbs");

Select Case (objExec.Status)
    case 0
        WScript.Echo "The script is executing"
    case 1
        WScript.Echo "The script is not executing"
 End Select
```

As you take a look at this code, you can see the simple logic being used here. The first statement, `Dim objExec`, is used to created a variable, or placeholder, for the object that you will be working with. In this case, it is a script that may or may not be executing.

We apply that script to the variable with the second statement that sets the script object to the `objExec` variable. Once this is complete, we can then use the much simpler `objExec` to refer to the script.

You then notice that the code runs a `Select Case` structure. A `Select Case` structure is a decision structure that allows us to determine which of a set of conditions is true at that moment. In this case, we are checking two conditions: Is the script running (0) or not (1)? When we determine which state it is in, we inform the user with a message box indicating the state by using the `Wscript.Echo` method.

Accessing the Input Stream of a Spawned Process

The `WshExecScript` object provides access to the `StdIn` stream that is useful for passing information between processes.

The first thing you need to do is to create an object variable to hold the `WshScriptExec` object so that you can pass the parameters in. Listing 2.7 shows an example piece of code that could be used for this purpose. This code is not meant to be executable.

LISTING 2.7 A Code Snippet That Demonstrates the Passing of Parameters Using the `StdIn` Stream with `WshScriptExec`

```
Dim objExec
Set objExec = WScript.Exec ("scriptname.vbs")
ObjExec.StdIn.Writeline (parameter)
```

Once you have the object variable declared and assigned to a script object, you can use the `WriteLine` method of the `StdIn` object to pass the parameters to the script process.

Accessing the Output Stream of a Spawned Process

The `StdOut` object can be used in conjunction with the `StdIn` object to accept parameters passed into a script. The `StdOut` object is read-only so you cannot write to it.

You gain access to the stream by using the `ReadLine` method of the `StdOut` object as in this example:

```
Dim objPassIn
ObjPassIn = ObjExec.StdOut.ReadLine
```

The parameter will be passed to the stream and read into the variable `objPassIn`. You can use this variable as you would any other. Some uses might be for decision making within a script, or you could check for it in a loop and hold execution of the script until the parameter was passed in.

Accessing the `StdErr` Output Stream of a Spawned Process

When `WshScriptExec` has executed a script using the `Exec` method, any errors that are generated by the `WshScriptExec` object are available in the `StdErr` object. If a script encounters an error, it will write to the `StdErr` stream and the `WshScriptExec` object will contain those error values.

To access the error messages you need to access the `StdErr` stream with the following syntax:

```
Dim objErr
ObjErr = WshScriptExec.StdErr
```

Terminating Spawned Process Scripts

If you have started a script with the `Exec` method of the `WshScriptExec` object, you have two choices when it comes to ending the execution of the script.

The first is the most recommended method and that is to allow the script to execute until completion. In this way, any clean up code that you have in the script will have a chance to execute and clean up any resources that you have may have used.

The second option is to use the `Terminate` method of the `WshScriptExec` object. There is a disadvantage to using this method however. It will stop the script from executing immediately. This means that any resource clean up code will not get a chance to execute and you may cause a memory leak situation if your script is executed multiple times and shutdown with the `Terminate` method.

Here is an example syntax of how to use this method to end the execution of a script.

```
Dim objScript
Set objScript = WScript.Exec("scriptname.vbs")
objScript.Terminate()
```

Accessing Command-Line named Arguments

The `WshArguments` object contains another object known as the `WshNamed` object. The `WshNamed` object contains a collection of arguments that are part of the `named` property.

You can further divide these arguments into `named` and `unnamed` arguments. Your script files can use either style and the `WshArgument` object allows access to them through the use of the `WshNamed` and `WshUnnamed` objects for their respective arguments.

Listing 2.8 shows an example of using two command-line arguments with a script and how the `WshArguments` object can return those arguments and display them.

LISTING 2.8   An Example of Accessing and Displaying Command-Line Arguments with the `WshArguments` Object

```
WScript.Echo WScript.Arguments.Named.Item("a")
WScript.Echo WScript.Arguments.Named.Item("b")
```

Figure 2.1 shows an example output of running this script from the command line and specifying two arguments for the script.

As you can see, the arguments that you specified are returned by the `WshArguments` object and displayed in the output of the script. You could have specified the arguments as `unnamed` as well.

For more information on the available properties of the `WshArgument` object, see Appendix A.

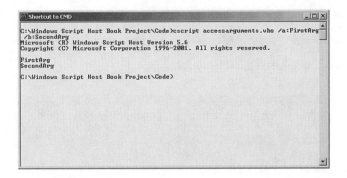

FIGURE 2.1
An example of executing the script in Listing 2.8 from the command prompt with CScript.exe and passing in two named arguments.

WshNamed Objects

WshNamed objects are actually arguments to a script file. These arguments have a name such as you saw in the example in the previous section. The use of named objects is a great help when your scripts contain arguments for optional choices. It is much easier sometimes to remember what an argument does or where it goes in the command line for the script.

Determining Whether Key Values Exist in a WshNamed Object

When you want to execute a script that contains arguments but you are not sure whether certain arguments are present, you can use a method of the WshNamed object known as Exists.

This method will return a Boolean result indicating True or False based on whether a named argument was used to execute a script or not. An example follows in Listing 2.9.

LISTING 2.9   An Example of Checking for named Arguments When the Script Is Called

```
If WScript.Arguments.Named.Exists("a") Then
    WScript.Echo "Argument 'a' was used"
Else
    Wscript.Echo "Argument 'a' was not used"
End If

If WScript.Arguments.Named.Exists("b") Then
    WScript.Echo "Argument 'b' was used"
Else
    Wscript.Echo "Argument 'b' was not used"
End If
```

Save the script in Listing 2.9 as `argumentsExist.vbs` and run the script with the command line

```
cscript argumentsExist.vbs /a:FirstArg
```

You will see the output displayed in Figure 2.2.

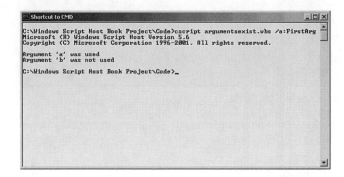

FIGURE 2.2

Executing the code in Listing 2.9 from the command line shows the use of the Exists *method.*

Determining the Number of Switches in a `WshNamed` Object or `WshUnnamed` Object

You can use the Count method to determine how many arguments were supplied at the command line for the script. This may be helpful if you are not sure how many named or unnamed arguments were used. An example follows in Listing 2.10.

LISTING 2.10   CountArgs.vbs Shows How to Use the Count Method to Determine How Many Arguments Were Used and Display Them Using a for Loop

```
Wscript.Echo Wscript.Arguments.Count
Wscript.Echo
For i = 0 to Wscript.Arguments.Count - 1
    Wscript.Echo Wscript.Arguments(i)
Next
```

By saving the code in Listing 2.10 and executing it from the command prompt, you will see output similar to that in Figure 2.3.

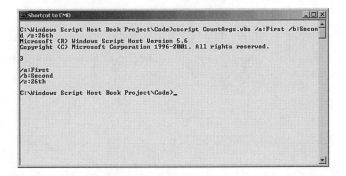

FIGURE 2.3
A command window showing the output generated by executing Listing 2.10 with three arguments.

Remote Scripting

WSH 5.6 offers you the ability to create and execute scripts remotely on other computers. This feature allows you to run multiple scripts on multiple systems and to get status information from those scripts as well such as whether they executed successfully or not.

Version 5.6 has added the `Controller` object that makes this possible. This object contains the `CreateScript` method that is used to create remote scripts on other computers.

WshController Object

The `WshController` object is a child object of the `WScript` object and therefore needs to be instantiated before you can use it. You instantiate the object in the following manner:

```
Dim objController
Set objController = Wscript.CreateObject ("Wscript.Controller")
```

This sets aside an object variable that will be used to access and work with the `WshController` object. Once you have the object created you can create and execute a remote script in the following way:

```
Dim objRemoteScript
Set objRemoteScript = objController.CreateScript
➥("scriptname", "\\computername")
ObjRemoteScript.Execute
```

This will create a script with the name you give it on the remote computer, specified using the Universal Naming Convention (UNC) name of the computer, and will then execute that script. (The UNC is used to name computers and their shares on a network.)

NOTE

You must be a member of the Administrator's group or have administrative rights on the remote computer.

NOTE

You need to open the registry on the remote computer as well and specify a new value for remote scripts to execute. Navigate to HKEY_LOCAL_MACHINE\Software\ Microsoft\Windows Script Host\Settings. Add a string value named Remote and give it a value of 1 if it is not already there.

CreateScript Method

As you saw in the section on the WshController object, you use the CreateScript method to create a remote script to be executed with the Execute method. The syntax of the CreateScript method is shown here:

```
object.CreateScript (scriptname, [computername])
```

Let's take a look at the syntax a little more closely. The object portion, seen above, is a WshController object. The WshController object is a child object of the root Wscript object and is required for remote scripts. There will be more discussion on this object later in the book.

The scriptname argument is required and specifies the full path name of the script that is to be executed.

The computername argument is optional. If you do not specify a computer name, the script will run on the local computer.

An example of using the CreateScript method follows:

```
Set objRemoteScript = objController.CreateScript
➥("createuser.vbs", "\\Celeron500")
```

WshRemote Object

The WshRemote object gives you access to the remote script that is executing either locally or on the remote computer by containing an instance of the remote script.

You need to use the `CreateScript` method to create the remote script that the `WshRemote` object will contain. An example is shown here:

```
Dim objController
Set objController = Wscript.CreateObject("WshController")
Dim objRemoteScript
Set objRemoteScript = objController.CreateScript
➥("createuser.vbs", "\\Celeron500")
```

As you can see, you must create a `WshController` object first. Then you create a variable to hold the remote script object and set it to the remote script that will execute.

The script will not execute until you call the `Execute` method of the object, which you will see in the next section.

Execute Method

This is a method of the `WshRemote` object that is used to start the execution of the script on the local or remote computer. Until you call this method, the script will not execute.

You can use this to your advantage in that you can create multiple remote scripts on various computers but hold the execution until you are ready. You may want to do this if you need to have all the scripts execute simultaneously.

Using the example given in the `WshRemote` section, you simply need to add the line

```
objRemoteScript.Execute
```

after the line that instantiates the remote script to have it execute. Until you call this method, the script will merely be copied to the remote computer.

WshRemote Status

The `Status` property of the `WshRemote` object allows you to determine the current status of the script that you have created with the `WshRemote` object. The script can be in one of three states:

- *No Task*—returns a numeric value of 0 to indicate that the script has been created but has not executed
- *Running*—returns a value of 1 to indicate that the script is currently running
- *Finished*—returns a value of 2 to indicate that the script has finished executing

The syntax for the `Status` property is shown here:

```
object.status
```

Where *object* is a WshRemote object and *status* is the property that will return one of the three values listed earlier.

WshRemoteError Object

If a remote script generates an error, such as terminating unexpectedly, you can use this object to see a brief description of the error that was generated.

You use the Description property of the WshRemoteError object to determine what the error was. The returned information is in the format of a string, and if no description is available, the string will be empty. An example follows:

```
Dim objError
objError = objRemoteScript.Error
```

This places the error description into the objError variable, provided you have created the objRemoteScript object from the WshRemote object. You can then use the error description in a more descriptive message to the user, such as the one shown here:

```
Wscript.Echo "The error occurred at line " &
➥objError.Line & " " & objError.Description
```

This will return a message to the user indicating that an error occurred and will list the line in the script that caused the error as well as a description of the error.

Description Property (WshRemoteError)

You have seen in the previous section that the WshRemoteError object returns error information from a script that terminates unexpectedly. You also saw a small example of the use of the Description property of the WshRemoteError object.

The Description property is a string data type that you can place into a variable for later use or you can display it in a message box to the user by using the dot syntax with the error object you created to hold a reference to the WshRemoteError object. An example of using the Description property in the dot syntax is shown here:

```
Dim objError
Set objError = objRemoteScript.Error
Wscript.Echo objError.Description
```

This code assumes that you already have an object objRemoteScript that was created using the WshRemoteExec CreateScript method.

Line Property (`WshRemoteError`)

When a script generates an error, the scripting engine knows which line was executing when the error occurred. A `long` data type will be returned indicating the line number that the error occurred on.

You can have an instance of an error that doesn't occur on a line. For example, if a piece of code is missing such as a closing `End If` or an `End Select` for a `Select Case` statement. In this case, there is an error in the script, but it doesn't occur on a specific line number because the code doesn't exist. In this event, the error line number returned will be zero (0).

The example shown in the `WshRemoteError` object section showed an example of using the `Line` property. The line of code is reproduced here for your convenience:

```
Wscript.Echo "The error occurred at line " &
objError.Line & " " & objError.Description
```

This code will display a message indicating the line number that the error occurred on.

Error Property (`WshRemoteError`)

This property is used to return a `WshRemoteError` object that contains information about the error or errors that caused the script to terminate abnormally.

The previous sections dealing with the `WshRemoteError` object and the `Description` and `Line` properties show examples of using the `Error` property; therefore, it will be shown here again.

Character Property

We have taken a look at how the `WshRemoteError` object can return the line number that an error occurred at in a script. The `Character` property works in conjunction with the `Line` property of the `WshRemoteError` object in that it will also return an unsigned `long` value that indicates the character in the specified line that caused the error.

The characters are counted from the leftmost character of the line indicated. The example shown here adds the character information to the line of code that was shown in the `Line` property section:

```
Wscript.Echo "The error occurred at line " & objError.Line
& " " & _   obrError.Character & " " & objError.Description
```

As you can see from this line of code, the `Character` property has been added to the message and will display showing the character at which the error occurred.

Number Property

Errors are also specified using numbers. These numbers are unsigned long integers that have specific meanings. If you are familiar with programming with Visual Basic or C++ in Windows, you will have seen error numbers that are used for specific errors. For example, in Visual Basic, if your code encounters an error while trying to access the floppy drive and there is no disk present in the drive, you will get this error returned:

```
Run-time error '68' Device Unavailable
```

The error number 68 is reserved for this specific error and should not be used by a programmer to indicate any other error.

Likewise, WSH uses reserved error numbers as well. Although they don't offer much in the way of an explanation as to what the error is, they can be checked reliably in code and faster than the error string values. You can refer to the references for the meaning of the error numbers.

As an example, take a look at this line of code that outputs the error number in place of line number:

```
Wscript.Echo "The error occurred at line " & objError.Number
```

Source Property

The Source property returns a string value indicating the COM object that is responsible for causing the error. As an example, if you do not have administrative rights on the computer that you are attempting to create a remote script on using the CreateScript object, you will receive an error to the effect that the ActiveX object can't create the component. This indicates that the WshRemote object cannot create the script.

You access the source of the error by using the objError.Source syntax. You can display this information using the sample line of code that we have been using in the previous sections.

SourceText Property

The WshRemoteError object can also return the line of source code that caused the error. This can be useful if you are using an editor to write your code that doesn't support line numbers. It will save you from having to count the lines to locate the statement that is causing the error.

The syntax for using the SourceText property is the same as for the other properties of the WshRemoteError object. It is shown here:

```
WScript.Echo objError.SourceText
```

> **NOTE**
>
> You may not always be able to retrieve the SourceText property depending on the state of the script. In this case, an empty string will be returned in SourceText property.

Remote Object Events

The WshRemote object supports three events that can be used in your scripts. These events will occur when the script starts, ends, or generates an error. We will look at each of these in turn.

Start Event

When you start the execution of a remote script with the Execute method, the Start event will fire. This is where you can place code that will notify you or the user that the script has started, and you can also place initialization code here as well.

End Event

The End event will fire whenever the script has terminated. This can be due to the script stopping normally, if it has timeout or if it has ended abnormally due to an error.

One of the reasons that you might want to use the End event in your code is to place notifications to users that the script has ended. It might not be the best place to have clean up code due to the fact that script can end unexpectedly and the code would not execute as anticipated.

Error Event

If the remote script terminates abnormally, an error is generated and sent back to the Error property of the WshRemoteScript object. This also generates an Error event for the script.

The error information will be contained in the Error property and can be read by using the WshRemoteError object.

Accessing Active Directory Information with the CurrentDirectory Property

When you execute a script, that script has what is known as a working directory. This is the directory that the script is located in.

There is another directory that is known as the current directory. This is the directory that you are currently in when you execute the script. This directory does not have to be the same directory that the script resides in.

You can access and even change the current directory by using the `CurrentDirectory` property of the `WshShell` object. When checking this property, a `string` value is returned that indicates the full path to the directory that you were in when the script was first executed. The syntax is

```
object.CurrentDirectory
```

where `object` is a `WshShell` object and `CurrentDirectory` is the `string` value indicating the directory that is current.

Scripting Security

Security is a major concern when it comes to executing scripts on your computer. Especially if that computer is a domain controller in a corporate network environment.

WSH 5.6 adds the ability to sign your scripts. You can sign script files by using a digital certificate. Digital certificates can be acquired from many different sources. These sources will be covered in more detail in Chapter 5, "Securing Your Scripts."

WSH can use CryptoAPI tools to aid in the security of script files as well.

By using the available tools for securing scripts, authors can ensure the end users that their scripts are safe for executing, and that they haven't been modified. This is accomplished by embedding the author's certificate as well as encryption information into the script file. By doing so the script file cannot be modified without affecting the digital signature.

Chapter 5 will discuss the procedures necessary for acquiring digital signatures and using the available tools for signing and verifying script files.

Summary

This chapter looked at the new features that have been added to version 5.6 of Windows Script Host along with some features that have been enhanced from other versions.

The addition of the `WshController` object gives version 5.6 the ability to create and execute scripts on remote computers. This allows you to create scripts on a computer other than the local computer and to access status information about those scripts.

With XML, you can create script files that contain multiple script languages, make use of include files for using pre-written code components and scripts and with the addition of the `<job>` element, you can create multiple jobs in one file and selectively execute the job or jobs you want.

WSH 5.6 also makes use of named and unnamed arguments at the command line and provides a mechanism for accessing that information.

One of the most important enhancements relates to script security. You can sign your scripts and users can verify that your scripts are safe and unmodified from their original version.

Of course all of these enhancements make for more learning, but the tradeoff with the added functionality is worth the time.

Creating Scripts

IN THIS CHAPTER

In this chapter, we'll take a look at what you need to create scripts. We'll examine the variety of tools and editors that are available, and then you can decide which one suits you best.

You will also learn how to create scripts for reuse, which is a great time saver as it eliminates the need to rewrite scripts endlessly.

Lastly, we'll look at the Windows Script Host Object Model, which is what you will use to access the functionality of WSH and the operating system.

Tools for Creating Scripts

The title of this section is a bit misleading, perhaps in the sense that there are no "special" tools for creating scripts. Most people use simple ASCII text editors such as Notepad or TextPad.

There are other editors that you can use, such as the Visual Basic IDE for creating VBScript code. The reasons for this will be apparent a little later in the chapter when you see the use of the VB IDE and how it displays syntax automatically, also known as *Intellisense*.

> **NOTE**
>
> You can also use a great debugging feature that helps to prevent errors up front by inserting an `Option Explicit` statement at the top of the code. This feature helps to reduce spelling errors in variable names that can be extremely difficult to locate. With scripts that contain many lines of code, this can be a great time saver.

Notepad as a Script Text Editor

For those who just want to create scripts with the minimum amount of fuss, you can use Microsoft's built-in text editor, Notepad. An example of a script in Notepad is shown in Figure 3.1.

The script file that you see here might be a typical login script file that you would use to map network drives for users when they log on.

As you will notice, `Option Explicit` was used even though Notepad was the editor of choice, and not the VB IDE. Even though Notepad has no way of doing any code syntax checks, WSH will provide the notification of any variable name errors when the script runs. We will go into this a little later when we start creating scripts.

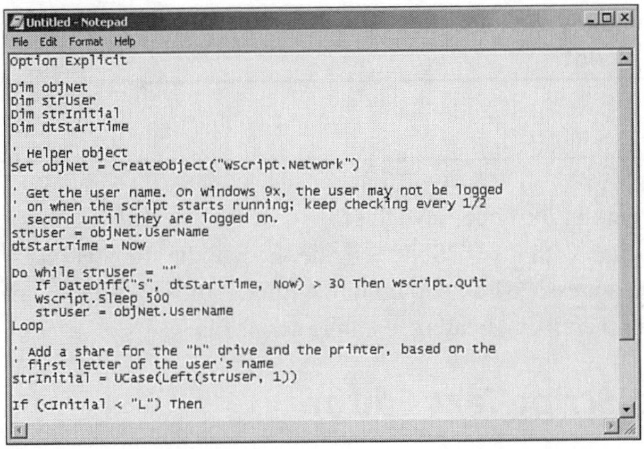

FIGURE 3.1
A simple script file that was typed into the Notepad text editor.

One nice thing about using Notepad is that any Windows-based computer automatically has a copy. Even though it doesn't include any special features for writing code in a clear manner, you can still make use of the basic editor features, such as tabs and white space. The real advantage that Notepad offers is that it will save your files as plain ASCII text files with no formatting codes in place. This is important, because WSH does not know how to interpret any special formatting codes.

TIP

For those who may not know, when you save a file in Notepad, the default file type is .txt. Notepad only offers two choices, .txt or all file types. If you want to include the file extension of your choice without having Notepad overwrite it, or add the .txt extension to it if you forget to change the file type to all, simply surround the entire filename with double quotes as in "script.vbs". Notepad will leave the extension alone and your file will be saved correctly.

Let's start out by creating the first script in Notepad. Open Notepad and type the code you see in Listing 3.1.

LISTING 3.1   A Simple VBScript Code That Displays a Message Box on Your Screen with the Words "Hello World!"

```
Option Explicit
Wscript.Echo "Hello World!"
```

When you finish typing in the code, save the file as Hello.vbs. This will create a VBScript file that WSH will associate with the VBScript engine. Locate the file you just saved and double-click it. You will see a message box pop up in the middle of your screen with Hello World! displayed. That is all there is to creating a simple script file.

TextPad as a Script Text Editor

As I mentioned earlier, there are other tools available for writing your scripts as well. There is a shareware tool called TextPad that you can download from the Web (see note). This tool enables you to create text files, but also provides you with the capability to customize the editor to display colors and other features based on the type of file you are creating. Figure 3.2 shows a VBScript file in TextPad using the VBScript syntax.

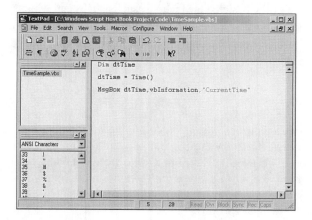

FIGURE 3.2

TextPad displaying a VBScript file using the VBScript syntax add-on for displaying the current time to the user in a message box.

NOTE

The TextPad program and support for it can be found at http://www.textpad.com. Here you can find various add-ons that make the program a breeze to use for your scripting needs. Once you have downloaded the program and are ready to set up some syntax definitions, go to the Add-Ons section and download the VBScript and JavaScript syntax definitions.

With these syntax definitions, keywords and other code aspects are displayed using colors. This can make it easier to read your code and work with it.

Writing Scripts with Microsoft's Visual Basic Integrated Development Environment

Another available tool to use for writing scripts is Microsoft's Visual Basic Development environment. Because VBScript is a subset of the Visual Basic language, the IDE for Visual Basic makes for a great script-writing tool that also provides code syntax coloring. Figure 3.3 shows an example of the VB IDE.

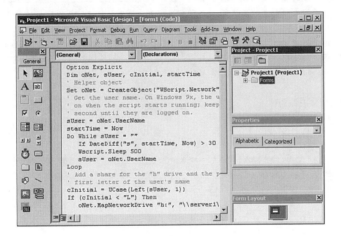

FIGURE 3.3
The Visual Basic IDE, where you can write VBScript code and have the keywords displayed in color.

Of course if you don't have Visual Basic or Visual Studio, the IDE is not an option for you to use. My suggestion is to find one tool that you are comfortable using and stick with it; as long as it saves the files as ASCII text with no formatting codes, you will be all right. My personal preferences are Notepad and TextPad, with a slight lean toward TextPad because of the syntax capabilities it has.

Creating Reusable Scripts

One of the greatest benefits that computer programmers have realized in a long time is the capability to create reusable components in their code. This capability has enabled them to build a library of reusable components and code snippets that can be "plugged into" their new or existing projects. This is a great time saver in that the programmer doesn't rewrite a functionality over and over for each project that requires it. WSH enables you to perform the same thing with your script files.

One example of this is the capability to map a network drive. Now, mapping one network drive doesn't seem like a big deal, but what if you had to do it for every login script? Would it make sense to write the same lines of code in every login script? Of course not. Listing 3.2 shows a simple script that is used to map a network drive. You can create this script and save it as `MapNetDrive` and it will be available whenever you need it. You can also link it into a WSH file with the extension .wsf, and it will be made available to any process that executes that .wsf file. We will create a couple of scripts that can be linked together and then demonstrate how to do this.

LISTING 3.2   Script for Mapping a Network Drive Shown in VBScript and JScript

```
'************************************************************************
' MapNetDrive.vbs
' This script maps a network drive on the server named celeron500
' It uses the Boolean value True to indicate a persistent connection
' It also passes the username and password to the server
'
' Author: Gerry O'Brien
' Date:    April 7, 2001
' Platform: Windows 2000/XP
' Language: VBScript
'************************************************************************
' Declare a variable to hold the Wscript.Network object
Dim objnet

' Set the object to the variable
Set objnet = CreateObject("Wscript.Network")

'Map the drive
objnet.MapNetworkDrive "S:", "\\celeron500\C","True","gobrien","dianne"
//************************************************************************
// MapNetDrive.js
// This script maps a network drive on the server named celeron500
// It uses the Boolean value True to indicate a persistent connection
// It also passes the username and password to the server
//
// Author: Gerry O'Brien
// Date:    April 7, 2001
// Platform: Windows 2000/XP
// Language: Jscript
//************************************************************************
```

LISTING 3.2 Continued

```
// Declare a variable to hold the Wscript.Network object
var objnet;

// Set the object to the variable
objnet = new ActiveXObject("WScript.Network");
// Map the network drive
objnet.MapNetworkDrive("I:", "\\\\celeron500 _ \\C","True","gobrien","dianne");
```

Both of these script files will perform the same task. The first step is to declare a variable to hold a reference to the `Wscript.Network` object. (We will look at the object model a little later in this chapter). Next, we assign the network object to the variable `net` and then use that variable to execute the `MapNetworkDrive` method.

This method takes some arguments, as you can see. The first is the drive letter that we want to use for the network drive. It is very important to keep track of the available drive letters so that you don't inadvertently overwrite one that is already in use. If you attempt to use a drive letter that is already assigned, you will receive an error message like that shown in Figure 3.4.

FIGURE 3.4

The Windows Script Host error message indicating that a drive letter is already in use when executing the `MapNetDrive` *script.*

After choosing a drive letter for the mapped drive, we specify the name of the computer or server and the share that we will map to. The last three arguments are optional. The "True" argument is a Boolean argument used to indicate whether the drive should be persistently connected, and the last two arguments are the username and password to use if necessary.

If the script executes with no errors, you will have a mapped network drive displayed in your Explorer or My Computer window, as shown in Figure 3.5.

Now, mapping network drives is not always the only thing you want to do when it comes to dealing with networks and connections. What if you want to add a printer? The code in Listing 3.3 shows how to connect to a network printer.

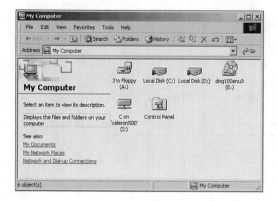

FIGURE 3.5
The My Computer window showing the newly mapped network drive with drive letter I.

LISTING 3.3   VBScript and JScript for Connecting to a Network Printer

```vbscript
'***********************************************************************
' MapPrinter.vbs
' This script maps a network printer on the server named celeron500
' It uses the UNC convention for the connection string
'
' Author: Gerry O'Brien
' Date:   April 7, 2001
' Platform: Windows 2000/XP
' Language: VBScript
'***********************************************************************

Dim objnet
Set objnet = CreateObject("WScript.Network")
objnet.AddWindowsPrinterConnection \\Celeron500\EPSON


//***********************************************************************
// MapPrinter.js
// This script maps a network printer on the server named celeron500
// It uses the UNC convention for the connection string
//
// Author: Gerry O'Brien
// Date:   April 7, 2001
// Platform: Windows 2000/XP
// Language: Jscript
//***********************************************************************
```

LISTING 3.3 Continued

```
var objnet;
objnet = new ActiveXObject("WScript.Network");
objnet.AddWindowsPrinterConnection ("\\\\celeron500\\EPSON");
```

Once again, either script will work in WSH, and you can choose the language of your choice. This script will add a printer connection to a client machine for a network printer.

> **NOTE**
>
> Although no network administrator I have ever encountered would provide a network printer share on a Windows 9x machine, it's worth noting here that this script will not work for printers shared on Windows 9x computers. The printers must be shared on a Windows NT/2000/XP server.

> **TIP**
>
> Although the previous note indicates that you cannot map to a printer shared on a Windows 9x computer directly, you can add a network printer to a server computer and share it. You can then map to that share as though it exists as a printer connected directly to the server.

Each of the scripts shown here is an actual functioning script that you can use as is or customize to suit your own needs. The main idea here is that you create these and save them for reuse later on. Any time you create a script that you can use over and over again, you have a reusable piece of code that is worth saving.

Linking Scripts

What do we mean when we talk about linking scripts? Well, for starters, we have just finished talking about reusable scripts and how we can save them for future use. Another way of using these scripts is to plug them into a .wsf file and have multiple scripts execute, one after another; or you can include a script in the middle of another to perform certain tasks during the processing of the original script.

One reason that stands out as an excellent use for .wsf files and linking your scripts is the situation where you have various script files already created from previous versions of WSH, or you have script files created in different languages, such as VBScript and JScript. With the use of a .wsh file, you can include a script that was written in JScript and call a function in that script from a VBScript file. Listing 3.4 shows an example of this usage.

To see how this linking works, first create the JScript file that is shown in Listing 3.5 and save it as FSO.js. Next, create the file shown in Listing 3.4 and save it as GetDriveSpace.wsh. This will cause it to be a WSH file with a job element.

LISTING 3.4   A WSH File That Contains a Code Snippet Written in VBScript and a Reference to an External JScript File That Displays the Free Drive Space for the C Drive

```
'*********************************************************************
' GetDriveSpace.wsh
' This .wsh file demonstrates calling a Jscript function from
' within a VBScript function and using the value returned
' from that function
'
' Author: Gerry O'Brien
' Date:    April 7, 2001
' Platform: Windows 2000/XP
' Language: VBScript/XML
'*********************************************************************

<job id="IncludeExample">
   <script language="JScript" src="FSO.JS"/>
   <script language="VBScript">
      ' Get the free space for drive C.
      Dim strSpace
      strSpace = GetFreeSpace("c:")
      WScript.Echo strSpace
   </script>
</job>
```

LISTING 3.5   The GetFreeSpace JScript Function Referenced in the Preceding .wsh File

```
//*********************************************************************
// FSO.js
// This script provides information regarding the path,
// volume name and drive space for the drive passed in from
// the GetDriveSpace.wsh file
//
// Author: Gerry O'Brien
```

LISTING 3.5   Continued

```
// Date:    April 7, 2001
// Platform: Windows 2000/XP
// Language: Jscript
//*******************************************************************

function GetFreeSpace(drvPath) {
    var fs, dDrive, strSpace;
    fs = new ActiveXObject("Scripting.FileSystemObject");
    dDrive = fs.GetDrive(fs.GetDriveName(drvPath));
    strSpace = "Drive " + drvPath + " - " ;
    strSpace += dDrive.VolumeName;
    strSpace += " Free Space: " + dDrive.FreeSpace/1024 + " Kbytes";
    return strSpace;
}
```

When you double-click the GetDriveSpace WSH file, the code inside the file sees that the JScript file FSO.js is to be linked to this file. This makes the function `GetFreeSpace` available to the WSH file, hence the VBScript procedure that calls it. Figure 3.6 shows the message box that you receive after running this script. Your drive's free space will likely differ.

FIGURE 3.6
A message box displaying the result of running the GetDriveSpace WSH file.

You don't have to use a WSH file to run multiple scripts. You can create the scripts you need and run those that are required one at a time by creating a batch file that contains the name of each script that you want to run. The scripts will run in the order that they are listed in the batch file. This of course defeats the purpose of a WSH file, and doesn't permit you to call procedures or functions between more than one script file. This is the power of the WSH file.

The ability to work with and manage multiple script files in this way gives you some idea as to how programmers make use of object-oriented techniques to make their lives much easier. Developers who code using OO principles create their software and components or objects with reuse in mind. This translates to time saved at a later time when they need to reuse the object in another application. By creating your script files to be reusable, you save yourself time later by eliminating the need to write the same code over again.

3

CREATING SCRIPTS

The WSH Object Model

As we have mentioned previously, you access the functionality of Windows Script Host through the use of an object model. The object model provides the means to gain access to the properties and methods of the various pieces of WSH. Figure 3.7 shows a picture of the WSH object model for a reference.

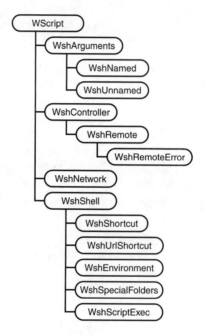

FIGURE 3.7

A pictorial representation of the WSH object model used to access the features of WSH.

This object model shows 14 objects with the root object being the WScript object. These objects are actually COM interfaces. They can be divided into two categories, Script Execution and Troubleshooting and Helper Functions.

The first category enables you to create scripts that can manipulate the WSH; you can use the CreateObject and GetObject methods, and you can output messages to the screen. Figure 3.6 shows an example of screen output by using a message box.

The Help Functions category contains properties and methods that you use to manipulate the registry and access network shares or environment variables.

Table 3.1 shows a breakdown of the objects in the WSH object model and the various tasks that you can perform with each object.

TABLE 3.1   WSH Objects and Their Tasks

Object	Task
WScript	Set and retrieve any command-line arguments
	Determine names of script files
	Determine whether CScript or WScript is the host environment
	Determine version information for the host being used
	Stop a script from executing
	Create COM objects as well as connect to and disconnect from them
	Output information to the screen, such as with a message box
WshArguments	Use to access the command-line arguments
WshNamed	Use to access the named command-line arguments
WshUnnamed	Use to access the unnamed command-line arguments
WshNetwork	Connect to network shares such as drives and printers (also used to disconnect from these devices)
	Map/unmap network drives
	Gain access to currently logged-on user
WshController	Uses the CreateScript method to create a remote script process
WshRemote	Manipulate scripts or programs
	Remotely administer network computers
WshRemoteError	Use to access remote script error information when that script terminates abnormally (as a result of an error)
WshShell	Run programs on the local computer
	Manipulate the registry
	Create shortcuts
	Gain access to the system folder
	Manipulate environment variables such as PATH
WshShortcut	Create shortcuts programmatically
WshSpecialFolders	Used to gain access to the Windows special folders
WshUrlShortcut	Create shortcuts to Internet resources
WshEnvironment	Access environment variables such as PATH or WINDIR
WshScriptExec	If you have run a script with Exec, use this object to determine status and error information about the script
	Gain access to stdIn, stdOut, and stdError

3

Although these are the objects available for WSH, you are not limited to using just these objects. Any ActiveX control that exposes a COM interface can be accessed and manipulated with WSH and the scripts that you write. This includes the Active Directory running on Windows 2000/XP.

Although you will find a complete reference in Appendix A for the objects exposed in the WSH object model, we will offer some examples here as to how each object might be used to help you gain a better understanding of each object. After you know how to work with the objects at a basic level, you can apply that knowledge to other properties or methods of the individual objects. We will start with the root object WScript and work down through the object model.

Using the WScript Object

The WScript object does not have to be instantiated with a Set statement before you use it. *Instantiating* an object simply means that you declare a variable name to hold a reference to the object and then you assign that object to the variable with a Set statement. This is the only way you can access the object for manipulation. Once the object is instantiated, you can simply call the WScript object and any of its properties or methods directly. Listing 3.6 shows the simplest of all uses for the WScript object.

LISTING 3.6   Using the WScript.Echo Method to Output Text to the Screen

```
Wscript.Echo ("Hello World!")
```

If you type this script into your script editor of choice and execute it, you will see a message box display on your screen with the text Hello World! displayed.

This particular script works as either a VBScript or JScript file.

You can combine text and variables in an Echo method call as demonstrated by Listing 3.7.

LISTING 3.7   Using a Variable to Determine the WSH Version Information and Then Concatenating the Variable and a Text String

```
Dim strVersion
strVersion = WScript.Version
WScript.Echo ("WSH Version is " & strVersion)
```

The output of this code snippet is shown in Figure 3.8.

FIGURE 3.8
A message box showing the results of running the code in Listing 3.7.

Using the WshArguments Object

The next object in the model is the WshArguments object. This object is used to access the list of command-line arguments that have been used in a script. The syntax for this usage can be best explained with a working example. Listing 3.8 shows the code to use.

LISTING 3.8   VBScript Code to Be Used for Enumerating and Displaying Any Arguments Passed in at the Command Line

```
Set objArgs = WScript.Arguments
For I = 0 to objArgs.Count - 1
   WScript.Echo objArgs(I)
Next
```

Save this script as Arguments.vbs in a directory called code, then enter the following text at the command prompt:

```
Wscript d:\code\Arguments.vbs /a:"This is argument 1" /b:"This is argument 2"
```

You will see two successive message boxes indicating the arguments that you just entered. This is known as *accessing the named arguments*. If you didn't give the arguments a name, they can still be displayed by issuing the following command at the command prompt:

```
Wscript d:\code\Arguments.vbs "Using an unnamed argument"
```

This will produce another message box with the text Using an unnamed argument in it, as shown in Figure 3.9. As you can see by these examples, the WshArguments object is used to enumerate the named or unnamed arguments passed to the script.

FIGURE 3.9
A message box showing the result of calling the script from the command prompt that doesn't use a named argument.

Using the `WshNetwork` Object

Next we will look at the `WshNetwork` object. For the network administrator, this is the object that will be dealt with the most.

The `WshNetwork` object contains a number of properties and methods that you can use to work with network resources. Some are included in the following list, but you can find a complete listing in Appendix A, "WSH Reference."

- `ComputerName`—Use this property to return a string value with the name of the computer.
- `UserDomain`—This property is a string value that returns the name of the domain that the user is currently logged in to.
- `Username`—This property will return the user's username.

The methods that are contained within this object deal with mapping network drives and connecting and working with network printers.

Listing 3.9 gives an example of using the `WshNetwork` object and some of the properties and methods that you can use with it. Once again, for a full reference of the properties and methods available, see Appendix A.

LISTING 3.9   A Script File Showing the Use of Some Properties and Methods of the `WshNetwork` Object

```
'*********************************************************************
' Network.vbs
' This script file demonstrates the use of the Network object
' of Wscript.  It enumerates the network drives and printers
' and displays that information along with the Domain name,
' username and computer name.
'
' Author: Gerry O'Brien
' Date:    April 7, 2001
' Platform: Windows 2000/XP
' Language: VBScript
'*********************************************************************

Set WshNetwork = WScript.CreateObject("WScript.Network")
Set objDrives = WshNetwork.EnumNetworkDrives
Set objPrinters = WshNetwork.EnumPrinterConnections
WScript.Echo "User Domain is: " & WshNetwork.UserDomain
WScript.Echo "Computer Name is: " & WshNetwork.ComputerName
WScript.Echo "User Name is: " & WshNetwork.UserName
```

LISTING 3.9 Continued

```
WScript.Echo "Network drive mappings on computer: "
For i = 0 to objDrives.Count - 1 Step 2
   WScript.Echo "Drive " & objDrives.Item(i) & " = " &
objDrives.Item(i+1)
Next
WScript.Echo "Network printer mappings on computer: "
For i = 0 to objPrinters.Count - 1 Step 2
   WScript.Echo "Port " & objPrinters.Item(i) & " = " & objPrinters.Item(i+1)
Next
//*******************************************************************
// Network.js
// This script file demonstrates the use of the Network object
// of Wscript.  It enumerates the network drives and printers
// and displays that information along with the Domain name,
// username and computer name.
//
// Author: Gerry O'Brien
// Date:    April 7, 2001
// Platform: Windows 2000/XP
// Language: JScript
//*******************************************************************
var WshNetwork = WScript.CreateObject("WScript.Network");
var Drives = WshNetwork.EnumNetworkDrives();
var Printers = WshNetwork.EnumPrinterConnections();
WScript.Echo("User Domain is: " + WshNetwork.UserDomain);
WScript.Echo("Computer Name is: " + WshNetwork.ComputerName);
WScript.Echo("User Name is: " + WshNetwork.UserName);
WScript.Echo("Network drive mappings on computer: ");
for(i=0; i<Drives.Count(); i+=2){
        WScript.Echo("Drive " + Drives.Item(i) + " = " + Drives.Item(i+1));
}
WScript.Echo("Network printer mappings on computer: ");
for(i=0; i<Printers.Count(); i+=2){
        WScript.Echo("Port " + Printers.Item(i) + " = " + Printers.Item(i+1));
}
```

3

CREATING SCRIPTS

When you run either of these scripts, you are presented with message boxes displaying the user's domain, computer name, and username, as well as the network drive mappings.

The WshNetwork object also enables you to add network printer mappings and to create mapped drives. An example of creating network drive mappings and adding a network printer is shown in Listing 3.10.

LISTING 3.10   Using the `WshNetwork` Object to Map Network Drives and Network Printers

```vbscript
'**********************************************************************
' MapNetDriveandPrinter.vbs
' This script file demonstrates the use of the Network object
' of Wscript.  It maps two network drives on the local computer
' that are shared on the server named celeron500 and ensures that
' the connections persist.  It also maps a network printer connection
'
' Author: Gerry O'Brien
' Date:    April 7, 2001
' Platform: Windows 2000/XP
' Language: VBScript
'**********************************************************************
Dim net
Set net = CreateObject("Wscript.Network")
net.MapNetworkDrive "S:", "\\celeron500\C", _
"True","gobrien","dianne"

net.MapNetworkDrive "X:", "\\celeron500\D", _
"True", "gobrien", "dianne"

net.AddWindowsPrinterConnection ("\\celeron500\Epson")
//**********************************************************************
// MapNetDriveandPrinter.js
// This script file demonstrates the use of the Network object
// of Wscript.  It maps two network drives on the local computer
// that are shared on the server named celeron500 and ensures that
// the connections persist.  It also maps a network printer connection
//
// Author: Gerry O'Brien
// Date:    April 7, 2001
// Platform: Windows 2000/XP
// Language: Jscript
//**********************************************************************
var net;
net = new ActiveXObject("WScript.Network");
net.MapNetworkDrive("S:","\\\\celeron500\\C", _ "True","gobrien","dianne");
net.MapNetworkDrive("X:","\\\\celeron500\\D", _ "True","gobrien","dianne");
net.AddWindowsPrinterConnection ("\\\\celeron500\\EPSON");
```

Running either one of these scripts will add two mapped network drives to the computer the script is run on, as well as map a network printer. This can be seen in Figures 3.10 and 3.11. In Figure 3.10, note the two network drives titled C on 'celeron500' (S:) and D on 'celeron500' (X:) in the tree view on the left of Explorer.

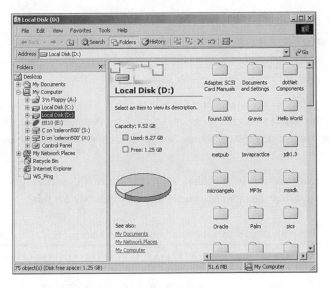

FIGURE 3.10
The two mapped network drives added to the Windows Explorer window.

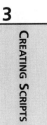

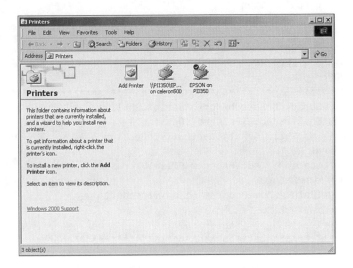

FIGURE 3.11
The network printer that was added after running the script.

This is just a small sample of the tasks that are available with the WshNetwork object. We will see some more as we progress through the book, and you can also find out the full usage of the available properties and methods in Appendix A.

Using the WshShell Object

The last parent object on the WSH object model is the WshShell object. This object contains some child objects, as can be seen in the object model diagram shown in Figure 3.7. We will start by taking a look at the WshShell object itself.

The main purpose of this object is to provide access to the native shell in Windows. The primary uses for this object are to run programs on the local computer, create shortcuts, manipulate the registry, access system folders, and look at environment variables. Let's look at each task here.

The first thing we will do with the WshShell object is create a shortcut on the desktop for Microsoft Word and give it an icon. Listing 3.11 shows the code for this.

LISTING 3.11   Using WshShell to Create a Shortcut to Microsoft Word on the Desktop

```
'*********************************************************************
' shortcut.vbs
' This script file demonstrates the use of the Shell object
' of Wscript.  It creates a shortcut on the Desktop for Microsoft Word
' and indicates the icon to use as well as the path to the executable
' file to run the application
'
' Author: Gerry O'Brien
' Date:    April 7, 2001
' Platform: Windows 2000/XP
' Language: VBScript
'*********************************************************************
set WshShell = WScript.CreateObject("Wscript.Shell")
strDesktop = WshShell.SpecialFolders("Desktop")
set oShellLink = WshShell.CreateShortcut(strDesktop & _
➥"\Microsoft Word.lnk")
oShellLink.IconLocation = "d:\Program Files\Microsoft
➥Office\Office\winword.exe ,0"
oShellLink.TargetPath = "d:\Program Files\Microsoft _
➥Office\Office\winword.exe"
oShellLink.Save
//*********************************************************************
// shortcut.js
// This script file demonstrates the use of the Shell object
// of Wscript.  It creates a shortcut on the Desktop for Microsoft Word
// and indicates the icon to use as well as the path to the executable
// file to run the application
//
// Author: Gerry O'Brien
```

LISTING 3.11 Continued

```
// Date:    April 7, 2001
// Platform: Windows 2000/XP
// Language: Jscript
//*********************************************************************
var WshShell = WScript.CreateObject("Wscript.Shell");
strDesktop = WshShell.SpecialFolders("Desktop");
var oShellLink = WshShell.CreateShortcut(strDesktop + _
➥"\\Microsoft Word.lnk");
oShellLink.IconLocation = "d:\\Program Files\\Microsoft
➥Office\\Office\\winword.exe ,1";
oShellLink.TargetPath = "d:\\Program Files\\Microsoft _\
➥Office\\Office\\winword.exe ";
oShellLink.Save();
```

This script has some interesting parts to it. Let's look at it one line at a time. First of all, we create an object WshShell to be used in the code. Then we declare a variable strDesktop to hold a reference to the Desktop as a special folder.

Next, we create the shortcut on the desktop by using the variable we just created, and give it the name Microsoft Word. The extension .lnk is used to indicate a shortcut style icon.

Following this we provide a location for the icon that will be used for the shortcut. The icon is located within the Winword executable file. This file contains many icons, and we choose to use the first icon in the available list by using the 0 at the end of the string. You can consider the icon list in the executable to be an array that is 0-based. This means that it is an array that starts at 0 for the first item. You could change this number to other values to see the other available icons.

The next line tells the shortcut where to go for the executable file that it is linked to, and the last line saves the shortcut. This is necessary to have the shortcut show up on the desktop or wherever you have chosen to place it.

Sometimes you might want to start a program automatically, or some users might even want a program to open when they log on. A co-worker at one of my jobs insisted on having her word processor, spreadsheet, and e-mail applications start automatically for her each time she turned on her computer. You could do this in the Startup folder for Windows, true, but we will take a look at how you can perform this using a script file in the event that you want to include this in a login script. The simple script file is shown in Listing 3.12.

3

CREATING SCRIPTS

LISTING 3.12   A Script That Will Open Microsoft Word in a New Window

```
set WshShell = WScript.CreateObject("Wscript.Shell")
WshShell.Run ("Winword.exe")
```

Another use for the `WshShell` object is to work with the command prompt. Listing 3.13 shows a simple use of the `WshShell` object to open the command prompt window, change to the C: drive, issue a `make` directory command, and change to that new directory.

LISTING 3.13   A Script That Uses the Command Prompt cmd.exe to Create a Directory and Switch to It

```
Dim objShell
Set objShell = WScript.CreateObject ("WScript.shell")
objShell.run "cmd /K CD C:\ & mkdir \newdirectory & cd newdirectory"
Set oShell = Nothing
```

Taking a look at this script, you can see we create the `WshShell` object at the top, and then using the `run` method, we manipulate the command prompt. The `/K` switch in the command prompt syntax is used to tell Windows to keep the window open after we have executed the command. We will show some of the command-line switches here that you might want to use. For a complete list, see the Windows online help files.

NOTE

These switches are used when calling the `cmd.exe` program from within a script, or from the `run` command found on the Start button menu in Windows.

- `/C`—This switch will cause `cmd.exe` to execute the command given and then shut down the window.
- `/K`—Using this switch will execute the command, but it will leave the command prompt window open for you to continue working with it.
- `/Q`—This switch will turn `echo` off (the command does not display when executing).

So far, we have taken a look at how to create shortcuts and open an application with the `WshShell` object. We also mentioned the fact that you can manipulate the registry with this object as well.

Working with Registry Methods and the WshShell Object

In almost any book or instruction that deals with registry manipulation, there are warnings of doom and gloom associated with modifying entries in the registry. This book will not be an exception, as the warnings have merit. Any changes to areas of the registry that you are not sure of are best left alone as they can render the computer unbootable or inoperable.

Having given you that message, however, the methods available for working with the registry are listed here:

- RegWrite—provides the capability to write a registry value to an existing key, create a new key, or modify an existing value/name pair
- RegRead—used to read the value of a key or value/name pair from the registry
- RegDelete—used to delete a key from the registry or a value from a key

We will look at the RegWrite method here; you'll find an example of using RegWrite, RegDelete, and RegRead in a code sample a little later in this section. The syntax for RegWrite is as follows:

```
object.RegWrite (strName, varValue, [,strType])
```

The arguments are described here:

- strName—used to indicate the key name, value name, or value that will be added
- varValue—used to create a new key or to name a value that you will add to an existing key
- strType—an optional string argument used to indicate the data type for the value (described later)

When you are indicating key names, you must use the abbreviated form. These abbreviated forms are used for all three registry methods and are displayed in Table 3.2.

TABLE 3.2 Registry Key Abbreviations to Be Used with the Registry Access Methods

Root Key Name	Abbreviation
HKEY_CURRENT_USER	HKCU
HKEY_LOCAL_MACHINE	HKLM
HKEY_CLASSES_ROOT	HKCR
HKEY_USERS	HKEY_USERS
HKEY_CURRENT_CONFIG	HKEY_CURRENT_CONFIG

I can't offer an explanation as to why the HKEY_USERS and CURRENT_CONFIG keys are not abbreviated.

3

CREATING SCRIPTS

Table 3.3 shows the available string types that you can use to specify data types for values.

TABLE 3.3   The Available Data Types for the Values to Be Used in the Optional `strType` Argument

String Type	Description	Data Type
REG_SZ	String	String
REG_DWORD	Number	Integer
REG_BINARY	VBArray of Integers	Binary
REG_EXPAND_SZ	Expandable String	String

Each string type is described here to help those not familiar with the registry and its data types:

- REG_SZ—This value is a fixed-length text string. The values are most commonly short strings but they can be Boolean values as well. The SZ on the end stands for String/Zero. This means that it is a zero (zero byte) terminated string. This is how Windows knows the string has ended.

- REG_DWORD—DWORD stands for Double Word. A Word is a 16-bit value; hence, the DWORD is 32 bits long (two 16-bit Words). This is the most common string type found in the registry and is used to store information for device drivers, Boolean values, and other information. The registry editor normally displays these values in HEX format.

- REG_BINARY—This string type is used mostly for storing hardware-specific information. It is stored in raw binary format. You can edit this information in the registry editor in either binary or HEX format.

- REG_EXPAND_SZ—You will find this string type used to store variables used by an application or the operating system such as %systemroot% or %windir%.

Let's take a look at adding some keys and values to the registry. These values are completely benign and will cause no ill effects to your system. Use the code shown in Listing 3.14 to see an example of how to add, read, and delete registry values.

LISTING 3.14   VBScript and JScript Files That Show How to Write, Read, and Delete Registry Values

```
'********************************************************************
' registry.vbs
' This script creates registry keys and values for those keys.
' It also reads the newly created values back in message boxes.
' Uncomment the WshShell.RegDelete lines to delete the entries made
'
```

LISTING 3.14   Continued

```vbscript
' Author: Gerry O'Brien
' Date:    April 7, 2001
' Platform: Windows 2000/XP
' Language: VBScript
'********************************************************************
' Create an object to hold a reference to the Wscript.Shell object
Dim objShell
Set objShell = WScript.CreateObject("WScript.Shell")

' Create some registry keys and values using RegWrite with objShell
    .RegWrite "HKCU\Software\GKComputerConsulting\Software\", _
➥1, "REG_BINARY"
    .RegWrite "HKCU\Software\GKComputerConsulting\Hardware\", _
➥1, "REG_BINARY"
    .RegWrite "HKCU\Software\GKComputerConsulting
➥\Software\ProductName", "ScriptExample", "REG_SZ"
    .RegWrite "HKCU\Software\GKComputerConsulting _
➥\Hardware\Mouse", "USBModel", "REG_SZ"
    ' Read the values back that were created and display in a message box
    .RegRead ("HKCU\Software\GKComputerConsulting\Software\")
    .RegRead ("HKCU\Software\GKComputerConsulting\Hardware\")
    Wscript.Echo .RegRead ("HKCU\Software\GKComputerConsulting
➥\Software\ProductName")
    WScript.Echo .RegRead ("HKCU\Software\GKComputerConsulting
➥\Hardware\Mouse")
End With
' Uncomment these lines to delete the previously created keys and values
' With objShell
    '.RegDelete "HKCU\Software\GKComputerConsulting _ \Software\ProductName"
    '.RegDelete "HKCU\Software\GKComputerConsulting _ \Hardware\Mouse"
    '.RegDelete "HKCU\Software\GKComputerConsulting _\Software\"
    '.RegDelete "HKCU\Software\GKComputerConsulting _\Hardware\"
    '.RegDelete "HKCU\Software\GKComputerConsulting\"
'End With
//********************************************************************
// registry.js
// This script creates registry keys and values for those keys.
// It also reads the newly created values back in message boxes.
// Uncomment the WshShell.RegDelete lines to delete the entries made
//
// Author: Gerry O'Brien
```

3

CREATING SCRIPTS

LISTING 3.14   Continued

```
// Date:    April 7, 2001
// Platform: Windows 2000/XP
// Language: Jscript
//*********************************************************************
// Create an object to hold a reference to the Wscript.Shell object
var objShell = WScript.CreateObject("WScript.Shell");
// Create some registry keys and values using RegWrite
objShell.RegWrite ("HKCU\\Software\\GKComputerConsulting
➥\\Software\\", 1, "REG_BINARY");
objShell.RegWrite ("HKCU\\Software\\GKComputerConsulting
➥\\Hardware\\", 1, "REG_BINARY");
objShell.RegWrite ("HKCU\\Software\\GKComputerConsulting
➥\\Software\\ProductName", "ScriptExample", "REG_SZ");
objShell.RegWrite ("HKCU\\Software\\GKComputerConsulting
➥\\Hardware\\Mouse", "USBModel", "REG_SZ");
// Read the values back that were created and display in a message box
var objKey1 = objShell.RegRead ("HKCU\\Software\\GKComputerConsulting _
➥\\Software\\");
var objKey2 = objShell.RegRead ("HKCU\\Software\\GKComputerConsulting
➥\\Hardware\\");
WScript.Echo (objShell.RegRead ("HKCU\\Software\\GKComputerConsulting
➥\\Software\\ProductName"));
WScript.Echo (objShell.RegRead ("HKCU\\Software\\GKComputerConsulting
➥\\Hardware\\Mouse"));
// Uncomment these lines to delete the previously created keys and values
//objShell.RegDelete ("HKCU\\Software\\GKComputerConsulting
➥\\Software\\ProductName");
//objShell.RegDelete ("HKCU\\Software\\GKComputerConsulting
➥\\Hardware\\Mouse");
//objShell.RegDelete ("HKCU\\Software\\GKComputerConsulting\\Software\\");
//objShell.RegDelete ("HKCU\\Software\\GKComputerConsulting\\Hardware\\");
//objShell.RegDelete ("HKCU\\Software\\GKComputerConsulting\\");
```

Both of these scripts perform the same task. They create some keys under the
HKEY_CURRENT_USER key and add some values to them. The scripts then read the values
back. If you uncomment the sections indicated in the code listing following the line that reads
// Uncomment these lines to delete the previously created keys, the scripts will
also delete the created values and keys.

NOTE

Notice that in order to delete the keys and values, you must delete the values first
and then the keys.

Using the `WshUrlShortcut` Object

We took a look at the capability of the `Shell` object to create shortcuts earlier. Another child object of the `WshShell` object is the `WshUrlShortcut` object. This object permits you to create a shortcut to a URL or Internet resource. The usage is identical to the code found in Listing 3.11. All you have to do is add these lines to the code to create the URL shortcut:

```
Dim objLink
set objLink = WshShell.CreateShortcut(strDesktop & "\Sams _ Publishing.url")
objLink.TargetPath = "http://www.samspublishing.com"
objLink.Save
```

This will create a link on the desktop to the Sams Publishing Web site.

Earlier, I made mention of the fact that you can read environment variables with WSH. The `WshEnvironment` child object of the `WshShell` object allows you to do this.

Using the `WshEnvironment` Object

The `WshEnvironment` object actually contains a collection of variables returned from the `WshShell`'s `Environment` property. (For more information on the `Environment` property, check Appendix A, "WSH Reference.")

For an example of how to use the `Environment` property with the `WshShell` and the `WshEnvironment` object, look at the code in Listing 3.15.

LISTING 3.15 VBScript and JScript Files Demonstrating the Use of Environment Variables and Displaying Them in Message Boxes

```
'**********************************************************************
' environment.vbs
' This script file demonstrates the use of the Environment property
' of Wscript.Shell.  It displays some environment variables in some
' message boxes that are returned by the Environment Property.
' The variables are returned from the Process and System categories
'
' Author: Gerry O'Brien
' Date:   April 7, 2001
' Platform: Windows 2000/XP
' Language: VBScript
'**********************************************************************
Set objShell = WScript.CreateObject ("WScript.Shell")
Set objProEnv = objShell.Environment ("Process")
WScript.Echo "Windows Directory " & objProEnv("windir")
WScript.Echo "System Path " & objProEnv("path")

' This set of environment variables will be empty for Windows 9x/ME OS.
Set objSysEnv = objShell.Environment("System")
```

LISTING 3.15   Continued

```
WScript.Echo ("Operating System " & objSysEnv("OS"))
WScript.Echo ("Temp Directory " & objSysEnv("TEMP"))
WScript.Echo ("Extensions in Path " & objSysEnv("PATHEXT"))
If objSysEnv("NUMBER_OF_PROCESSORS") = 1 Then
    WScript.Echo "Your system has 1 Processor"
Else
    WScript.Echo "Your system has " &
➥objSysEnv("NUMBER_OF_PROCESSORS") & " Processors"
End If
//********************************************************************
// environment.js
// This script file demonstrates the use of the Environment property
// of Wscript.Shell.  It displays some environment variables in some
// message boxes that are returned by the Environment Property.
// The variables are returned from the Process and System categories
//
// Author: Gerry O'Brien
// Date:   April 7, 2001
// Platform: Windows 2000/XP
// Language: Jscript
//********************************************************************
var objShell = WScript.CreateObject("WScript.Shell");
var objProEnv = objShell.Environment("Process");
WScript.Echo ("Windows Directory " + objProEnv("windir"));
WScript.Echo ("System Path " + objProEnv("path"));
// This set of environment variables will be empty for Windows 9x/ME OS.
var objSysEnv = objShell.Environment("System");
WScript.Echo ("Operating System " + objSysEnv("OS"));
WScript.Echo ("Temp Directory " + objSysEnv("TEMP"));
WScript.Echo ("Extensions in Path " + objSysEnv("PATHEXT"));
WScript.Echo ("Your system contains " +
➥objSysEnv("NUMBER_OF_PROCESSORS") + " processor(s)");
```

Note the use of a decision structure at the end of the VBScript file that determines the number of processors returned by the variable and displays a different message based on that value. This is a prime example of one of the added benefits that scripting has over batch files. Decision structures permit you to run certain pieces of code based on conditions you specify.

The WshSpecialFolders Object

The next object in the model is the WshSpecialFolders object. This object is used to return the Windows Special Folders collection for your use. Examples of Special Folders are the Desktop, Start Menu, and Personal Documents. For an example of using the Special Folders, see the code in Listing 3.11. This code uses the Desktop Special Folder to hold the shortcut that we create. For more information, refer to Appendix A.

The `WshScriptExec` Object

The final object in the model is `WshScriptExec`. This object is used to return status information about a script that is running or has been executed with the `Exec` method. The most common use is to provide a variable in which to store the status information, as shown in this line of JScript code:

```
var ScriptStatus = WshShell.Exec("%comspec% _ /c scriptname.js");
```

After you have the status assigned to the variable, you can display it with the `Echo` method if you want.

Summary

This chapter has presented an overview of the tools you can use to create your scripts as well as information about how you can reuse your scripts.

You can create Windows Script Host files with a .wsf extension that include XML markup along with script code based on the supported script languages in WSH. This enables you to create multiple jobs in one script file and provides a method to use functions from other scripts as well by incorporating include statements and function calls within the .wsf file.

You can also link your script files using the .wsf files or even calling them with batch files.

The WSH object model provides you with access to the various objects exposed by WSH for manipulating the operating system, user and group accounts, and even the registry. You can also inspect environment variables and execute scripts remotely on other computers using the various objects in the model.

Further information on each of the available objects along with their properties and methods can be found in Appendix A.

3

CREATING SCRIPTS

How to Use Your Scripts

IN THIS CHAPTER

This chapter will take a look at how you can use the various features of WSH to use your scripts. You will learn about the support that is offered for WSH files, which contain a .wsf extension and provide the capability to use include statements and multiple languages. You will also look at the support for drag-and-drop in your scripts, as well as how to set script properties.

You will then move on to CScript, the command-line script interpreter, and WScript, the Windows script interpreter. You will see the differences between the two, and learn when to use each one.

.wsf File Support

So, what exactly is a WSH file? It is an ASCII text file that can be created with any text editor, like Notepad or TextPad, and contains XML code as well as script code. These files are not classed as engine-specific; therefore, they can contain script code from multiple WSH-supported script languages.

The use of the .wsf file can save you a great amount of time when it comes to your scripts. For instance, if you have scripts that you have already created previously, or even scripts written in different scripting languages supported by WSH, you can place them in a .wsf file and use them as one script job.

Listing 4.1 shows an example of a .wsh file that includes some VBScript and some JScript code. Take note of the XML tags used to indicate the job ID.

LISTING 4.1 An Example .wsh File with Mixed Script Code and XML Tags

```
<job id="JscriptandVBS">
   <script language=Jscript RUNAT=Server>
      function Hello(strArg) {
         WScript.Echo(strArg);
      }
   </script>

   <script language="VBScript">
      WScript.Echo "Calling VBScript"
      Hello "Calling Jscript"
   </script>
</job>
```

This script file, when executed, will run the VBScript code followed by the JScript code, proving that the two languages can exist in the same .wsf file and execute together. You will be given two message boxes each displaying the appropriate message for the language executing at the time.

> **NOTE**
>
> When you save a WSH file, make sure that you give it the .wsf extension, even though it might contain VBScript or JScript code, or both.

Use Statements and Include Statements

Another use for .wsf files is that you can create multiple jobs in one file and run only the job you want. This is a nice feature that is implemented using the XML tags within the file. You can also use *use* statements to include other scripting files in the execution of the .wsf file. We will take a look at an example of each of these in this chapter.

With .wsf files, you can also make use of *include* statements. These statements enable code reuse. If you have programming experience in the C or C++ programming languages, you will recognize the include statement as a preprocessor directive.

In these two languages, developers have long had the capability to create code components that can be reused in other programs. What this means is that you can create scripts that are tested, debugged, and certain to work. Once you have created these script files, you can save them for later use whenever you need them.

An example of this is if you have created a script file that creates registry entries and you need to reuse that script on other systems, or you need to use it repeatedly. You can save that script file and use it again later by executing it as many times as you want.

The real power and flexibility of the include statement is that you can reuse that same script from within other scripts. You could call it from another script, but the easiest way is to include it in a .wsf file with the include statement. An example was given in Chapter 3 where we used a .wsf file to include a function written in JScript into the .wsf file. We then called that function from a VBScript function written directly in the .wsf file. The code is reproduced in Listing 4.2 for your convenience.

4

LISTING 4.2   An Example of a .wsf File That Uses the Include Statement to Include a JScript File

```
drive
'*****************************************************************
' GetDriveSpace.wsh
' This .wsh file demonstrates calling a Jscript function from
' within a VBScript function and using the value returned
  from that function
'
```

LISTING 4.2   Continued

```
' Author: Gerry O'Brien
' Date:    April 7, 2001
' Platform: Windows 2000/XP
' Language: VBScript/XML
'**********************************************************************

<job id="IncludeExample">
    <script language="JScript" src="FSO.JS"/>
    <script language="VBScript">
        ' Get the free space for drive C.
        Dim strSpace
        strSpace = GetFreeSpace("c:")
        WScript.Echo strSpace
    </script>
</job>
//**********************************************************************
// FSO.js
// This script provides information regarding the path,
// volume name and drive space for the drive passed in from
// the GetDriveSpace.wsh file
//
// Author: Gerry O'Brien
// Date:    April 7, 2001
// Platform: Windows 2000/XP
// Language: Jscript
//**********************************************************************

function GetFreeSpace(drvPath) {
    var fs, dDrive, strSpace;
    fs = new ActiveXObject("Scripting.FileSystemObject");
    dDrive = fs.GetDrive(fs.GetDriveName(drvPath));
    strSpace = "Drive " + drvPath + " - " ;
    strSpace += dDrive.VolumeName;
    strSpace += " Free Space: " + dDrive.FreeSpace/1024 + " Kbytes";
    return strSpace;
}
```

Running the code listed here will cause WSH to include the FSO.JS file into the .wsf file, and permit the VBScript code to call the GetFreeSpace function in the JScript file. This produces the output shown in Figure 4.1.

FIGURE 4.1
A message box displaying the free drive space on my computer using the code in Listing 4.2.

In order to include a file in a .wsf file, all you have to do is to place a tag in the file as shown in the following line of code, as well as in Listing 4.2:

```
<script language="jscript" src="fso.js"/>
```

This line has a couple of things worth mentioning. First of all, it is placed between a set of XML tags used to define the language. If you are not familiar with XML, let's briefly cover some of the requirements here.

XML and WSH Files

There are two compelling reasons to use XML in script files. First of all, XML is becoming a part of all Microsoft technologies and products and is integrated into SQL Server 2000 and all newer developer products such as Visual Studio .NET.

The second reason is that it is a good fit in .wsh files in that it allows you to specify various jobs using XML tags for job IDs. This gives you the ability to create a generic .wsh file that can be used for multiple purposes by simply specifying an ID on the command line when calling the file.

XML is a meta-markup language. This means that it contains data that describes itself. There are no set tags in XML. You make up the tags that you need to complete a job. However, each tag must follow a set of rules.

Much like most tags in HTML, you must have an opening and closing tag. XML permits you to specify your closing tag in one of two possible ways. Let's look at an example of creating a tag for something like a person's name:

```
<name>
```

This is the opening tag. It contains two angle brackets plus the tag name. When an XML parser sees this tag, it knows that it is an opening tag. It will then look for a matching closing tag. Normally a closing tag should look like this:

```
</name>
```

As you can see, there is great similarity with HTML. One difference from HTML is that XML requires the closing tag to be present at all times. HTML has elements that don't require closing tags to work, such as <p> or <br> tags.

As I mentioned, there is another way to display a closing tag. Besides using the method of the previous example, you can use the same syntax as shown in Listing 4.2, where you end the opening tag with a forward slash / before the closing bracket. XML permits this, although some consider it bad practice. The choice is yours.

XML Attributes

Much like HTML tags, XML tags can have attributes added as well. You see one attribute in Listing 4.2 that specifies a source for the JScript file. The attribute tag is `src` and means to include a file. The file to be included is the `fso.js` file.

This property of the source is an absolute reference to the file to be included. That means that unless the *include* file is in the same directory as the script, you will have to provide the correct path to the filename. Table 4.1 supplies you with some more common XML tags you can use in your scripts.

TABLE 4.1 Common XML Tags Used in .wsh and .wsf Files

Tag	Description
`<description>`	Used to specify descriptive text that will be displayed when a user issues the `Showusage` command-line argument.
`<example>`	Used to create self-documenting scripts by inserting comments that tell the user how to use the script.
`<job>`	Use this tag to indicate a job within your script file. You also give the `<job>` tag and attribute of `id` if you have more than one job specified in the file (for example, `<job id="job1">`).
`<?job?>`	Used to specify attributes for error handling.
`<named>`	Used to indicate the names of named arguments to the script.
`<object>`	Used to define an object in your script file. Takes an object ID as an `id` attribute with optional GUID or progID.
`<package>`	Used to enclose multiple jobs within one .wsf file.
`<reference>`	Used to indicate a reference to an external type library that is used by your script.
`<resource>`	Used for text or numeric data that needs to be isolated from the rest of the script so as not to be included as part of the script processing. These resources are normally text or numbers that you need to reference in your scripts for various reasons (for example, strings to be used for localized languages).

TABLE 4.1 Continued

Tag	Description
`<runtime>`	Used to group together a set of runtime arguments such as those used for named and unnamed arguments.
`<script>`	Used to indicate the script language for the script file (for example `<script language="VBScript">`).
`<unnamed>`	Used to indicate the unnamed arguments for a script.

Using Multiple Languages in a WSH File

Earlier you discovered that the use of .wsf files also enables multiple languages in one file. In this way, you can mix your scripting languages, such as having VBScript and JScript in the same file together. Listing 4.3 is a snippet of code that will display the current system date and time using two different languages in the same file.

LISTING 4.3   A Code Segment That Shows the Use of JScript and VBScript in the Same .wsf File

```
//*****************************************************************
// multi.wsf
// This file demonstrates the use of multiple scripting languages
// within one .wsf file.  It uses a Jscript file to display the
// system date and time as well as a message telling you the
// portion of the code that is running.  A VBScript procedure then
// executes giving you the system time only and a message telling
// what portion of the code is executing.
//
// Author: Gerry O'Brien
// Date:   April 9, 2001
// Platform: Windows 2000/XP
// Language: JScript and VBScript
//*****************************************************************

<job id="MultiLanguage">
    <script language="Jscript">
    var lReturn;
    lReturn = fDate();
    function fDate(){
        var lngReturn;
        WScript.Echo ("Entering Jscript portion");
        Wscript.Echo ("Your current date is " + Date());
    }
```

LISTING 4.3   Continued

```
  </script>

  <script language="vbscript">
  sTime

  Sub sTime()
     Dim lngReturn
     Wscript.Echo "Entering VBScript portion"
     Wscript.Echo "Your current time is " & Time
  End Sub
  </script>
</job>
```

If you run this code on your computer, you will see four message boxes altogether. The first message box will inform you that it is in the JScript section of the code. The second message box will display the current date and time on your computer.

Next you will see a message box indicating that the VBScript code is executing, followed by a final message box that just displays the current time.

The contents of the message boxes are not that important and don't do anything fantastic. They are just used to show you how the code is working, and that each procedure written in the code is actually executing.

Object-Oriented Capabilities in WSH Files

Something that might not be familiar to those used to writing batch files is the concept of *components* and *type libraries*. Components and type libraries are associated with what is called *object-oriented programming*.

Almost all software written today is done using the object-oriented concept. Everything one programs is an object. An object is designed with specific functionality in mind and is reusable for future items you create that will need similar functionality. What this means is that programmers are trying to write their software based on real-world objects translated into software terms. For example, when writing an application for a company to use in their Human Resources department, a developer will create objects related to the employees in the company. These objects will hold information and provide access to that information as it relates to employees (Social Security number, employee number, address, and so on). The Employee object will be written in code and will provide the properties to store the needed information along with methods that are executed to update and retrieve that information. In this way, the developer doesn't lose sight of what the software is intended for, and the software can perform the necessary tasks and store the necessary information that relates to an actual person.

Each object created has attributes, known as *properties*, and can also contain *methods* and *events*. Methods are things that the object can do. Using a person as an example, a method would be to walk or run. Events are things that happen, such as a person falling down. The software component can be written to react to events, and can perform tasks by using methods.

Type Libraries

Within this same idea of object-oriented programming is another concept, known as a *type library*. A type library is essentially a collection of attributes, methods, or events related to an object. A type library is used to indicate all these properties to the user of the object. You can consider it to be an appendix in an owner's manual for the object. You look at the type library to see what the object is capable of.

WSH offers support for type libraries. When a developer creates a component in C++ or VB, the available information that makes up the type library is stored in a file with a .lib extension. Let's look at a textual example of a component that might open a window at a certain size based on the screen resolution.

Within this component, there is a property that holds the screen resolution value. For the purposes of this control, we'll say that the developer wanted to indicate 640×480 as a value of 1, 800×600 as a value of 2, and 1024×768 as a value of 3. The component is called ResizeMe. Within the ResizeMe code, the property that holds this resolution value is called ResValue.

In order to use that component's property in the script, we need to instantiate an object variable to hold an instance of that component. We can then access the properties of the generic component. Listing 4.4 shows the code for this.

LISTING 4.4 An Example of Reading the Property from a Component Created Outside of WSH Using the Type Library Information

```
<job id="TypeLibraryExample">
   <reference progid="ResizeMe.ResClass">
   <script language="VBScript">
      Dim objResizer
      Dim lngReturnValue
      Set objResizer = CreateObject("ResizeMe.ResClass ")
      lngReturnValue = objResizer.ResValue
      WScript.Echo lngReturnValue
   </script>
</job>
```

This code is not intended to be executed, because you do not have any component installed on your computer. It is here just to give you an idea as to how you can use an outside component and its type library.

Drag-and-Drop Support in Files

WSH enables you to make use of drag-and-drop support. When you perform a drag-and-drop operation onto a script file, the filename that you dropped will be an argument to the script file.

A simple way to demonstrate this is through the use of an example that will show how a script file can receive a drag-and-drop event, and even determine information from the file that was dropped. Look at the code in Listing 4.5.

LISTING 4.5   A Script File Used to Demonstrate Drag-and-Drop by Opening a Database File in Access When It Is Dropped on the Script File

```
' ************************************************************************
' dragdrop.vbs
' This script file demonstrates the ability of a script file to make
' use of drag-and-drop within the Windows environment.  If you drag
' a Microsoft Access database onto the script file and drop it there,
' the script will check the file extension to determine if it is an
' Access file and then, will append the complete absolute filename
' to the MSAccess command to start Access and open the database.
'
' Author: Gerry O'Brien
' Date: April 11, 2001
' Platform: Windows 2000/XP
' Language: VBScript
' ************************************************************************

Set WshShell = Wscript.CreateObject("Wscript.Shell")
Set objArgs = WScript.Arguments
Dim strStartString
'If Right(objArgs.item(0),3) = "mdb" Then
If fso.GetExtensionName(objArgs.Item(0)) = "mdb" Then
    strStartString = "Msaccess.exe " & chr(34) & objArgs(0) & chr(34)
    Wscript.Echo strStartString
    WshShell.Run strStartString
Else
    Wscript.echo "Unknown File Type"
End If
```

Create this file on your computer and save it as dragdrop.vbs. Then locate a Microsoft Access database file and drag and drop that file onto the script icon. You will see a message box displaying the filename of the Access database, and then the database will open in an Access window.

Notice that one line in this code was commented out. This is the line that used the `Right` function to determine what the filename extension was. The reason for this is to show you two possible ways of performing this check on filename extensions. You can comment the line using the `GetExtensionName` method, and uncomment the `Right` function line to check this out.

The `Wscript`.Arguments collection returns the filename in a zero-based array. That is why `item(0)` was chosen. Because only one file was dragged onto the script, you only need to be concerned with the first element in the returned array.

Note that the three rightmost characters with the `Right` function were checked to determine the file type. If it is "mdb," you know it's an Access file. If you drag another type of file onto the script, you will receive a message box telling you that the file is not recognized.

Now you are likely saying "Big deal, I can double-click a .mdb file and it will open in Access anyway." You are correct, but I merely used this as an example to show you how drag-and-drop works. You can extend this example by looking at Listing 4.6, which uses a Microsoft Word document filled with comma-separated information that adds user accounts, full names, and passwords.

LISTING 4.6   A Script File That Pulls Information from a Word Document and Uses It to Create User Accounts

```
' ************************************************************
' DragDropWord.vbs
' This file demonstrates the ability of a script to make
' use of drag and drop within the Windows environment.
' If you drag a Microsoft Word document onto the script
' file and drop it there, the script will check the file
' extension to determine if it is a Word file and then,
' will append the complete absolute filename
' to the the Word command to start Microsoft Word and open
' the document.
'
' It will then take the comma separated information and use
' that to create user accounts on the computer complete
' with full name and password
'
' Author: Gerry O'Brien
' Date: August 25, 2001
' Platform: Windows 2000/XP
' Language: VBScript
' ************************************************************
```

LISTING 4.6   Continued

```
Dim objWordApp
Dim strNames
Dim arrUserNames
Dim intCounter
Dim strUserName
Dim strPassword
Dim strFullName
Dim fso
Dim strStartString
Set WshShell = Wscript.CreateObject("Wscript.Shell")
Set objArgs = WScript.Arguments
Set fso = CreateObject("Scripting.FileSystemObject")
If fso.GetExtensionName(objArgs.Item(0)) = "doc" Then
    Wscript.Echo "Valid Word document."
Else
    Wscript.echo "This is not a valid Word document."
End If
Set objWordApp = CreateObject("Word.Application")
objWordApp.Visible = False
objWordApp.documents.Open objArgs(0)
strNames = objWordApp.ActiveDocument.range
arrUserNames = Split(strNames, ",")
objWordApp.Quit
intCounter = 0
If Not arrUserNames(0) = "" Then
    Dim i
    i = UBound(arrUserNames)
    For intCounter = 0 to i -1
            strUserName = arrUserNames(intCounter)
            intCounter = intCounter + 1
            strFullname = arrUserNames(intCounter)
            intCounter = intCounter + 1
            strPassword = arrUserNames(intCounter)
            CreateUser strUserName, strFullname, strPassword
        Next
Wscript.Echo "User accounts added."
End If
Public Sub CreateUser(strUserName, strFullname, strPassword)
    WScript.echo strUserName & " " & strFullname & " " & strPassword
    set objServer = GetObject("WinNT://PIII500")
    set objUser = objServer.Create ("user", strUserName)
    objUser.Fullname = strFullname
    objUser.setPassword strPassword
    objUser.SetInfo
    Set objServer = Nothing
```

LISTING 4.6   Continued

```
    Set objUser = Nothing
    WScript.echo "User account added"

End Sub
```

This particular script file shows some of the various methods of working with the file system object, Office application automation, and working with arrays that don't have predefined upper limits. The script is explained here.

Directly after the introductory comment section, the code declares the variables that will be used in the script. Note that we have some string variables to hold our character data, some object variables to hold the references to the Microsoft Word application and the WSH objects, an integer variable, and a file system object variable.

After the declarations, we set the WshShell object and the objArgs object to work with the drag-and-drop operation of the script file. These are necessary for the drag-and-drop to work; they allow the filename to be passed to our script when it is dropped onto the script icon.

The If decision structure is designed to check the extension of the file that is dropped onto the icon and verify that it is a .doc extension, indicating a Microsoft Word file. Note that this doesn't verify that the file is an actual valid Microsoft Word file; it merely checks the extension then sends the appropriate message to the user.

Once you are notified that the document is a valid Word document, the script assigns a Word application to the objWordApp object variable. This is used to open the document that was dropped onto our script. Note that the Word application is not actually shown onscreen because the script set the Visible property to False. You don't need to see Word on the screen as we only need it to contain the document long enough to get the text from it.

Once the document is open, the text is extracted using the Range property of the active document, and is assigned to a string variable called strNames.

There is a new built-in function introduced next: the Split function. This function will take a text string and split it into its individual words based on the separator used. By default, Split uses a space as an indicator of where one word ends and the next one starts. Because you will have full names with spaces in them for users, you need to use another separator so that the full name is passed in as one entity. For this reason, the Split function makes use of the comma separator, as you can see in the code listing.

An example of how the Split function works is shown here. Suppose you have a text string "This is a text string". Split will break the string up into its individual words and place them in an array like this:

```
"This"
"is"
"a"
"text"
"string"
```

Each word is a member of a string array. The word `"This"` starts the array off and has an index value of zero (`0`). (Remember our discussion of arrays. They are zero-based, which means that they start counting at 0 instead of 1.)

Once the values from the text in the document are separated into an array, you no longer need Word, so it is shut down with the `Quit` method. (No need to take up system resources that are not needed, right?)

Following this, the variable `intCounter` is initialized with a value of `0`, the start value of the array, in preparation for looping through the values in the array. The next line tests to make sure that there are actually values in the array before the loop starts. After all, there is no need to run the script if there are no entries to add to the user account database.

The next couple of lines of code declare another variable called simply `i` and then the `Ubound` built-in function assigns the variable to the upper bound, or highest value in the array. `Ubound` is used to determine the upper limit of an array if it is not known in advance. This is done so that the loop will stop at the end of the array.

The loop is then set up starting with the `For` keyword. The `intCounter` variable is assigned a value starting at `0` and will continue until we reach the upper limit of the array minus one. The `-1` is used so that we do not generate an error on the last entry. If you leave it off, the last account will not be added, as the loop will attempt to run one more time where there isn't a valid username, causing a runtime error.

The loop is responsible for stepping through the array and assigning the username, full name, and password values to variables. Note that you have to use an increment before each assignment to ensure that you are assigning the correct value from the array.

After each variable is assigned the correct information, the subprocedure `CreateUser` is called and is passed the variables to use for the information we want to assign to the user accounts.

The `CreateUser` procedure takes each variable's value and creates a user account using the `strUserName` variables as the user account name and then assigns the fullname and password values to that account. The `SetInfo` method is used to write the values to the user account database. Once this is accomplished, the user object and server object are set to nothing to prevent unnecessary resource usage and you are informed that the user account has been added. Execution then returns to the loop for the next entry.

When the loop has finished (that is, there are no more values in the array), the message "User accounts added" is displayed to tell you that the script has completed successfully and the user accounts have been added.

> **NOTE**
>
> The file used here is rather crude; it is simply a string of values separated by commas (gjones,George Jones,password,fflint,Fred Flint,password,jhannah,Jack Hannah, password...). This will work in Microsoft Word as long as you do not place any hard returns in the document. The text must be one long string. If there are any hard returns, ADSI will return an error about an invalid username because the hard return code will be interpreted as a value.

Set Script Properties

WSH enables you to set the properties for script files. This is done so you can execute a script using different parameters if you have a need to do so. For example, you might want to have a script execute for a specific time period before it ends because of a timeout. This might be because you don't want a script file to continue executing if there is a problem, such as a file not found error, or a network connection being down. You can specify different timeout periods in different .wsh files and execute the script with the timeout you want by executing the .wsh file of your choice.

Setting Script File Properties to Create a .wsh File

As you have learned previously, the .wsh file is an ASCII text file that you can create on your own with your favorite text editor, or you can set the properties for the script file itself, which will create the file for you automatically.

Let's use the latter method first and create a .wsh file for the script that we have in Listing 4.5. Locate the script file on your computer and right-click it. This will bring up a dialog box similar to that shown in Figure 4.2.

As you can see from this image, there are only two options available on this tab. You can choose to have the script timeout after a specified period of time, and you can choose to have the script display a logo when you execute from within a command prompt window.

Listing 4.7 shows an example of the .wsh file that was created as a result of setting the properties for the dragdrop.vbs file.

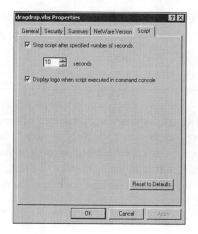

FIGURE 4.2

The dragdrop.vbs Properties dialog box, showing the Script tab selected and the options available for customizing the script.

LISTING 4.7   An Example .wsh File Showing the Properties Set Using the Dialog Box in Figure 4.1

```
[ScriptFile]
Path=C:\Documents and Settings\student\Desktop\dragdrop.vbs
[Options]
Timeout=10
DisplayLogo=1
```

The first entry in the file is the [ScriptFile] section. This section is used to indicate the path location for the script file.

> **TIP**
>
> If you are running your script file from a .wsh file and the script does not execute, check the path in the [ScriptFile] section of the .wsh file to ensure that it is pointing to the script file.

The next section of the .wsh file shows the values for the timeout and the DisplayLogo parameters. When the .wsh file is double-clicked, WSH checks these parameters.

The `timeout` parameter is measured in seconds, whereas the `DisplayLogo` parameter is a Boolean value, with `1` indicating yes, and `0` indicating no. For this particular file, it will set the timeout at 10 seconds and will display a logo when it happens.

Other Properties

If you want to, you can set some other properties for the script file as well while you have the Properties dialog box open. Figure 4.3 shows the Summary tab opened, with information already filled in for the available options.

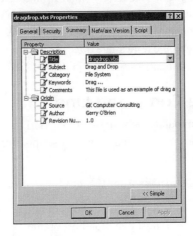

FIGURE 4.3
The Summary tab enables you to add more information to the script file, such as author and version information.

The first option available is the Title option, where you can specify a title for the script file. Next, you can specify a Subject that will tell users of the script what it deals with. You can also enter a Category if you want to categorize your scripts. Also note that File System is the category of the drag-and-drop example.

You can enter a list of keywords as well that can be used in search criteria when you want to locate a script that is based on keywords. This is a list of keywords that you can enter that pertain to what the script is working with.

TIP

When you want to add multiple keywords in this list, hold down the CTRL key when you press ENTER after each word. The list will remain open until you are finished entering keywords. When you are finished, press ENTER at the end of a line, and the list will close with all entries added.

The Origin section enables you to specify an origin for the script file, along with an author. You can also specify a version number in here as well. It is important to keep the version numbers up-to-date as you make revisions to a script file. That way you can be certain of using the latest version of the script.

Running Script Files from CScript.exe and WScript.exe

Windows Script Host enables you to run scripts either from the command prompt or from within Windows itself, as a GUI. Whichever method you choose depends on your needs. You can run scripts from the command prompt that don't require user intervention or any graphical elements. If you want to use graphical message boxes to ensure that users see a message or prompt, then you should run your scripts within a Windows GUI environment.

Scripting from the Command Line with CScript.exe

We will take a look at the command-line scripting tool CScript.exe in this section. CScript.exe enables you to enter parameters when you are running scripts from the command line. The syntax for CScript.exe is shown here:

```
cscript [host options] scriptname [script options or parameters]
```

The first parameter deals with any host options, and is optional. The host options begin with two forward slashes (//). The two most common host options that you will encounter are the //logo and //nologo options that specify whether to display a logo when the script is executing or not to display it.

The next requirement for CScript.exe is the script name. You must supply the name of the script that you want to run, and it must include the correct path to the script file if you are not already in the directory that contains the script.

After the script name has been supplied, you can then enter optional parameters that apply to the script, such as named arguments or other options that the script may require. An example of running a script from the command line is given here:

```
cscript multi.wsf
```

The resulting display is shown in Figure 4.4, where you can see that the same script we used earlier that showed the use of multiple languages in one script file can be executed from the command line as well. It will produce the same results as that of the GUI execution, with the exception that everything is executed at once without requiring the user to press anything.

FIGURE 4.4
A command prompt window displaying the output from executing the multi.wsf file from the command prompt.

As you can see, not only can you run script files with the .vbs or .js extension, but you can execute WSH files with a .wsf extension as well.

Using CScript.exe is a great way for network administrators to execute scripts that don't require user intervention. These can be login scripts or any other scripts that you want to execute that don't require a graphical interface. An example is shown here:

```
Dim objNetWork, strUser
Set objNetWork = CreateObject("WScript.Network")
strUser = objNetWork.UserName
Wscript.Sleep 500
objNetWork.MapNetworkDrive "h:", "\\servername\sharename\"  strUser
objNetWork.AddWindowsPrinterConnection "\\printer1\hp", "HP LaserJet 4"
```

This little login script creates a network object variable and a user string. It then assigns a WScript network object to the `objNetWork` variable and assigns the username of the currently logged on user to the `strUser` variable.

The next line, `Wscript.Sleep 500`, causes the script to pause for 500 milliseconds to ensure that a user has indeed logged on and then maps a network drive on the computer using the username and maps a printer from the server to the user's computer.

If you execute this script using CScript.exe, there is no visual interface at all and it will execute without the user knowing it is even there.

You can still provide feedback to the user or to yourself with the use of the `Echo` method, as illustrated by the multi.wsf example, where you still see the lines output to the screen indicating which procedure is executing.

4

**HOW TO USE
YOUR SCRIPTS**

Running Script Files with WScript.exe

As you have already seen, you can run your scripts from within Windows by double-clicking the file icon in Explorer. This causes the script to execute using GUI features, such as message boxes for feedback to the user. Your scripts will still execute in the same manner and all procedures will complete normally.

WScript is like CScript in that you can apply properties to your scripts as well. We will take a look at a table shortly that will display the available options that you can use with your scripts, both with CScript and WScript.

One of the advantages to using WScript is that, as we have already mentioned, you get the Windows features such as message boxes that provide a much more "in your face" style of feedback. Not only that, but you can double-click the icon or file anywhere it is displayed: in Explorer, on the Desktop, or even in the Find dialog box.

You set the properties for the script file that WScript will use by following the procedure mentioned earlier in the chapter in the section titled "Setting Script File Properties to Create a .wsh File." Right-click the file and choose Properties to set the timeout and logo options from the script tab.

Table 4.1 shows the available options that you can set for your scripts and differentiates between CScript and WScript.

TABLE 4.1   Script Options for CScript and WScript

Option	Description
//B	Used to indicate batch mode. This will cause your scripts to execute with prompts and error messages suppressed.
//D	Used to turn on the script debugger, which can aid in debugging errors in your scripts.
//E:engine	This will cause the script to execute with the specified script engine.
//H:cscript, //H:wscript	Sets the default scripting engine. If none is specified, WScript is the default.
//I	Used to turn on Interactive mode, where you will get screen prompts and error messages.
//Job:<jobID>	Used to run a specific job (jobID) from the .wsf file.
//logo	Use this option to have WSH display the logo when the script is executed.
//nologo	Prevents display of an execution banner at runtime.
//S	Saves the current option for the user that is executing the script.
//T:nn	Used to specify a timeout that the script will run before it ends.

TABLE 4.1   Continued

Option	Description
//X	Will launch the program in the debugger.
//?	Used to display help about the script that you specify in the command line.

Summary

The support for use of .wsf files within WSH 5.6 permits you great flexibility in how you execute your scripts. Permitting multiple jobs to exist in one file gives the user the capability to call the appropriate job when needed by specifying the jobID in the command line options when the script is executed.

The .wsf files also permit you to use *include* statements, which is a great way of reusing code that has been previously written by other authors, or even yourself. In this way, you can create reusable scripts that can serve you over and over again.

Windows is built heavily on the concept of drag-and-drop, and WSH enables you to use this feature as well. You can use decision structures within your code to determine what type of file was dropped on the script and take appropriate action.

Setting script properties permits you to perform some customizations with your scripts that enable the setting of timeout values, and even for including information with the script file, such as author name and company information. You can also place keywords in a list that will aid in searching for just the right script file for your needs.

WSH gives you the option of executing your scripts from the command line with no user interaction or intervention by using the CScript engine. You can provide the user with GUI-based visual feedback by using message boxes within your scripts. All these features give you a little more control over your scripts and how you work with them.

Securing Your Scripts

IN THIS CHAPTER

Earlier in the book you touched briefly on the topic of how powerful scripting languages have become. With this power, you discovered how users could exercise this power to create vicious code. You also explored some examples that showed malicious use of VBScript in the form of macro virus programs written to perform mass mailings, such as the Melissa macro virus. Once people heard about the havoc created by this virus, and the language that was used to create it, a few more people decided they would like to try it.

Because scripting languages are easy to learn, more and more non-developers can create scripts that will wreak havoc much easier and faster than ever before. Thus, the need to be able to secure your scripts from malicious users is imperative.

Accessing the File System with Malicious Code

The fact remains that the most potent viruses are still being created with lower level languages, such as C and Assembly. These virus programs are certainly most destructive when they gain access to the binary representations of a file, attach themselves to the file, and hide within it. This makes the virus extremely hard to eliminate without causing file loss.

Yet, one is able to access file system attributes via scripting languages using the Windows Script Host File System Object. Because of this, any script that can be written in VBScript or JScript, or any other WSH-compliant scripting language for that matter, can wreak havoc on your files by deleting, copying, renaming, and so on. This makes WSH a threat to your system if not used correctly.

Accessing Registries with Malicious Code

WSH also allows you access to the registry. Any person with malicious intent can destroy your registry settings, making your computer non-bootable. The scripts can create, access, read, and delete registry settings on the computer that it is executed on.

For the preceding reasons, version 5.6 of WSH has added some features that allow authors to sign their scripts (see more on this later in the chapter), ensuring end-users that the script has not been modified and is safe for execution on their systems. Of course, a malicious script writer can sign a script as well, but the intent is that you will run scripts from trusted sources.

Administrators can also set permissions that allow only certain users to execute scripts. In this way, the network administrator can ensure that those users who are administrators, or who understand what the scripts are used for, can only execute scripts.

Scripting with the CryptoAPI Tools

In order for you to sign your scripts, you need to utilize the CyrptoAPI tools. Microsoft makes the documentation for the CryptoAPI available in the Platform SDK and also on the Web at `http://msdn.microsoft.com/library/psdk/crypto/portalapi_3351.htm?RLD=290`.

The actual signing of your scripts is done with a digital signature. Digital signatures will be covered later in the chapter, but a brief explanation is presented here for you. Digital signatures provide a means of protecting a document or other entity such as code with an encrypted portion or signature that is created using a specific mathematical algorithm that takes some of the original as a part of the key to decrypt it. If there is a change in the original and the same algorithm is run on the signed document, the algorithm will fail, indicating tampering.

> **NOTE**
>
> This book will not provide a complete tutorial on the CryptoAPI, but will offer an introduction as to what it is and some of the concepts behind using it.

The API portion tells you that it is an Application Programming Interface. For those not familiar with APIs, they are a set of interfaces to functions that enable you to gain access to functionality that is not built into the tool you are using for development. An example follows.

The example we will use here is known as `SendMessage`. This API function is used to send a message within Windows to a control on a form for the purpose of getting the control to do something. One common use would be to redraw a control if the form were resized. For instance, if the control had a picture or graphic element on it, `SendMessage` would require it to redraw that element at the new coordinates that changed as a result of the resize. The API function looks like this:

```
Public Declare Function SendMessage Lib "user32" Alias "SendMessageA"
➥ (ByVal hWnd As Long, ByVal wMsg As Long, ByVal wParam As Long,
➥ lParam As Any) As Long
```

As you can see, it looks quite cryptic. To help you understand it a bit, let's dissect it.

The first portion of the function is `Public`, which merely indicates that the function can be called from other functions. The `Declare` keyword is required in Visual Basic as a means of declaring the function for use.

You then see the word `Function`, indicating that it is indeed a function, and then the name `SendMessage`, which is the name of the function. Next you see `Lib "user32"`, which goes together to tell the VB compiler that this function is found in the user32 library (a part of Windows).

After the "user32" entry you see the word Alias and the name "SendMessageA". This provides the function with another name that can be used in Visual Basic. The reason behind the need for this second name is based on the way VB handles function names, spaces, and so on. It is not important for our discussion here.

The next things you see are more entries within parentheses. These are the arguments that the function takes to provide the correct functionality. hWnd is known as a handle to a window and is what Windows uses to keep track of which window, or form, caused or sent the message. It also allows you to take control of a window or form.

The next argument is wMsg. This is an identifier for the message that you wish to send. The last two arguments are parameters that depend on the message and are not important here.

Visual Basic and C++ developers have long accessed a set of APIs for manipulating the Windows operating systems. They are especially useful for Visual Basic developers in that they provide functionality that is not native to Visual Basic.

The CryptoAPIs are useful for the same purpose. They serve to provide cryptographic functions that you can use for your own purposes. This means that you have access to special functions, such as those used to encode or decode data by simply calling them, providing the necessary input information, and receiving the completed product back.

You do not need to know how the function works. All you need to be aware of is how to call the built-in functions and what parameters to provide with those calls.

> **NOTE**
>
> Currently in version 2.0, the CryptoAPI provides functions for encoding and decoding from ASN.1 (Abstract Syntax Notation .1). There are also functions for hashing, for encrypting and decrypting your data, and for providing authentication with digital signatures.
>
> ASN.1 is a method for describing data types such as integers or bit strings. It can also be used to describe collections of data types. For more information on ASN.1, visit the RSA Web site at http://www.rsa.com.

Public and Private Keys

The CryptoAPI can utilize *session keys* or *public/private keys*. Public/Private keys are perhaps most recognizable if you have used PGP (Pretty Good Privacy). PGP is a software application that can integrate into e-mail and other applications and provide a means to encrypt your text or data using encryption keys. It can also be used to decrypt that data. This style of key is based on the use of a private key that only you know and a public key that you distribute. With this setup, when you need to encrypt some data, you do so with your private key. When a user of that data needs to read it, they must decrypt it with the public key that you provided. If they wished to encrypt data for only you, they would do so with the public key that you provided. When you wish to decrypt that data, you would do so with your private key.

Some say that there is an inherent weakness with this method in that there is always one key known and given enough time and resources, you could decipher the private key. That may be so, but it is also dependent on the strength of the key that you use. The higher the encryption strength, the harder it is to decipher a key. The most common key strengths are 40-bit and 128-bit, but keys with 256-bit encryption are also available.

Session keys are also known as *symmetric keys*. The reason for this is due to the fact that the same key is used for encryption and decryption, unlike the public/private keys.

You can create keys in the CryptoAPI by using the CryptGenKey function. This function will generate a random key which is either a session key or a public/private key pair. For more information on using this function, see the Platform SDK.

Securing Scripts with Signing

What exactly do I mean when I talk about signing a script? To put it simply, signing a script involves placing a digital signature block consisting of comments within the script.

Within this signature exists some encoded information that contains the identity of the author of the script. It also contains encoded information about the script file. By including this encoded information in the script file itself, it can be determined if the script was tampered with because the signature would no longer validate. An example signature block is shown here:

```
'' SIG '' Begin signature block
'' SIG '' MIIHyQYJKoZIhvcNAQcCoIIHujCCB7YCAQExDjAMBggq
'' SIG '' hkiG9w0CBQUAMGYGCisGAQQBgjcCAQSgWDBWMDIGCisG
'' SIG '' AQQBgjcCAR4wJAIBAQQQTvApFpkntU2P5azhDxfrqwIB
'' SIG '' AAIBAAIBAAIBAAIBADAgMAwGCCqGSIb3DQIFBQAEEMtO
'' SIG '' i/AfxcxD6Dj8e6wArXL7MDY=
'' SIG '' End signature block
```

The actual signature block is much larger than this and takes about two pages, so I truncated it to save space. You can see that there is a begin statement and an end statement, both of which are plain text. The information in between is encrypted data and as such is not readable until decrypted.

5

Acquiring a Digital Certificate for Script Signing

The first thing that you need to do before you can sign a script is to acquire a *digital certificate*. A digital certificate is a means of ensuring that you are who you say you are.

Webmasters may be familiar with certificates as they are used for Web sites that employ Secure Sockets Layer (SSL) for secure transaction and handling of sensitive information.

If you are working in a Windows 2000/XP environment, you can talk to your network administrator about acquiring a certificate from the system. For the most part, you can request a certificate by using Internet Explorer, or if you have administrative rights on your Windows 2000 Professional computer, you can request a certificate using the User and Passwords applet in the Control Panel. We will look at using the Internet Explorer method next.

Acquiring a Ticket via Internet Explorer

Open IE and browse to the Root CA (Certificate Authority) server on your network. This is usually in the form `http://servername/certsrv`. When you run IE on your computer and execute the URL in this manner, you will be greeted with the screen shown in Figure 5.1. Take note that certificate services must be installed and running on the server before you can request certificates.

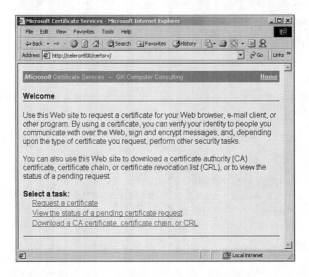

FIGURE 5.1
Internet Explorer showing the Certificate Request page.

Select the Request a Certificate hyperlink under the Select a Task section. This will take you to the Request a Certificate screen where you choose the type of certificate you want to request. This screen is shown in Figure 5.2.

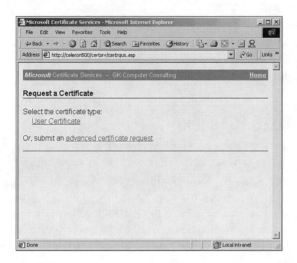

FIGURE 5.2

The Request a Certificate screen where you choose the type of certificate to request.

You can choose one of two possible options on this screen. The first option allows you to request a User Certificate. If you choose this option, you are not prompted for any more information and the Certificate Authority will generate a certificate for you and prompt you to install it. This certificate is useful for identification on the network only.

The next type of certificate is one that will allow you to use it for signing code. Select the Advanced Certificate Request option. This will advance you to the next screen, which is shown in Figure 5.3.

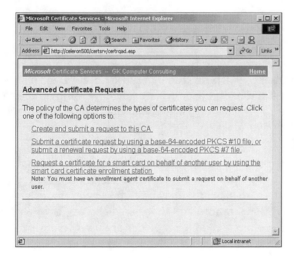

FIGURE 5.3

The Advanced Certificate Request page where you can choose to request a more advanced type of certificate.

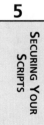

5

SECURING YOUR SCRIPTS

The next step is to select the first option, Create and Submit a Request to This CA. Select that hyperlink to advance to the next screen. Here is where you will make the choices that will determine what certificate template to use as well as determine options relating to the key (PKI) and the hash algorithm.

Public Key Infrastructure (PKI)

It's important to take a moment and look at the options that are available here, especially for those not quite familiar with Public Key Infrastructure (PKI).

PKI is a method of using two keys for the purpose of encrypting and decrypting data or information. With this scenario, the two keys are known as *private* and *public*. When you generate a key pair by using a PKI method, whether it is a certificate or some other means, such as Pretty Good Privacy (PGP), you create a set of keys that together provide the necessary encryption and decryption seeds.

A private key is created for you and is never given out. You should at all times protect your private key. If it is ever compromised, you should create a new key pair or request a new certificate.

The second key is the public key. This is the key that you can freely distribute to intended recipients. It doesn't matter if this key is stolen because it is meant to be public and used by all who need to encrypt or decrypt data with you.

The keys will work in pairs as you might have guessed. When you want to encrypt data, or in our case sign a script file, you use your private key to do so. When you send the data or script to another user who wishes to decrypt the data or verify the script file, you also send your public key. With the use of the public key, the end user can decrypt the data and view or verify its contents.

If a user wanted to send you a script or data and wanted to ensure that only you could decrypt it, they would employ your public key to encrypt the data. In this way, only your private key can decrypt the data.

There are some who believe that even if you only have the public key, you can determine what the private key is. This is true in a sense because given enough time, somebody could determine what your private key is by using data encrypted with the private key and reverse engineering, if you will, the data with the public key to determine what the private key is.

This would obviously take considerable time and resources to accomplish but it can be done. This is why there are various *strengths* of keys. The strength of a key is measured in terms of its bit length. Some of the most common bit lengths in use today for certificates are 512 and 1024. You may be familiar with Internet Explorer using 56-bit and 128-bit encryption strength and those are valid values as well, but for the purposes of digital signatures, the higher values are used to ensure more security. The greater the key strength, the longer it will take to break it.

NOTE

If you want more information on encryption and key strength, visit the RSA Web site at http://www.rsasecurity.com/.

Windows 2000/XP supports five standard certificate formats. These are listed here:

- *Personal Information Exchange*—These certificates are also known as PKCS #12 or Public Key Cryptography Standards #12. This is an industry standard format for certificates that allow for the backup and restoration of the certificate and its keys. It is also independent of any vendor so it can be transferred from computer to computer. Windows uses this format when exporting certificates due to the fact that the private keys are not exposed to unintended persons.

- *Cryptographic Message*—Also known as PKCS #7.

- *Syntax Standard*—With this standard, you can also transfer certificates to other computers or removable media. These certificate files have an extension of .p7b.

- *DER Encoded Binary X.509*—Mostly used by certification authorities on the Internet. It is not Windows specific but is supported for interoperability.

- *Base64 Encoded X.509*—Another format common on the Internet. It is also supported by Windows for interoperability. Files contain a .cer extension.

NOTE

For more information on these types of certificates, see the RSA Web site URL mentioned earlier.

Now that you know some options Windows makes available for certificates, it's time to continue your certificate request. On the Advanced Certificate Request page, select the Administrator certificate template. Scroll down to the Key Options section.

Here you are given a choice to create a new key set or utilize an existing one. You will create a new key set, so ensure that option is selected.

The CSP drop-down box is where you will select a provider. CSP stands for Cryptographic Service Provider. At present, the only available choice is the Microsoft Base Cryptographic Provider v1.0. You can safely ignore the Exchange option that is grayed out here as well.

The next option to look at is the key size. You can see that the minimum size is 384 and the maximum is 1024. This will determine how strong the key is. The higher the number, the

5

stronger your key will be. Make your choice and enter it in the box provided. I chose the default of 512 for my key for this demonstration.

The remainder of the options on this page are not of any concern for your purposes so you will leave them all at the default settings. You can review the online help for Windows to gain a better understanding of these settings.

Click the Submit button at the bottom of the page and you should see the Certificate Issued screen that indicates success in creating the signature.

When you reach this screen, the certificate has been created and is ready to be installed onto your computer. Select the Install this certificate link, and the Certificate Services will install the newly created certificate to your local computer.

You now have a certificate that you can use to digitally sign your script code. There is one disadvantage to this style of certificate, if you can call it a disadvantage. The fact that you have created it from a local CA means that everyone may not accept the certificate. The main reason is because your organization may not be recognized as a trusted CA.

To resolve this issue, you can obtain a certificate from Verisign or another trusted CA. In this way, your certificate can be verified to be valid from a trusted source. The downfall is that Verisign certificates for code signing are $400.00 US at present. If you are a developer who writes code for organizations outside of your own, this would be the ideal path to take for a certificate, and $400 is not really a large sum of money when it comes to providing security and insurance to users of your code.

Using Certificates to Sign Scripts

Now that you have generated a certificate, you can begin to sign the scripts. WSH makes this a really simple process with the use of the `Scripting.Signer` object. The Signer object has four methods and they will be discussed in this section.

The `Scripting.Signer` Object

The first thing that you need to do regarding the `Scripting.Signer` object is create a .wsf file that will store some named arguments you will pass in at the command prompt. Listing 5.1 is an example of such a file.

LISTING 5.1   A .wsf File That Specifies Named Arguments to Be Used at the Command Prompt for Signing a Script File

```
<job>
<!-- signtest.wsf.
    This file is designed to demonstrate the use of the
```

LISTING 5.1   Continued

```
        Scripting.Signer object for the purposes of signing
        script files with a digital signature.

        Author: Gerry O'Brien
        Date:    April 18, 2001
        Platform: Windows 2000/XP
        Language: JScript
 -->
<runtime>
   <named name="file" helpstring="script filename"
 ➥required="true" type="string"/>
   <named name="cert" helpstring="certificate name"
 ➥required="true" type="string"/>
   <named name="store" helpstring="[optional] certificate store name"
 ➥required="false" type="string"/>
</runtime>
<script language="JScript">
   var objSigner, objFile, objCert, objStore;
   if (!(WScript.Arguments.Named.Exists("cert") && _
 ➥ WScript.Arguments.Named.Exists("file")))
   {
      WScript.Arguments.ShowUsage();
      WScript.Quit();
   }
   objSigner = new ActiveXObject("Scripting.Signer");
   objFile  = WScript.Arguments.Named("file");
   objCert  = WScript.Arguments.Named("cert");
   objStore = WScript.Arguments.Named("store");
   objSigner.SignFile(objFile, objCert, objStore);
</script>
</job>

<job>
<!-- signtestvb.wsf.
     This file is designed to demonstrate the use of the
     Scripting.Signer object for the purposes of signing
     script files with a digital signature.

     Author: Gerry O'Brien
     Date:    April 18, 2001
     Platform: Windows 2000/XP
     Language: VBScript
 -->
<runtime>
```

5

LISTING 5.1   Continued

```
    <named name="file" helpstring="script filename"
    ➥required="true" type="string"/>
    <named name="cert" helpstring="certificate name"
    ➥required="true" type="string"/>
    <named name="store" helpstring="[optional] certificate store name"
    ➥required="false" type="string"/>
</runtime>
<script language="VBScript">
    Dim objSigner, objFile, objCert, objStore
    If Not WScript.Arguments.Named.Exists("cert") And
    ➥WScript.Arguments.Named.Exists("file") Then
        WScript.Arguments.ShowUsage
        WScript.Quit
    End If

    Set objSigner = CreateObject("Scripting.Signer")
    objFile  = WScript.Arguments.Named("file")
    objCert  = WScript.Arguments.Named("cert")
    objStore = WScript.Arguments.Named("store")
    objSigner.SignFile objFile, objCert, objStore
</script>
</job>
```

This listing shows an example of signing a file using JScript and VBScript. When you execute this script file, you use the command line and supply a command like the following:

```
cscript signtestvb.wsf /file:HelloW.vbs /cert:Gerry O'Brien /store:my
```

This command line specifies the CScript engine, using the signtestvb.wsf file that is included in Listing 5.1. You then provide the named arguments for the file, such as the name of the file to sign which in this case is a file called HelloW.vbs that resides in the same directory. You then specify the cert argument, seen as Gerry O'Brien in Listing 5.1, which is the name of the certificate that I am using to sign the file.

The last argument specifies the store that the certificate is stored in. By default, your certificates are stored in the my store. If you are storing your certificates in a different store, specify that name here.

This will generate a signature block in the script file as shown in Figure 5.4.

You can only see the partial file and signature block here due to the constraints for the image size but when you run the command yourself, you will see that the signature block is added to the file.

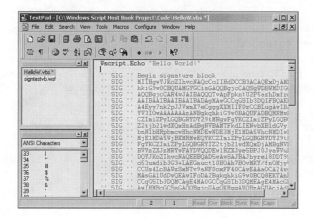

FIGURE 5.4
The HelloW.vbs file shown in TextPad with the signature block added.

With this signature added to the script file, an end user can verify the security of the script by running the `verify` method. If the script is not correct or even if the script itself has been modified after it was signed, the verification process will fail indicating that the script is not secure and should not be executed.

Verifying Scripts with the `Scripting.Signer` Object

When you need to verify that a script file is secure and has not been modified, you use the `VerifyFile` method of the `Scripting.Signer` object. This method will verify the signature that was encapsulated in the script file with the `SignFile` method. The syntax for the `VerifyFile` method is shown here:

```
object.VerifyFile (filename, ShowUI)
```

object is the `Scripting.Signer` object and *filename* is a string value indicating the name of the script file to verify. The last argument is `ShowUI`, which is a Boolean value.

If you set the value of `ShowUI` to `False`, the `Scripting.Signer` object will determine if the signature was provided by a trusted source without requiring intervention from the user. If the value is set to `True`, the `Scripting.Signer` object will prompt the user with dialog boxes for information to help it determine if the signature is from a trusted source. An example is shown in Listing 5.2.

LISTING 5.2   An Example VBScript File That Verifies the Digital Signature of a Script File

```
'***************************************************************
' verifyHelloW.vbs
' Demonstrates the use of the VerifyFile method of the
```

LISTING 5.2   Continued

```
' Scripting.Signer object.
'
' Author:    Gerry O'Brien
' Date:      April 18, 2001
' Platform: Windows 2000/XP
' Language: VBScript
'*****************************************************************

Dim Signer, File, UI, OK
If Not WScript.Arguments.Named.Exists("file") Then
     WScript.Arguments.ShowUsage
     WScript.Quit
End If
Set Signer = CreateObject("Scripting.Signer")
File = WScript.Arguments.Named("file")
UI   = WScript.Arguments.Named.Exists("ui")
OK = Signer.VerifyFile(File, UI)
If OK Then
     WScript.Echo File & " is trusted."
Else
     WScript.Echo File & " is NOT trusted."
End If
```

When you run this script on your computer with the command line

wscript verifyHelloW.vbs /file:HelloW.vbs /UI:True,

you get the results displayed in Figures 5.5 and 5.6.

FIGURE 5.5

An example screen showing the prompt that informs you that the script signature cannot be verified.

FIGURE 5.6
The message box displayed after I verified that the script was secure in the previous screen.

Choose the Yes option on the screen shown in Figure 5.5 to tell the system that the script signature was verified. If you didn't choose Yes, the script would not be verified and you would receive a message indicating that the script signature was not valid.

If you eliminate the UI argument on the command line, you will not be prompted with the screen in Figure 5.5 and the system will determine whether the script signature is valid or not.

The reason that the example certificate failed is because the contents of the file were altered after it was signed. The alteration merely consisted of deleting an extra line in the file. You can see that something as little as that will cause a failure of the signature verification.

With a properly signed file that hasn't been altered, you will receive the screen shown in Figure 5.7.

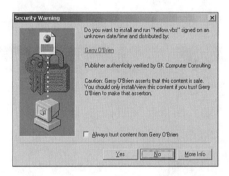

FIGURE 5.7
The screen you will see if the signature has been verified and is from a trusted source.

This screen should look familiar if you are used to downloading ActiveX components from the Internet. You can select Yes if you are sure that you trust the person and the organization that the signature is from. You can also choose in advance to trust everything you receive from this person by checking the Always Trust Content from Gerry O'Brien option.

Establishing Trusts Within Scripts

WSH 5.6 also allows administrators to determine the trust policy when it comes to running scripts. The options available for trusts are described in the next two sections.

Trust Policies

Trust policies are a method used by administrators to determine how scripts will be executed based on signature verification. The administrator can turn signature verification on or off.

With signature verification turned on, only scripts with signatures from trusted sources will be allowed to execute on the computer. With signature verification turned on, the system will verify if a trust has been determined for the script's signature.

If the script can't be trusted, the user can be prompted to decide whether the signature is a trusted signature or not before the script is executed.

You can also set the trust policy in such a way that it doesn't run a script or prompt the user at all if the signature cannot be verified.

These settings are made through the Local Security Policy editor or through the Registry. I will show the Registry method here.

Open the registry editor and navigate to HKEY_CURRENT_USER\Software\Microsoft\ Windows Script Host\Settings. Add a REG_DWORD value called TrustPolicy. This value will apply Hexadecimal values and you can set the value to one of three possible choices: 0, 1, or 2. Each value is explained next:

- 0—Setting the value to 0 will allow all scripts to run (see Figure 5.8).

FIGURE 5.8
An example of trying to run a script with the value set to 0.

- 1—This setting will prompt the user if a script is not trusted, as noted in Figure 5.9.

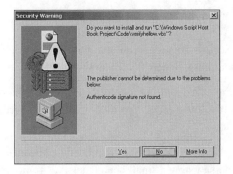

FIGURE 5.9
A Security Warning screen that shows what the user will see when the value is set to 1.

- 2—This setting will only allow trusted script to execute and will not prompt the user, as shown in Figure 5.10.

FIGURE 5.10
An example of the warning message displayed when the value is set to 2.

Each of these screens display the results of setting the `TrustPolicy` value to each of the respective settings in the Registry. In this way, you can set the policy for the users that are working on the computers and prevent the unauthorized execution of scripts on those computers.

WinTrust

WinTrust is actually a function that includes some structures for the purpose of verifying trust contained within files, certificates, or signatures. It makes use of the CryptoAPI functions to perform its tasks.

You will use the `WinVerifyTrust` function to perform the verification on the specified object.

WinTrust is part of the Security functions of the Platform SDK and more information can be found in that documentation relating to the use of WinTrust. Most of the documentation is intended for those familiar with C and C++, so I won't cover it any further here. You don't need the functionality for your purposes. I only mentioned it for the sake of completeness in this discussion of the security model for WSH.

Summary

This chapter looked at the security features available with WSH 5.6. You covered some information on security when dealing with certificates and what PKI is about and how it functions.

You also examined an example of acquiring a certificate from a Windows 2000/XP Certificate Authority for the purposes of code signing. You then applied that certificate to the signature of a script file.

Once the signature was in place, you looked at the procedure to verify the signature and the script after it was signed and saw how a small change such as removing a blank line after the script was signed caused the verification process to fail.

You then performed a successful verification and execution of a signed script.

You also saw the various messages displayed while trying to execute signed scripts. Finally, you examined the ability of an administrator to determine and enforce policies related to the execution of trusted and not trusted scripts.

Security is a major concern when it comes to executing scripts on a computer system, and any network administrator will have concerns when it comes to allowing users to run scripts on the local computer and networks. With these security features built into WSH, the fears can be relaxed somewhat when these procedures are applied.

Introduction to ADSI

Directory Services as a concept has been around for some time now. Novell uses a directory service that used to be known as NetWare Directory Services (NDS) and is now known as NDS eDirectory. With the advent of Windows 2000, Windows users now have a directory service known as Active Directory (AD).

For those maybe not familiar with Directory Services, you can consider them to be a method of defining resources on a network that consists of users, print queues, documents, or almost any other administrative resource that a network contains.

For the most part, there are various directory services available and in use today. We already mentioned that Novell has NDS eDirectory, which is the directory service available on NetWare 4.11 and higher.

NOTE

For previous versions of NetWare, the directory service was known as the NetWare Bindery.

Another directory service that has been around for some time is X.500. X.500 is an international message-handling standard. It is used for directory services and some of you may be familiar with using X.500 mail messages prior to widespread use of the Internet. X.500 is a standard that was published by the International Telegraph and Telephone Consultative Committee (CCITT). The X.500 syntax is illustrated here:

```
[X.500:/C=Country Code /O=Organization /OU=OrganizationUnit /CN=CommonName
```

Lotus also has a directory service available as well in the form of Lotus Notes. Many organizations may use Windows as an operating system but rely on Lotus Notes for group collaboration and e-mail.

There are still other directory services, such as Microsoft Exchange, Microsoft Mail, CC:Mail, and Banyan Street Talk. All of these directory services have one thing in common. In order to program access to the objects contained within them, you need to utilize the vendor-specific Application Programming Interfaces (APIs). If you have a wide range of directory services running in your organization, this means you will have to learn all of the necessary APIs so that you can programmatically access their objects and functionality. The Active Directory Service Interfaces (ADSI) aim to prevent this.

> **NOTE**
>
> The features and advantages of ADSI you will be exploring in this book will be from
> the perspective of a network administrator. Therefore the discussions seen in this
> book are aimed at using scripting languages to access and manipulate the various
> ADSI objects for administrative purposes. I will not talk about the advanced ADSI fea-
> tures nor will I discuss writing services that will work with ADSI . For more informa-
> tion on these features or how you might create applications and services to work
> with ADSI, be sure to check out *Active Directory Programming* by Gil Kirkpatrick
> (Sams Publishing, ISBN 0-672-31587-4).

The Active Directory Service Interfaces (ADSI)

Active Directory provides the Active Directory Service Interfaces (ADSI) for programmatically
administering and manipulating the Active Directory. Just because ADSI runs on Windows
2000 and deals with Active Directory, doesn't mean that you can only access AD. ADSI brings
directory services together from different network vendors. This results in a single set of interfaces that you can manipulate to manage network resources.

ADSI is implemented as a set of COM interfaces that provide this functionality to the developer. Therefore, in order to use ADSI effectively, you should have some knowledge of how
COM works and how to access COM-based interfaces.

By using ADSI, network administrators and developers can enumerate network resources
regardless of the network they are on. As long as these networks and their resources are a part
of the distributed network, they will appear as though they exist as one network.

What Is ADSI Used For?

If you are a network administrator, you can use ADSI for your administrative purposes. With
ADSI you can work with users and groups on your network as well as other resources. The
ADSI interface that exposes the user and group management functions allows you to add and
delete users. You can create new groups and assign membership to those groups for user
accounts.

With ADSI, you can also manage, install, and remove network print resources. These resources
can reside on multiple servers and even on multiple platforms. Because ADSI brings all directory services into one, users are not aware of these resources being spread over multiple
servers and platforms. They only see the resource available in one place. That makes searching
for and using these resources much easier for the end user.

Once you have created the resources on your network, you can employ ADSI to set and manage permissions on those resources. ADSI exposes interfaces that eliminate the need to go to each server or platform that is sharing the resources.

If you are a software developer, you can directory-enable your applications. What this means is that you can take your application and design it to run as a service. In this way, you can have the service publish itself in a directory. This allows end users to locate your service within the Active Directory and use its features and functions.

Another advantage that ADSI offers you as a developer is the ability to develop in the language of your choice. As long as the language supports automation, you can develop applications and access the features of ADSI.

Some of the languages that are supported are listed here:

- Visual Basic
- Visual Basic Scripting Edition (VBScript)
- JScript
- Java
- Visual C++
- C

Benefits of ADSI

In the early days of database application development, developers faced a steep learning curve due to the fact that they had to learn so many different API calls. Learning these calls sometimes took longer than the actual development of the software that they were trying to write. Having to learn the different API calls for each platform was like having to learn to speak another language before visiting a foreign country.

A technology known as ODBC (Open DataBase Connectivity) helped to solve these issues for developers of database applications. ODBC provided a common set of interfaces that the developer could use in applications to gain access to the underlying tables, queries, stored procedures, and other aspects of the database systems. ODBC's popularity increased, and database vendors began ensuring that their products supported ODBC. This meant a great benefit to developers, who now only had to worry about learning one set of interfaces and methods in order to work with any database that supported ODBC.

ADSI offers this same benefit. For directory service vendors, it makes sense to ensure that their products can work with a common interface that all programmers can learn and use to access these directory services. After all, it is much easier to learn one interface than it is to learn multiple interfaces. Let's take a look at two graphics that offer a comparison of the two methods of accessing the various directory services.

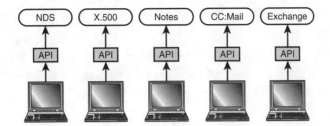

FIGURE 6.1
An example of the interface APIs that a developer would have to learn to access each of the available directory services.

As you can see from looking at Figure 6.1, the programmer has to call a separate set of API functions to access each of the various vendor-specific directory services. As we mentioned previously, it is time-consuming for the developer to have to learn multiple API calls and conventions. Take a look at Figure 6.2 for a comparison.

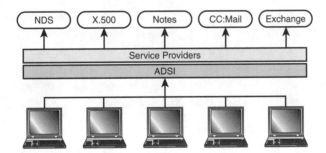

FIGURE 6.2
ADSI provides a common interface that shields the developer from the various APIs and calls the service providers internally.

Figure 6.2 depicts a different story. Here you can see that ADSI utilizes service providers that are written by the directory service vendor to be compliant and work with ADSI. In this way, ADSI deals with the providers internally and the developer only has to know one set of interfaces. This reduces the learning curve and makes development faster. Because ADSI exposes its functions through the ADSI services, developers don't have to worry about going through a plethora of hard-to-read API calls that are prone to errors. Any developer who has had to use the Windows Win32 APIs or the Network APIs knows all about the issues involved with those APIs. One of the biggest issues when dealing with APIs involves the data types that are used by the function and the language calling the API. For example, Visual Basic and C++ do not use the same data types when it comes to integers and strings. There are subtle differences that cause issues when the VB programmer calls the API functions, which are written in C++. The

VB programmer needs to know what type of data to pass to the function and also what data type will be returned.

Visual Basic contains rules regarding the naming of functions that don't apply to C++. Therefore, when you encounter an API function that contains spaces in the name, you have to provide an alias for that function name so that VB can use it.

Another major issue for VB programmers when calling APIs is that all of the API documentation is written for C++ developers. The VB programmer needs to be able to understand some C++ in order to be able to translate the functions to VB.

Although Visual Basic does come with an API text viewer applet, that allows the developer to search for the function they want to use and then paste that function's declaration into their code, there are some of these declarations that contain mistakes in them. What this means is that if you unknowingly paste a declaration into your code that contains an error, you can face the possibility of causing system lockups when you call that function from within your application.

Most of these issues may be changed in the very near future as Microsoft brings its .NET initiative into play. With the advent of the new Common Language Runtime (CLR), the data types used by the three languages in Visual Studio .NET, C++, C# (C sharp), and VB, will be exchangeable across all of the languages with no conversion necessary. This will of course translate into a new learning curve for existing VB developers. More on these developments can be found in Chapter 13, "WSH and the .NET Framework."

Accessing the Functionality of ADSI

When you want to access the functionality of ADSI, you do so by calling on the services and interfaces that it exposes. In this way, you are using a familiar COM automation style of programming that employs the (.) dot notation for the objects that you work with. An example is shown here:

```
Dim MyObject
Dim Child
Dim Container

On Error Resume Next
Set MyObject = GetObject("LDAP://celeron500/DC=Printers")
Set Container = MyObject

If Err = 0 Then
    For Each Child in Container
        WScript.Echo Child.Name
    Next
End If
```

This code example will be covered in a later chapter but you can see that in the For Each
Child section, we use the term Child.Name to display the name of an ADSI element.

> **NOTE**
>
> This also means that you don't have to learn a programming language like C++ or
> Java just to be able to access ADSI and all it provides. For the most part, without
> COM, you would have to resort to one of those languages for ADSI programming.

Support for Scripting Languages

Another advantage is that in order to access the functionality of ADSI, you don't have to write
complete standalone applications. ADSI supports the use of scripting languages, which means
that you can write scripts to do the work for you. If you have network administrators who are
familiar with writing batch files to perform common administrative tasks, their knowledge
transfers easily to scripting languages such as VBScript.

Scripts are good because they take up far less room than full applications. This is due partly to
their small size, and partly to the operating system having built-in support for the script languages. With WSH installed, you can write scripts in VBScript or JScript, which are two of the
best-supported and easiest scripting languages to learn.

> **NOTE**
>
> As was mentioned in earlier chapters, WSH also supports other scripting languages
> such as Perl, Python, and REXX. This means that you don't have to learn new scripting
> languages to make use of the ADSI architecture.

Built-in OLE DB Support

ADSI also makes us of OLE DB, which is built in. What does this mean to you? If you have
any clients that are already using OLE DB, such as those that have ActiveX Data Objects
incorporated into them, these same applications can use the OLE DB interface to access ADSI.

Other ADSI Advantages

Some other advantages of using ADSI are listed in Table 6.1.

TABLE 6.1   Advantages of Using ADSI

Feature	Benefit
Open architecture	Because ADSI is an open architecture, directory service providers can implement ADSI in their products. This allows the end user or network admininstrator to choose their directory services knowing that they will interact and function with other ADSI-enabled directory services.
Directory service independence	Because the platform is supported by multiple vendors or directory services, development time can be effectively reduced by only requiring the developers to concentrate on one common platform rather than multiple vendor-specific requirements.
Security	ADSI makes two programming models available in relation to security. A developer can choose to employ the authorization model or the authentication model.
Wide language support	The built-in support for OLE automation makes ADSI available to developers in their language of choice. As mentioned earlier in the chapter, support is present for VB, Java, C++, REXX, and Python. This helps to reduce development time for custom applications, because developers can program in the languages that they already know without the need to learn a new language.
Simple programming model	As was apparent in Figures 6.1 and 6.2 earlier, developers can utilize a common interface to access the objects within the various directory services without the need to learn and program multiple vendor-specific APIs.
Rich functionality	Throughout this book, we will show you how to program ADSI using scripting languages. ADSI provides the ability for developers to create robust full-fledged applications and services that use ADSI as well.
Extensibility	Developers can extend ADSI by adding custom objects and functions that can extend ADSI to suit an organization's needs specifically.

Summary

Directory services take all of the resources available in distributed network environments and bring them together into one central repository, making it easier for users to locate and use those resources. They also make administration of distributed networks much easier for the administrator.

Although this is a short chapter, it has given you an introduction to ADSI with an explanation of what it really is. By providing a common set of interfaces with which developers and administrators can gain access to directory services, ADSI provides a quick and efficient means of working with the various directory services available in networking products today.

Most of the features in ADSI are aimed at making it much easier to work with the various directory services that you may find within your networking environments, especially if you have mixed networks that utilize Windows NT/2000 and Novell NetWare.

ADSI Architecture

IN THIS CHAPTER

In this chapter you are going to take a look at the architecture of ADSI. The information presented will give you a better understanding of how ADSI is put together and how you can write script code to access the underlying structure of ADSI and manipulate the objects that it exposes.

Because most directory services are implemented in a hierarchical fashion they can be exposed to programmers in an Object model. With ADSI, you can make use of the COM object model, because ADSI uses the COM technology.

Various ADSI objects are classified as *containers*. Containers are objects that are used to hold other objects that relate to the container itself. You will see examples of these as you go through this and the other chapters on ADSI.

ADSI uses root namespaces to contain the objects that directly relate to each directory service that is implemented through ADSI. Not all directory services are exposed or work with ADSI. These namespaces are objects that are specified as root objects in the various directory services.

ADSI Objects

As was mentioned in the chapter introduction, ADSI uses COM interfaces to expose its objects to the programmer. Within the ADSI object model, you will find ADSI objects and child objects. You can work with these objects through interfaces in much the same way as you work with real-world objects using interfaces. An example would be the computer itself. You manipulate the various objects, the memory, the screen, and the disk drive objects, through the interface, which is the keyboard or speech recognition technology.

ADSI objects can be classified in two different groups: *leaf objects* and *container objects*. One of the biggest differences between the two is that the container object can contain other objects, such as other containers or leaf objects. The leaf objects cannot contain other objects and are essentially just objects.

Object-Oriented Programming (OOP) Fundamentals

For those who may not be familiar with the terminology used in object oriented programming (OOP), we will take a brief look at it here.

> **NOTE**
>
> OOP is beyond the scope of this book, but if you are inclined to continue down that path after you complete this book, you can find information on OOP in *The Object-Oriented Thought Process* by Matt Weisfeld (Sams Publishing, ISBN 0-672-31853-9).

There has been quite a bit of talk about objects in this book and sometimes the concept is not quite clear. I have read many books on OOP theory and have come across some good definitions of objects and some bad ones.

One of the definitions that I found extremely helpful is the one I will share with you here. To gain an understanding of what an object is in the world of programming, you only have to look at what an object is in real life. That is why OOP makes programming real-world applications easier than it used to be; you can model your software after real-world objects.

Let's look at an automobile as an example object. An automobile is a real-world object. Software objects behave and act like their real-world counterparts, sort of. You can't really drive a software car object. The point to be made here is that an automobile has some distinct features known as *properties* or *attributes*. These can be thought of as the color, the type of automobile, the number of doors, the size of wheels, and so on. The combination of each of these properties gives a particular automobile its own characteristics.

The automobile also has some *functionality* built in. Things like go, stop, and start the engine are functions cars can do. This functionality is equivalent to being known as *methods*. The user starts the engine and makes the automobile go and stop. The user of a software object invokes the methods of the object, such as start and stop, to make it do something.

There is one last piece of functionality that an automobile, or any object for that matter, can have. This is known as an *event*. An event is something that happens as a result of something else happening. An example would be if the driver of the car stepped on the accelerator. The engine's RPMs increase and, if the car is in gear, it moves on down the road. In the OOP world, the actual movement of the car can be considered an event that might be called *accelerate*.

Now, an automobile is quite far removed from the discussion of ADSI for sure, but, as I stated earlier, this is one of the best definitions that I have come across in a long time, and I find it makes it much easier to understand the concepts surrounding objects.

OOP Terminology

ADSI is built on objects and interfaces, so it is recommended that you have a good understanding of these two terms (objects and interfaces). The objects that make up ADSI are known as COM objects. COM stands for Component Object Model. COM is a technology that fits nicely with object-oriented programming. The reason for this is that when you create objects in a programming language, you are actually creating software components. COM allows these components to communicate with each other. Microsoft also has an updated version of COM known as COM+. COM+ is simply COM with added extensions that provide a runtime engine and various services that can be utilized by any programming language. It also allows for interoperability among components. You may have also heard of DCOM, which stands for Distributed Component Object Model and allows the use of COM over networks.

COM allows this communication to take place across multiple platforms, computers, and development languages, provided each is COM compliant. This is why you can access the various network resources with ADSI. The network service providers have written their software to be COM compliant; therefore, the interface is available to you for manipulation.

Current systems that are COM-compliant include the family of Windows operating systems along with Microsoft Transaction Server, a software package that controls software transactions across networks, as well as development tools such as C++, VB, and Java.

There is also another advantage to using COM and OOP. The objects that are created contain the properties, methods, and events that were talked about earlier in this section, in a *protected state*. What this means is that the internal workings of the object are *abstracted*, or hidden, from the user. Why is this good? There are actually a couple of reasons for this.

First, when you create an object, you may set properties that require validation before they are actually set within the object. Programmers deal with data types that are intrinsic within the programming language. These data types are fixed and can contain only certain data. An example is the use of an `integer` data type. Depending on the language you are using, an `integer` data type can be a 16-bit value or it can be a 32-bit value. Obviously the 32-bit value will not fit into the 16-bit value. Also, you cannot place a `string` value such as a letter or punctuation symbol into an `integer` value. This will cause an error.

You can see here that the programmer must provide a validation routine to ensure that the correct data is passed into the property before that property is changed. By making the property hidden, the user cannot change it directly, but must use what is known as an `accessor` method. This method can contain the necessary functionality to validate the data and change the property appropriately. This prevents any unwanted errors in the object. If any errors are detected, the developer can take the appropriate action necessary such as alerting the user to the error and recommending a way to rectify the error.

The second reason for using abstraction is to provide the means necessary to change or enhance the internal workings of the object without breaking the interface of it. This means that you can enhance functionality and replace the component without the user needing to acquire a new interface or change the way they access the object's methods and properties. This makes applications easier and cheaper to maintain.

Imagine, if you will for a moment, that you have written some WSH scripts that access your Windows 2000 Active Directory domain for the purposes of running backup jobs or enumerating user and groups on a regular basis. You have been using the necessary ADSI objects for these processes. During this time, Microsoft may have decided to enhance one of the objects or fix a bug in one. Then, the next service pack that you install contains this enhanced or fixed object and it overwrites the original. If the interface hasn't been changed, which it is not supposed to be, then your code will continue to function and you won't have to rewrite your scripts based on a new interface or changed methods.

This scenario can happen with any of the vendors that provide ADSI compliant services. If they write their objects and interfaces to the COM standard and employ the ADSI functionality, your code should never break. This is of course in a perfect world, and that just doesn't exist at the moment, but, for the most part, you should find that your code will continue to function with changes to the objects. If a vendor does make a change that affects the way you interface with an object, they will normally keep the programmers and end users aware of these changes.

The objects that you will be working with in ADSI will be used to represent the following types of network resources:

- Users
- Computers
- Printers
- Print queues
- Files
- Services

This is, of course, not a complete listing of the objects available as that depends on the provider. Each ADSI provider will make available to you, a list of the objects that you can work with and manipulate. This information can be found in the documentation for the particular directory service.

Working with Dot Notation

When you work with an object, you will access the various properties and methods of that object by using a dot notation. This means that you will refer to the object itself followed by a dot, which in turn is followed by the property or method. Listing 7.1 demonstrates setting the full name of a user object in ADSI.

LISTING 7.1 An Example Script That Is Used to Set the Full Name for the gobrien User Account

```
'****************************************************************
' userfullname.vbs
' This script demonstrates using object properties to set the full
' name of a user account.
'
```

LISTING 7.1 Continued

```
' Author: Gerry O'Brien
' Date:    May 6, 2001
' Platform: Windows 2000/XP
' Language: VBScript
'*************************************************************************
Dim objADSIObject
Dim strUserName

strUserName = "gobrien"
Set objADSIObject = GetObject("WinNT://gkcomput/PIII500/" & _
strUserName & ",user")
objADSIObject.FullName = "Gerry A. O'Brien"
WScript.Echo "The full name for " & strUserName &
➥" is " & _ objADSIObject.FullName
```

The result of running this script with the WScript engine is shown in Figure 7.1.

FIGURE 7.1

A message box displaying the result of setting the FullName *property of the* gobrien *account to* Gerry A. O'Brien.

Taking the code one line at a time, you will see how the property is manipulated. We first declare two variables that will be used to hold the data we will work with. The first variable is the objADSIObject. We will use this variable to hold a reference to the ADSI user object that we need to work with. The second variable is just used to hold the name that we will pass in as the username. You could have hard-coded, or written the value gobrien, in the username but that would make the script only usable for one user. This way, we can change the string stored in the variable to reflect different users or set the variable string using a loop that works its way through an array of names or even a tab- or comma-delimited file.

Next, the strUserName is assigned the value gobrien. The next line of code sets up the object that we need to work with the ADSI user object. The Set command is used here, because we are dealing with an object rather than a data type such as a string or integer. Anytime you want to assign an object to a variable, you must use the Set statement. This line of code is worth breaking down a little further.

The GetObject function is responsible for requesting the ADSI object for your script. Within the brackets you will notice that the provider is specified as WinNT. This provider is indicated as being used for Windows NT 4.0 networks, but you need to use it when you are working with ADSI on a Windows 2000 Professional workstation or a Windows 2000 Server that does not have Active Directory installed.

The next part of the function call contains the name of the domain, gkcomput and then the name of the computer in the domain that you want to contact, PIII500 in this case. You may notice that I am not particularly creative in the naming of my computers.

You will notice the use of ampersands (&) and the variable name strUserName next. This is a little concatenation that is used to provide a variable name in place of a hard coded value. This will insert the gobrien value that the strUserName variable was set to earlier.

The last piece of this function call is user. This is an optional argument to the function, but it is a good idea to use when you make these function calls. The reason for this is that if you have any duplicate names within your network such as a user and computer with the same name, this argument tells ADSI which object type you want to work with. In this case, you are telling ADSI that you are working with the user gobrien.

Once you have the object variable assigned to the appropriate object, you can then begin to manipulate the object's properties. That is what the next line does; it sets the FullName property for the gobrien user account to Gerry A. O'Brien. This is where you see the use of the Dot notation. The object we are working with is objADSIObject and the property that we are manipulating, which comes after the dot, is the FullName property. You can see how the property and the object that it belongs to are separated by the dot (.). Methods follow the same syntax.

The last line of code simply confirms this for you by displaying the value for the full name in a message box as was displayed in Figure 7.1.

The objects that you work with in ADSI are a part of a namespace. Namespaces will be discussed in the next section.

Namespaces

ADSI providers, for the purpose of defining the objects that are contained within their specific directory service, use namespaces. Windows Active Directory uses its own namespace for the purpose of allowing users to resolve an object in the namespace by specifying that name within the namespace.

The namespace that I'm referring to is merely a collection of related objects and their methods and properties, which are collectively placed under one umbrella. With .NET coming out later this year, the term *namespace* will see more widespread use as the object models in .NET are considered namespaces.

7

ADSI
ARCHITECTURE

Different providers will use different naming schemes for their namespaces and the objects within them, which can make life a little more difficult for you when it comes time to work with different providers in one network. One of ADSI's goals is to make this easier for you by providing a naming framework that makes it easier to access the various network providers' namespaces.

ADSI does this through the use of ADsPath strings. These strings contain an identifier that tells you and ADSI which provider you are working with. The following list shows the available ADsPaths for the providers that are currently supported by ADSI out of the box:

- Ads://
- LDAP://
- WinNT://
- NDS://
- NWCOMPAT://

The provider names will be included within a set of double quotation marks and will include the necessary object names. For example, look at this line of code:

```
GetObject ("LDAP://Celeron500/CN=Gerry O'Brien,
➥CN=users,DC=gkcomput,DC=com")
```

> **NOTE**
>
> The names that you see here are case sensitive, meaning that they must be specified exactly as you see them here.

You saw an example earlier in the code of Listing 7.1. The line following has been changed a bit to reflect the correct use of the namespace without the addition of the variable name that was used in the code.

```
"WinNT://gkcomput/PIII500/gobrien"
```

Here you see that we are using the WinNT provider which deals with Windows NT and Windows 2000 non Active Directory networks. The full namespace specifies the provider, the domain, the computer, and then the user account.

ADSI Providers

As mentioned earlier in the chapter, each directory service provider makes the necessary namespace available to ADSI. By doing so, ADSI handles all of the necessary inner workings to connect to the provider's implementations and exposes the necessary interfaces for you to work with. The directory service or ADSI provider would be a company such as Microsoft or Novell that would write the necessary implementations. An example of how this works is illustrated in Figure 7.2.

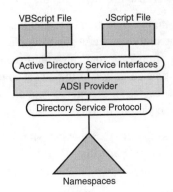

FIGURE 7.2

An example of how a directory service provider's namespace is accessed via ADSI.

As you can see from Figure 7.2, your script files communicate through the ADSI interface to the ADSI provider. From there, the ADSI provider uses the underlying directory service protocols supplied by the ADSI provider. These protocols know how to talk to the various namespace objects of that provider. This shows you that you don't have to know or understand these protocols as long as you can write your scripts to work with the ADSI interface.

It is the responsibility of the various directory service providers to ensure that their protocols and interfaces are compliant with the ADSI architecture. This means that you can be assured that your code will work within a heterogeneous network environment. You can access and manipulate objects using ADSI in a network that contains Windows 2000 Servers in an Active Directory domain with NetWare Bindery and NDS servers as well as Windows NT 4.0 servers. All of this using a common interface.

Of course, these network OS vendors are not the only providers of ADSI interfaces. Microsoft offers two more that you can use with the same techniques that you are learning here. Microsoft Exchange and Internet Information Server 5.0 have ADSI interfaces, as they are directory services as well. You can use these techniques in this book to gain access to the objects within the Exchange directory to manipulate user mailboxes, messages, and other Exchange objects. You can also access and manipulate Web sites and services on Internet Information Services.

ADSI Schema Model

The term *schema* has never really set well with me for the simple reason that it sounds too much like *scheme*. *Schema* sounds like a sneaky person trying to devise some method of swindling me out of my money. The tax man and my wife take care of that without any scheming.

In terms of ADSI, schema refers to the collection or model that contains the various objects' definitions that are part of the directory service. As an example for those familiar with programming, the schema would be similar to what you would see in the Object Browser with Visual Basic or by checking the type definition of the objects. For those not familiar with Visual Basic's Object Browser, consider the schema to be a dictionary of sorts that contains the definition or explanation of the various objects.

You can create client applications or script files that can search through a schema and determine the features that are present in that particular ADSI implementation. This is also known as enumeration and will be covered in Chapter 10, "Enumerating ADSI Objects."

Some providers will make their schemas extensible. This means that they can publish new interfaces or add new objects to their schema at any time. This allows you to access the new objects or work with the new interfaces while you can continue to use the schema as it existed before the upgrade.

Schema objects are divided into three types: classes, properties, and syntaxes. Each of these objects has its own interface as outlined and described here:

- IADsClass—Used for schema class objects. These objects must provide class definitions for the ADSI objects.

- IADsProperty—Used to manage the attribute definition of an ADSI object. This definition indicates values such as minimum and maximum as well as the syntax for the object.

- IADsSyntax—This interface is used to determine the methods that can be used with the object for identification and modification of the data types that the object uses for representation of its data.

Programming Language Support

In this section, you will see some discussion on the support that is available in ADSI for the languages that we talked about earlier in the book. As was mentioned then, ADSI is available to any language that is COM compliant, such as Visual Basic and Java.

Although ADSI allows you to create full-fledged computer applications and Microsoft Management Console (MMC) snap-ins to access and manipulate ADSI objects, that won't be covered here as your goal is to administer your distributed network with the help of scripting and the ADSI objects. With scripting, you will create applets, which are small applications that are not compiled into a binary form like standalone applications are.

You already know that you can use VBScript and JScript as languages for creating your scripts in WSH. What you may not know is all the possibilities that exist for creating and executing scripts.

Throughout the book you have seen most of the examples set as standalone scripts that you execute from a command line using CScript.exe or by double-clicking the script file name in Explorer view to execute the script using WScript.exe. This is likely the most common style of ADSI scripting that you will use. You can write these scripts in any supported language of your choosing such as VBScript, or even Perl.

You saw in Chapter 3, "Creating Scripts," and Chapter 4, "How to Use Your Scripts," how you can create a Windows script file that contains XML and a combination of scripting languages such as VBScript and JScript. Some of these examples also showed you how to call a function written in one language from another language. This support for multiple languages is a benefit to you in terms of being able to write your scripts in the language you prefer while still reusing scripts that may have been written by someone else on another supported language.

Another advantage of the various languages supported by ADSI is the ability to create Web-based front ends or Active Server Pages that can access your ADSI objects over a TCP/IP connection and display those objects and results using an HTML page displayed in your browser. Of course there are security implications by doing this so you need to take caution when exposing your ADSI in this way. That is one reason why ASP was mentioned. By running the scripts in ASP pages on your server, you can control the access to the ADSI objects and ensure that the ASP pages are not exposed.

Even though you are learning scripting with this book, you may have a need to develop a standalone application for accessing ADSI. Most of the time this will be accomplished by software developers. ADSI includes support for full programming languages such as Visual Basic, Java, and C++. VB and Java can access ADSI through the standard COM interfaces that you are accessing with your scripts, but developers using C++ need another mechanism to gain access to the ADSI schema.

ADSI makes a set of APIs available that C++ developers can call and work with that provide the necessary access to the ADSI schema. These APIs are not COM compliant but are actually wrappers for the COM interfaces that are not native to C++.

Also remember that Microsoft built ADSI to be extensible and also published the necessary information for other script and programming language vendors to use as a guideline for making their languages work with ADSI. Chances are that if your favorite scripting language is not supported yet, it may very well be supported in the future.

With the range of languages already supported and with two of the easiest to learn already incorporated into WSH, you don't really have any excuse for not using it for your repetitive and time-consuming administrative tasks.

Summary

ADSI consists of objects that are accessed through their various namespaces. Using this architecture, ADSI makes available to you the necessary mechanisms to access the underlying structures and objects to perform your administrative tasks.

Each namespace that you work with is provided from the directory service vendor. These vendors make their internal protocols and access mechanisms available to a common ADSI interface, which reduces or eliminates the need for you to understand multiple interfaces and complicate API syntax just to access your network resources. This translates into lower learning curves, which further translates into savings in reducing the amount of time and resources required for learning these interfaces.

The support that ADSI has for programming languages covers the range of the most popular languages used today. Visual Basic and VBScript, as well as Java, Jscript, and C++ mean that you can create scripts, ASP pages, and full-fledged standalone applications that can all access and manipulate ADSI and its objects.

This all translates into a little more work up front, but a great time saver, because you can create scripts and applications that can take away the repetitive and mundane administrative tasks that you need to deal with on a daily basis.

Using ADSI

So far you have heard a great deal about what ADSI is and what you can do with it. You have read through chapters that talked about the interfaces that ADSI provides and the various languages it supports. This chapter will start you on your way to becoming proficient in using WSH and ADSI for your administrative needs. You won't rehash what has been covered thus far; instead, you will get started right away by learning how to access the ADSI features you need.

Binding to ADSI Objects

In order for you to work with ADSI, the first step you must perform, after learning the scripting language and reading this far in the book, is to bind to an ADSI object. What does binding mean? To bind to an ADSI object means that you must make a connection to that object using a binding string that associates a variable with the ADSI object you want to work with.

As you might remember from our discussion on objects and variables, a variable is a location in memory that stores the data you need to work with. In this case, the variable contains a reference to the actual ADSI object that you have specified making access to the object and its underlying structures easier. Once you bind the ADSI object to the variable, you will use the variable to refer to the ADSI object rather than referring to the object itself directly.

This actually has a benefit and that will be explained here, because I know you must be thinking, "Why not just refer to the ADSI object directly? Why all this fooling around with another name for something?" The reasoning behind it is so that you can access the same ADSI objects from multiple scripts at the same time if you want to. This provides a mechanism for you to know which object you are dealing with and can help to reduce confusion. It also ensures that changes made during one script session do not inadvertently affect any other sessions.

As you will see when working with various ADSI providers, the syntax of the binding string may vary. Each provider may require different information to be supplied in the binding string. Some of that information may be what is shown in this list:

- *Username*—Used to verify access to the object.
- *Password*—Used in conjunction with the username when security is set on the ADSI objects and authentication is required.
- *Server name*—Obviously a much needed piece of information to ensure that you are communicating with the correct server.
- *Encryption*—If encryption has been used you can specify the methods used.

These are just a few of the possibilities ,and, as was mentioned earlier in this section, each provider is free to implement their own requirements for the binding string. They will be documented so that you will know what is required when you write your binding strings.

Throughout the examples given in this book, you will see examples of binding strings that relate to WinNT for use on Windows NT 4.0 servers, NT workstations, and Windows 2000 Professional workstations, as well as LDAP for use with Active Directory on Windows 2000 and Windows 2002 domains.

The ADSI Binding String

The ADSI binding string is what you use to bind to an ADSI object. Binding strings apply to the various directory service providers. There are two that will be discussed here as they relate to the Windows Active Directory (AD) directory services.

WinNT Binding String

The syntax for the WinNT binding string is shown here:

```
WinNT:[//DomainName[/ComputerName[/ObjectName[,className]]]]
```

Note that the square brackets indicate the information contained within is optional. This means that you can specify just `WinNT://` for binding or add the other optional parameters. If you leave the optional parameters off, you will connect to the `root` object on the server and all objects will be available as a result.

An example is shown here:

```
Set objADSIObject = GetObject("WinNT://DomainName/
➥ComputerName/ADSIObject", class")
```

Breaking this string down into its parts will allow you to see what is required. The first word in the string is `Set`. This is a keyword that is used to assign the ADSI object to the variable that you have created. In the world of programming, any time you want to assign an object to a variable, you use the `Set` keyword.

The next part of the string is `objADSIObject`. This is the name of the variable that you wish to assign the object reference to. This variable name should be descriptive enough that you or another user will understand its purpose just by looking at its name. Variables also must adhere to naming conventions. These are simple and are listed here:

- Must begin with a letter or an underscore
- Can contain numbers
- May contain special characters

One thing that you may notice about my sample name here and those used throughout my code is the way I write my variable names. This convention comes from many years of programming that started out with lessons from some of the best-known programmers and authors. It's a great habit to get into, and I tell all my students to start it at the onset and it will be second nature every time you code.

The first part of the variable name is `obj`. This is used to represent the fact that it will hold a reference to an object. If it were to hold an integer value, you would use `int`, or for a string value I would use `str`. A big advantage is the fact that this can help to make your code self-documenting to a certain degree. When looking at variable names, you instantly know what type of data is stored in them.

> **NOTE**
>
> You can also use what is known as *camel notation*. This is where you capitalize initial letters of words in the name, which usually makes the variable name look like a camel's hump with a capital letter in the middle. You are free to choose your own naming conventions.

The next part of this string is the = symbol. It is easy to call this an equals symbol, which for all intents and purposes it is. In the world of coding, however, it is referred to as an assignment statement, unless it is being used in a mathematical expression. What it is saying here is, "Take what is on the right side of me and assign it to what is on the left side of me." You will see that the right hand side must equate to a single entity before this assignment can take place. This simply means that nothing will be assigned to the variable until the object is retrieved using the `GetObject` function.

Speaking of `GetObject`, this is the next part of the string. This is actually a function that is built into WSH as a result of its COM implementation. There are two methods to get an object. The first, `CreateObject`, is used to create an instance of an object that does not exist. For our purpose we don't need to be concerned with this. You will work with the `GetObject` function, which will return an object that already exists. ADSI objects are already created, hence they already exist, which is why we only need to *get* the object rather than *create* it.

The `GetObject` function requires certain arguments to complete its task. These are found in the string that is contained within double quotes in the parentheses. This string is known as the ADsPath and it consists of two parts, the Provider and the path to the computer or object. As mentioned earlier in the chapter, you will only be looking at two providers, WinNT and LDAP. In the example string, WinNT has been specified as the provider.

The second part is the path to the object that you want to work with. This path can contain something as simple as a domain name where it will return the domain as the root and allow access to all ADSI objects in the domain. Such a binding string might look like this:

```
Set objMyObject = GetObject("WinNT://gkcomput")
```

When used in an enumeration script, this binding string produced the following output:

```
Microsoft (R) Windows Script Host Version 5.6
Copyright (C) Microsoft Corporation 1996-2001. All rights reserved.

Administrator
bobrien
dobrien
gobrien
Guest
HelpAssistant
IUSR_CELERON500
IWAM_CELERON500
krbtgt
NetShowServices
SUPPORT_388945a0
DnsUpdateProxy
Domain Admins
Domain Computers
Domain Controllers
Domain Guests
Domain Users
Enterprise Admins
Group Policy Creator Owners
Schema Admins
Administrators
Users
Guests
Print Operators
Backup Operators
Replicator
Remote Desktop Users
Network Configuration Operators
Server Operators
Account Operators
Pre-Windows 2000 Compatible Access
Cert Publishers
RAS and IAS Servers
NetShow Administrators
IIS_WPG
HelpServicesGroup
WINS Users
DHCP Users
DHCP Administrators
DnsAdmins
BRANDON
CELERON366
CELERON500
```

```
P3
PII350
PIII500
PPRO
Schema
```

As you can see from this list, there are quite a few items in my Active Directory domain. The list starts off with users, then groups, and finally computer accounts that reside on my domain controller. This is also an example of how you can enumerate a directory service or domain to determine what objects are available to work with.

If you wanted to, you could bind to a specific computer within the domain as well. All you would have to do is extend the path to include the computer name, as shown here:

```
Set objMyObject = GetObject("WinNT://gkcomput/PIII500")
```

Note the difference between the previous output and the output listed here when I enumerate the objects on a specific computer:

```
Microsoft (R) Windows Script Host Version 5.6
Copyright (C) Microsoft Corporation 1996-2001. All rights reserved.
Administrator
gobrien
Guest
IUSR_PIII500
IWAM_PIII500
SQLDebugger
VUSR_PIII500
VUSR_PIII5001
Administrators
Backup Operators
Guests
Power Users
Replicator
Users
Debugger Users
PIII500 Admins
PIII500 Authors
PIII500 Browsers
VS Developers
Alerter
AppMgmt
aspstate
Browser
cisvc
ClipSrv
CORRTSvc
```

```
DbgProxy
Dhcp
dmadmin
dmserver
Dnscache
Eventlog
EventSystem
Fax
IISADMIN
lanmanserver
lanmanworkstation
LmHosts
MDM
Messenger
mnmsrvc
MSDTC
MSFTPSVC
MSIServer
NetDDE
NetDDEdsdm
Netlogon
Netman
NtLmSsp
NtmsSvc
PerfCounterService
PlugPlay
PolicyAgent
ProtectedStorage
RasAuto
RasMan
RemoteAccess
RemoteRegistry
RpcLocator
RpcSs
RSVP
SamSs
ScardDrv
ScardSvr
Schedule
seclogon
SENS
SharedAccess
SMTPSVC
Spooler
SysmonLog
TapiSrv
```

```
TlntSvr
TrkWks
UPS
UtilMan
Visual Studio Analyzer RPC bridge
W32Time
W3SVC
WinMgmt
Wmi
```

The objects you see here are the ones that are available on my Windows 2000 Professional computer. If you were to enumerate objects on your computer, you would no doubt come up with some different objects, but there would be similar objects as well that most Windows 2000 computers have (for instance, the W3SVC object, which indicates that IIS is installed and running).

The LDAP Binding String

The LDAP binding string is used to bind to a Windows 2000 or later Active Directory. The syntax for the LDAP binding string is shown here:

```
LDAP://HostName[:PortNumber][/DistinguishedName]
```

When you take a look at this binding string you will notice first of all the provider name at the beginning specified as LDAP://.

The HostName portion can have one of three possible values. It can be a computer name, an IP address for a computer, or a domain name.

You will also notice that there are two optional parameters in this binding string. The first of these is the PortNumber parameter. The port number can be specified if you have multiple directory service providers installed on the same server that use the same port number. For example, Active Directory uses port 389 by default. Exchange Server also uses this port by default. This means that your scripts could communicate with the wrong provider. By specifying a port number that has been assigned to the provider, you can be assured that your scripts are working with the correct provider.

NOTE

If you are using SSL for secure communications then the default port for AD is 636.

If you want to bind to a specific object using the LDAP binding string, you must specify the object's Distinguished Name (DN). A DN is the full path to an ADSI object.

> **NOTE**
>
> Distinguished Names are unique in Active Directory and point to one and only one object within the directory.

LDAP uses abbreviations for the naming attributes of the various components of the object and its path. Active Directory does not use the same abbreviations for some of these attributes. The naming attributes are listed in Table 8.1 with the LDAP and Active Directory equivalents side by side.

TABLE 8.1   Naming Conventions for LDAP and AD Objects and Paths

LDAP	AD	Description
cn	cn	Common name of an object, normally a user object
ou	ou	Organizational unit
dc	dc	Domain component
o	dc	Organization (AD uses the domain component in place of the organization)
c		Country (AD does not use a country name attribute)

The DN for an object works its way from left to right starting with the object itself. An example is given here:

```
cn=gobrien,ou=ppro,dc=gkcomput,dc=com
```

This DN specifies the `gobrien` user account found in the `ppro` organizational unit in the `gkcomput.com` domain.

Binding Types

The WinNT and LDAP binding strings are the two that you will likely use the most, but we will discuss two other binding methods in the sections "Serverless Binding and RootDSE" and "Binding to the Global Catalog (GC)."

Serverless Binding and RootDSE

What is meant by serverless binding? This term refers to binding to a server without explicitly setting that server name in the binding string. Specifying the server name in the binding string is known as hard coding. This means that the server name is fixed in the binding string, and it cannot be changed without changing the script file to update the server name.

Active Directory allows you to use serverless binding by binding to the *best* server in the AD domain. It does this by choosing the server that best fits in the security context of the calling computer. This means that AD will search for the domain controller in the currently logged on domain. If there is more than one domain controller present, AD will attempt to select the server based on other criteria, such as IP address subnets. If a domain controller cannot be found in the current subnet, AD will select the first available domain controller.

RootDSE refers to the root of a directory information tree that resides on a directory server, normally a domain controller. The rootDSE is used to provide information about the directory server only and is not considered a part of any namespace.

The syntax for rootDSE is shown here:

```
LDAP://rootDSE
```

As you can see, the server name is not specified; therefore, ADSI will search for a domain controller as mentioned earlier.

Table 8.2 lists the properties that are associated with the rootDSE.

TABLE 8.2   Properties Associated with the RootDSE

Property	Description
CurrentTime	Current time for the directory server that you are connected to.
SubschemaSubentry	This is the DN for the subschema object. For more information on this property, search the Internet for RFC 2251.
DsServiceName	The DN used for the NTDS settings for the directory server.
NamingContexts	The DNs for all naming contexts that the directory server stores. Windows 2000 servers contain at least three, Configuration, Schema, and for the domain of which the server is a member. This is a multi-value property.
DefaultNamingContext	This stores the DN for the domain of which the server is a member.
SchemaNamingContext	This is the DN for the schema container.
ConfigurationNamingContext	The DN for the configuration container.
RootDomainNamingContext	DN for the parent domain, or first domain within the forest of which this server's domain is a member.

TABLE 8.2 Continued

Property	Description
SupportedControl	Another multi-value property used for specifying controls that are supported by the directory server. (These controls are mostly used by C++ developers. For an overview of them, search MSDN for the phrase "Binding Types Specific to Active Directory.")
SupportedLDAPVersion	This property contains multiple values used to specify the LDAP major versions supported on the directory server.
DnsHostName	DNS address for the connected directory server.
LDAPServiceName	Active Directory uses a Service Principal Name (SPN) for mutual authentication. This property returns this value for the directory server.
ServerName	The DN for the directory server.

This type of binding is more suited for building applications that will access ADSI rather than administrative tasks using WSH so we won't cover it in any more detail than what is presented here.

Binding to the Global Catalog (GC)

This section will briefly discuss binding to the global catalog (GC) in terms of the theory only. The main reason for binding to the GC is to enable applications written in C/C++ or Visual Basic to enumerate the objects in the catalog. The main purpose of this book is to teach you scripting for administrative tasks and not application development, so this section will be informational only.

The GC is itself simply a namespace. Within the GC you will find directory information from all of the domains that reside in your forest. It does not contain every property that exists for all of the objects. Only those properties that have been specified to be included in the GC will be listed and available.

The location of the GC is on domain controllers within the network. Only domain controllers can contain the GC. You can determine which domain controllers will participate as servers for the GC by configuring those servers' participation in the AD Sites and Services Manager.

You can search across all domains that exist in your forest by binding to the root object in your enterprise. This would be similar to binding to the root domain controller that resides in your forest and obtaining all of the objects that exist in the entire Active Directory.

You can also bind to a specific object, such as a domain controller within the forest, and enumerate all of its objects along with its child objects' objects. To bind to the root of the GC you use GC: in the binding string in the same way as you would use LDAP: or WinNT:.

Binding Programmatically

You can choose two methods of binding to ADSI objects. The first method is likely the one you will use most often and is one you have seen in the book so far. It is known as binding directly to an object using the ADSI functions. The other method is to use ADO, also known as ActiveX Data Objects. You will see each of these in the next sections.

Binding Directly to an Object

If you want to bind directly to an ADSI object, you can do so with any language that supports automation. Languages such as JScript and VBScript come to mind again because they are included with WSH, but you can also use languages such as Java and Visual Basic.

There is an ADSI function that allows you to bind to the objects from these languages. This function is called GetObject. You have already seen examples of using this function in the book so far. The most recent example is in Chapter 7, "ADSI Architecture," in Listing 7.1, where you used a script called userfullname.vbs to get a user account object and set the full name for that user.

The line of code containing the GetObject function from that listing is shown here for your convenience:

```
Set objADSIObject = GetObject("WinNT://gkcomput/PIII500/" & _
➡strUserName & ",user")
```

As you can see by this line of code, the GetObject function is using a full ADsPath to reach the user object. Remember that strUserName is a variable that was used to hold the actual username that you wanted to request. The ADsPath is always enclosed in parentheses as you see here.

The first part of the code is responsible for setting the result of the GetObject function, or in other words, the object returned by the function, to an object variable called objADSIObject. An object variable is simply a variable that is capable of holding an object.

NOTE

This style of binding to an ADSI object will use the current logged on user credentials for authentication. If the user does not have sufficient privileges to access the object or to execute the script, the operation will fail. In this case, he will have to use the ADsOpenObject function described in the following section.

ADsOpenObject

As mentioned in the note regarding the user credentials and the GetObject function, if the currently logged on user does not have the necessary permissions to access the object, he must use the ADsOpenObject function instead. The ADsOpenObject function is a part of the IADsOpenDSObject interface. An example of using this is shown here. This code is not intended to be executable:

```
Dim objIADsObject As IADsOpenDSObject

Set objIADsObject = GetObject("LDAP:")

objIADsObject.OpenDSObject("LDAP://CN=gobrien,DC=gkcomput,DC=com",
                    ➥ "Administrator", "password",
                    ➥ ADS_SECURE_AUTHENTICATION)
```

Following this code snippet, you can see that we declare an object variable to hold a reference to the IADsOpenDSObject object. We then use the GetObject function to return the LDAP namespace to our object.

Don't get confused by the fact that we are using GetObject here. It is still necessary to return the namespace object.

Once you set the namespace to your object in line two, use the OpenDSObject function of the IADsOpenDSObject interface and pass it some arguments. These are found within the parentheses.

The first argument is the ADsPath that you are familiar with by now. We are binding to the gobrien user account on the gkcomput.com domain. The next two arguments are the user account and password that you want to use for the operation. The last argument is the ADS_SECURE_AUTHENTICATION flag. This last argument will be discussed in the next section.

For the most part, you will be logged in as an Administrator or have Administrator rights when you are executing scripts but this example can be utilized for a couple of purposes.

One, you may be logged on to a user's workstation with his or her credentials to resolve an issue, and you may need to execute a script that requires higher privileges than the user has.

The second instance might arise where you have delegated a specific user to run certain scripts on your behalf, but you don't want that user to have elevated privileges outside of the scripts. When you use the ADsOpenObject you are communicating with an AD Domain Controller. This is discussed in the next section.

Communicating with an AD Domain Controller

As you saw in the preceding section dealing with the ADsOpenObject function, you must provide a username and password to use the GetObject function when you are logged in using an account that doesn't have the appropriate permissions.

8

USING ADSI

As the title of this section indicates, this is known as communicating with the AD domain controller. You can use one of three possible username types when you communicate this way. These are listed here:

- *Downlevel logon*—This style allows the use of an organization name and username such as gkcomput\gobrien or simply the username.
- *Distinguished name*—A full distinguished name such as CN=Gerry O'Brien, OU=Marketing, DC=GKComput, or DC=COM.
- *User principal name (UPN)*—An example would be gobrien@gkcomput.com.

Any one of these username styles may be used in the place of the username entry in the arguments list for the ADsOpenObject function.

The last argument used earlier in the function call was one of many flags that you can use as well with the ADsOpenObject function. All available flags are listed in Table 8.3.

TABLE 8.3   Available Flags for the ADsOpenObject Function

Flag	Description
ADS_SECURE_AUTHENTICATION	Use this flag to request secure authentication for the function call. If you are using the WinNT provider, the NTLM (NT Lan Manager) will be used to authenticate the call. If you are using LDAP for Active Directory, the Kerberos protocol will be used.
ADS_USE_ENCRYPTION	In order to use this flag, ensure that your server has SSL installed and configured correctly. For Active Directory, this will also require the installation of Certificate Services.
ADS_USE_SSL	This flag indicates that the data will be encrypted using SSL.
ADS_READONLY_SERVER	This has two different meanings depending on whether you are using WinNT or LDAP for AD. If you are using WinNT, this will cause an attempt to connect to a PDC or BDC. If you are using LDAP, this flag will only be used if you are performing serverless binding.
ADS_NO_AUTHENTICATION	This indicates that no authentication is required. If you are using LDAP, the provider will connect to the server but no binding will occur.

TABLE 8.3 Continued

Flag	Description
ADS_FAST_BIND	When you set this flag, only the base interfaces will be exposed. This can be used to increase performance, but there is a trade off. ADSI will not verify the objects, because not all of the objects are returned.
ADS_USE_SIGNING	This flag must be used in conjunction with the ADS_SECURE_AUTHENTICATION flag. This flag is used to verify the integrity of the data sent.
ADS_USE_SEALING	This flag will cause the data to be encrypted using Kerberos. Once again the ADS_SECURE_AUTHENTICATION flag must be set as well.
ADS_USE_DELEGATION	If you will be moving objects across domains, this flag must be set. It will cause ADSI to delegate the logged on user account's security context.
ADS_SERVER_BIND	This flag is used for Windows 2000 Service Pack 1 and later systems. If you have an LDAP provider and you have specified the server name in the binding string, use this flag to avoid unnecessary traffic.

8

Binding to ADSI with ActiveX Data Objects

Microsoft introduced a new data access mechanism known as ActiveX Data Objects. This object model is enjoying wide spread use due in part to its simplicity. Ask any programmer who has had to deal with Data Access Objects which they prefer, and you are sure to hear that ADO is the preferred method.

Another advantage of ADO is that it can be used to access Object Linking and Embedding DataBase (OLE DB) data sources. OLE DB is an open set of interface standards that allow access to relational data in various data stores. ADSI is an OLE DB provider therefore, you can access ADSI as an OLE DB interface using ADO. Are there enough acronyms for you in this paragraph?

In order to access the data using ADO, you must create a connection string. This connection string sets up the necessary parameters needed to connect to the data source. These arguments are normally the data store name and any credentials that may be needed. An example is shown here:

```
Dim objConn As New Connection
Set objConn = CreateObject("ADODB.Connection")
```

```
objConn.Provider = "ADsDSOObject"
objConn.Properties("User ID") = "gobrien"
objConn.Properties("Password") = "password"
objConn.Properties("Encrypt Password") = True
objConn.Open
```

In this example, a variable was created to hold a reference to a connection object. The connection object is then set to reference the `ADODB.Connection` object that is created using the `CreateObject` function.

You will notice that there are properties set before the connection is opened. These are only necessary if the currently logged on user does not have sufficient privileges to create the object.

You may also have noticed that we have not tried to bind to a specific object in ADSI. This is because using ADO and OLE DB does not allow binding to a specific object directly. You have to run a query on an object to return what is known as a resultset that contains the properties of the object. Normally this is not required with WSH and scripting access to ADSI, because you will use binding strings in your code.

Connection Caching

As with all networks today, yours will likely be congested, and the last thing you want to do is to add more traffic to that congestion. Some networks are running high speed backbones, but not all have the high speed connections available within subnets or domains. Also, for anyone operating in a WAN environment, the need to transfer large amounts of data across that WAN connection is neither advisable nor wanted. ADSI offers you the ability to cache your connection information preventing the need to make that round trip to the server.

With ADSI, once you have established the connection, that connection is cached on the client that requested it. Once you have created a connection and have created objects that make use of that connection, ADSI uses handles to keep track of the objects. These handles are what are cached and will remain on all objects that have not been destroyed.

As you read earlier in the book, objects take up memory when they are created and release that memory when they are destroyed.

When you create a connection to a server, you have connected using three parameters, the server name, a port number, and credentials. Remember from earlier in the chapter that we talked about the port numbers for ADSI. The default port is 389, and port 686 is used for SSL connections.

If you happen to set all of your objects to nothing, which destroys them, you will lose your connection handles. When this happens, you must bind to the server again. When you do this, you must make a trip to the server to return the information on the objects again. This is where your network traffic can increase. This doesn't mean that you have to cache every connection that you make. Listing 8.1 is an example of a script that makes use of caching.

LISTING 8.1 An Example of Using Caching on a Connection

```
Dim objCacheConn
Dim objIADs
Dim strCacheName
Dim strName
' Connect to the server and maintain the handle in order to cache the
' connection.
Set objCacheConn = GetObject("LDAP://celeron500/DC=gkcomput,DC=com")
strCacheName = objCacheConn.Get("distinguishedName")
WScript.Echo (strCacheName)
' Reuse the connection to celeron500 opened by objCacheConn.
' This line will execute faster because it doesn't
' have to go across the network a second time.
Set objIADs =GetObject("LDAP://celeron500/CN=Users,DC=gkcomput,DC=com")
strName = objIADs.Get("distinguishedName")
WScript.Echo (strName)
' Destroy the second connection's object.
Set objIADs = Nothing

' Reuse the connection to celeron500 opened by objCacheConn again.
Set objIADs = GetObject("LDAP://celeron500/
➥ CN=Administrator,CN=Users,DC=gkcomput,DC=com")
strName = objIADs.Get("distinguishedName")
Wscript.Echo (strName)
' Destroy the second connection's object again.
Set objIADs = Nothing
' Destroy the first connection's object.
Set objCacheConn = Nothing
```

When you run this script, replace the domain names and computer names with those on your network. Running the script on my computer produces the message boxes shown in Figures 8.1–8.3.

FIGURE 8.1

The first message box displayed as a result of the objCacheConn *object.*

FIGURE 8.2

The next message box displayed has the Users group added but is still using the object created earlier.

FIGURE 8.3

The result of destroying a connection object and then reusing it.

> **NOTE**
>
> When you run this script, be sure to run it across the network to reach a remote server. An example would be to execute the script on a workstation so that it is contacting an AD Domain Controller. This will show the true reason for caching.

Run the script from Listing 8.1 and note the time that it takes to display the first message box. Then, compare that with how quickly the two remaining message boxes are displayed. If that still doesn't convince you, try this. Comment out the lines in the script that set the objects to nothing. Execute the script one more time to create the objects and the cache. When it has finished executing, run it again. Note how fast the first message box is displayed in comparison to previously. This shows an example of how maintaining a handle to an object will keep that information in the cache. The script didn't have to back to the server to retrieve it.

The only advantage that you gain is when you are executing scripts that will be communicating with the server on a constant basis requesting ADSI objects. For the occasional script, caching is not really necessary as the data is only retrieved on a sporadic basis rather than continuously.

Summary

In this chapter, you have been presented with a fair bit of material on using ADSI. You learned that in order to access the objects that reside in ADSI you must bind to them using a binding string. You learned what binding strings are composed of and how to create them.

Next, you took at look at the different types of binding available. We talked about serverless binding and how it causes the system to go out and look for the closest server to connect to when no server name is given. You also saw how to programmatically bind to the ADSI objects from outside the scripting environment.

You saw how to bind to objects using the `GetObject` and `ADsGetObject` functions, and you learned the differences between the two. `GetObject` is the most commonly used function for connecting to the objects, and is used in WSH.

There was a brief discussion on using ADO to connect to and request information from ADSI using the OLE DB set of interfaces.

The chapter finished off with a discussion and demonstration script on the use of caching the connections to help reduce the amount of traffic needed to pass across the network.

The information learned here will present a good foundation for you to continue through the rest of the book and learn more about connecting to and manipulating the ADSI objects available using WSH.

8

USING ADSI

Accessing Data with ADSI

IN THIS CHAPTER

The first thing to note about this chapter is the fact that it is not about accessing data from databases but accessing the data that resides in ADSI. As mentioned in previous chapters in the book, ADSI objects have properties. It is these properties that you will access using ADSI. This chapter will discuss how you go about doing that.

The ADSI objects that you will be working with contain what are known as *interfaces* to their properties. These interfaces are not a visual interface such as you might see in a Windows application, but rather a logical interface that provides the necessary mechanisms for accessing the underlying data. These mechanisms are known as *methods*.

There are four different ways to gain access to the data in the objects in ADSI. These are listed here with a brief explanation of each:

- `IADs` interface—This interface has two methods, `Get` and `GetEx`, that you can use to retrieve a specific property by name. Every ADSI object that is a COM object has an IADs interface.

- `IDirectory` object—This method uses the `GetObjectAttributes` function to retrieve a list of values. These values are returned in an array of structures that hold the values you requested. You must supply a list of the names of the properties that you want to retrieve.

- `IADsPropertyList` Interface—You can use this interface for enumerating all properties of a given object. You specify the object that you want to return the properties for.

- `IADs` special interfaces—These are used to return special properties that are not stored in an object. Some of these methods are the `Get_Name` method which will return the objects relative distinguished name (RDN). The `get_Class` method will return the object's class, and the `get_Parent` method will return the path to the object's parent object.

ADSI allows you to cache the properties that you have read from the server. This cache resides on the local computer and can provide a performance increase by not requiring round trips to the server when you want to read the data that resides in the object properties.

You can also choose the properties that you want to cache as well as update the cache. You may not want to cache all of the objects that are returned for various reasons. The most obvious is to prevent the cache from taking up too much RAM on the local computer. If the local computer does not have sufficient RAM, the caching can offset the performance increase gained on the network side.

You must retrieve the properties first before you can read the values associated with those properties. The data types that are returned will be dependant on the property that you are reading the value from.

ADSI Properties and Attributes

Sometimes the documentation can get confusing when there are different terms used for the same concept. One area that is most confusing is when authors write about information that is to be passed to functions. The placeholders in the function are known as *parameters* and the information that is passed is known as *arguments*. A fair bit of people use these two terms interchangeably. I have a habit of doing so as well.

The reason I mention this is that there is also another situation where there are two terms used to describe the same concept. These two terms are *properties* and *attributes*. The terms are used to refer to the describing aspects of the objects you work with in ADSI. A property or attribute is a physical describing piece of information about that object. An example is the name of an object. This can be classified as the Name property or the Name attribute. Both terms will be used interchangeably, both in this book and in other documentation that you will read, so hopefully this helps to clear up any confusion that you may have regarding these terms.

Working with ADSI Objects and Their Properties

Earlier on in the book you learned how to bind to ADSI objects. Once you have bound to the objects, you can then return the required information from those objects by querying the properties and then reading the values. For the most part, you will be accessing these properties to manipulate them in some way. You may be setting properties for user accounts or mapping network drives.

> **NOTE**
>
> Appendix A, "WSH Reference," lists all the properties that are a part of the ADSI objects that you will be working with. You can use this reference to determine what properties are available for you to work with but the list only refers to Active Directory objects for Windows 2000/XP.

If you are using a different directory service provider or a combination of providers you will need to bind to the provider namespace and enumerate the objects and their properties. You saw an example of enumerating directory service objects in Chapter 8, "Using ADSI."

The ADSI interfaces will expose some of the properties for you, such as the Name and Class properties. For some of the other properties, you will have to use other methods such as the IADs Get and Put methods, which allow you to retrieve and set, respectively, the properties of ADSI objects.

Property Cache

Chapter 11, "Searching Active Directory," will discuss some performance issues when it comes to searching ADSI objects, and one of the topics presented will be caching. ADSI uses client-side caching to provide performance enhancements for searching and manipulating ADSI objects.

As was mentioned earlier, the cache can provide performance gains to your ADSI searches and property setting by holding a copy of the data in memory on the local computer. In this way, you can make changes to multiple objects' properties and then upload the changes in a batch style.

By using the cache in this way, you reduce the amount of network traffic that is generated by the ADSI searches and property manipulation. If you were making numerous changes and searches without using batch mode, you could cause excessive traffic on the network.

NOTE

Although you will be using WSH and scripting languages mostly for your administrative tasks, you may write standalone applications as well in languages such as Visual Basic. The unfortunate part is that VB does not have any native batching capabilities for setting properties, so you would have to use the caching features of ADSI and upload the settings when all changes are complete.

Caching Internals

So how does this caching work? Envision a table or multidimensional array in the local computer's memory. This table or array provides storage location for the names and values of the object's properties.

When you first create the object that will return the properties with the `Dim` and `Set` keywords, as you have seen throughout the book, this virtual table is created in memory but contains no information. It is just a location for storing the information. You need to load the object's properties from the directory service by calling the `IADs GetInfo` function.

Once you have retrieved all of the object's properties and they are placed into the cache, all calls to the `Get` and `Put` functions will cause the data stored in the local cache to be affected. When you want to write out the changes to the directory service, you use the `SetInfo` method to cause the changes to be written to the directory service that you called it from. See Figure 9.1 for a visual representation of this concept.

NOTE

It is important to note that even though you have called the SetInfo method, this does not guarantee up-to-date information in the local cache. The values that you have modified will be reflected, but any values modified by another process or user will not be reflected. You must call the GetInfo method again to refresh the contents of the local cache.

In a sense, this is like a cursor that is used in database applications for working with records. The cursor determines where in the set of records, or recordset, you currently are. If changes are made prior to the location you are at, you will not see those changes reflected until you refresh the recordset.

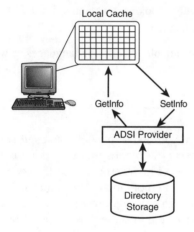

FIGURE 9.1
An example of the local cache and how the GetInfo and SetInfo methods work.

9

Single and Multiple Value Attributes

The Schema for the directory service is where the attributes are defined for the objects available in that directory service. For the most part, the attribute's definition indicates the data type of the attribute and whether or not it can contain multiple values.

If an instance of an attribute is indicated as containing only single values, that attribute can have either zero or one value. This means that the attribute is only allowed to contain one value or none at all and does not support more than one value.

On the other side, if an instance of an attribute supports multiple values, it can have zero, one, or more than one value. The order in which the multiple values exist in the attribute is not specified.

One of the advantages of using ADSI is that it can determine the data type of the value for you and you don't have to write special code to retrieve it. ADSI provides the functionality. The only exception to this rule is if the directory service you are using does not provide Schema that describes the objects and their attributes; you will have to determine the data type yourself.

IADs and IDirectoryObject Interface

The directory service objects that you access using ADSI are manipulated by the COM interfaces IADs and IDirectoryObject. The IDirectoryObject interface is usable only by programming languages that support vtable binding such as C or C++. The IDirectoryObject interface will not be covered in this book as you cannot use it with scripting languages. Therefore, it is not usable within WSH.

However, the IADs interface is available to scripting languages as well as Java, and it is the interface that you will use with WSH.

> **NOTE**
>
> The scripting languages that you use with WSH such as VBScript and JScript are considered *late-bound languages*. This means that they don't bind explicitly to an object before they create it and use it. The interpreter for the scripting language cannot set aside the required amount of memory in advance and cannot check for the proper use of object variables with late binding, but that is not a major concern with scripting. It plays a more important role in standalone applications.

The IADs interface allows the scripting languages to take advantage of some of the housekeeping tasks that are included with ADSI, such as the cache that we talked about earlier. It also allows clients written in script languages to utilize a set of user interface and ActiveX technologies in a set of libraries. This provides for a simpler programming model.

Using IADs

Every ADSI object must support the IADs interface so that its properties and methods are available from scripting languages running under WSH. This means that the object's interfaces

- Provide a method of identifying objects by name, class, or the ADsPath
- Provide the ability to retrieve the Schema definition of the object
- Provide the communication necessary to transfer the object's attributes between the cache and the persistent data store
- Identify the containers for the objects that provide the means for managing the creation and deletion of the objects
- Provide the ability to access the attributes in the local cache

This next list shows the available properties of the IADs interface:

- Name
- Class
- GUID
- ADsPath
- Parent
- Schema

This list shows the available methods for the IADs interface. These methods and properties are explained in the sections that follow with some examples of how to use them:

- SetInfo
- GetInfo
- Get
- Put
- GetEx
- PutEx
- GetInfoEx

The properties that were previously listed represent the data that is held in the ADSI object. They are the attributes that are used to describe the object.

The methods are used to retrieve and to set the properties of the objects. All of these properties and methods are accessed through the COM interfaces that you instantiate and use in your scripts.

The ADSI objects themselves can contain other objects. These are known as *container objects*. When the ADSI object is a container object, it contains additional properties and methods that pertain to being a container object. These properties and methods appear in the following bulleted lists:

- Count—the number of objects in the container
- _NewEnum—property used to enumerate through the collection of objects within the container
- Filter—used to set a filter when searching ADSI objects
- Hints—can be used with ADSI queries to speed searches by providing hints as to the object you are looking for

The IADs container methods are listed next:

- GetObject—used to return an ADSI object
- Create—used to create a new object in the container
- Delete—used to delete an object in the container
- CopyHere—creates a new copy of the specified object in the current container
- MoveHere—moves the specified object to the current container

You will find that almost all of the ADSI objects are contained within other ADSI objects. The most notable exception is the ADSI namespace object ADS, which is the top-level object in the hierarchy.

Accessing Attributes

In order for you to access the various attributes for the ADSI objects, you need a method to work with. This is because the attributes are not available to you directly for manipulation without going through an interface. The methods are the interfaces.

The reasons for this actually stem from the concepts used in object-oriented programming. There is a term used in OOP known as *encapsulation*. Encapsulation is the concept of hiding something within an interface. Hiding doesn't mean that it is not available, but merely that you can't access it directly.

Why is this such as good idea? The main reason is that if you were to allow programmers to directly access the property, there is a good chance that they might corrupt it or, if they are trying to modify it, they may pass in an incorrect data type or invalid data for that property.

By hiding or encapsulating the property and exposing it only through an access method, you can provide a means of checking the value before it gets assigned to the property. You can essentially validate the data. This is what ADSI provides with the access methods that will be discussed in this and the following sections. You will look at the methods to extract the property values next, and the following section will look at modifying the values.

Get Method

The Get method is used to retrieve an individual property value from the directory object that you specify. An example is shown in Listing 9.1.

LISTING 9.1 Using the Get Method to Return a Common Name Property from a User Object

```
Dim objUser
Dim objComName
' Bind to a user object.
set objUser = GetObject("LDAP://CN=gobrien,DC=gkcomput,DC=com")
' Get the common name property
objComName = objUser.Get("CN")
Wscript.Echo objComName
```

In this code example, we create two variables at the onset to hold two objects returned. The first variable, objUser, will hold a user object that pertains to the gobrien user in the gkcomput.com domain.

Once we have returned the object, we can then query and return the properties that are a part of that object. This is what the second variable is responsible for. It will hold the common name for the object that is returned by assigning that property value to the objComName variable by executing the Get method of the objUser object.

You may notice that the method is called by specifying the object name and then the method name after the dot. This is known as dot notation and is used extensively throughout COM and object programming. Each object's methods can be called in this fashion.

The last line will cause the common name to be displayed in a message box.

Accessing ADSI Properties Directly

Now, having rattled off a spiel concerning the merits of encapsulation and why data hiding is such a good idea, I must also inform you of another way to access the properties of the ADSI objects that doesn't require the use of the Get method. It involves using the dot notation and is described in the following paragraph.

With languages that support automation such as Visual Basic and Java, you can access the property values of the object directly. You do this with the same dot notation form that we just talked about, but rather than using the method name Get after the dot, you use the name of the property. In Listing 9.1 you would simply change the second to last line that makes use of the Get method to read like the following:

```
objComName = objUser.Name
```

GetEx Method

Some of the ADSI object's attributes may contain more than one value. If that is the case with the object that you are working with, you will need to use the GetEx method to return the available values. You can still use the Get method if you wish, but the GetEx method is much easier to work with when there are one or more values, which is why it is the preferred method.

The GetEx method will return the values in an array that you can work with. An *array* is a structure used in programming to hold multiple items. You can access the items in the array only by their index.

An example of an array could be a list of names or addresses. For this little example, consider a list of names and picture an array containing those names to look something like this:

```
0 Gerry O'Brien
1 Fred Rogers
2 Bill Clinton
```

That is essentially what an array might look like when it is displayed in a list. Note the numbers in front of each name. These numbers are the index numbers and are the key to working with arrays. You can only access the values in an array by using the index of that value.

If we wanted to return the second item in the array, which in this case is Fred Rogers, we would have to access it using the index value of 1. The array would then return the name Fred Rogers to us.

You may notice a peculiarity to where the array starts it's numbering. Most numbering schemes place a start point at one (1). Arrays are considered to be *base zero (0)*, which means that they start at 0 and not 1. This can get confusing when it comes time to work with the total amount of values in an array.

All arrays have an upper bound, which is specified in code with the use of the UBound keyword, which stands for upper bound. The UBound of an array will always be one number less than the actual number of values due to the fact the array starts counting at 0 and not 1. Keep this in mind when you are enumerating through any arrays returned so that you are sure to get the correct value from the array.

One other thing to keep in mind is that the GetEx method only queries the local cache. If the requested objects are not in the local cache then the GetEx method will perform an implicit call to the GetInfo method to refresh the cache.

Listing 9.2 is an example of using the GetEx function to return the available values in the otherPhones property of the user object specified.

LISTING 9.2 Example Code Using GetEx to Return Multiple Values

```
'**************************************************************
' GetExSample.vbs
' This script file is used to demonstrate how the GetEx
' method of the
' ADSI object will return multiple values if they exist in
' the object's property.
'
' Author: Gerry O'Brien
' Date: June 20, 2001
' Platform: Windows 2000/XP
' Language: VBScript
'**************************************************************
Dim objUser
Dim objList
Set objUser = GetObject("LDAP://Celeron500/
➥CN=Gerry O'Brien,CN=Users,DC=gkcomput,DC=com")
objList = objUser.GetEx("otherTelephone")
For Each Desc In objList
    WScript.Echo (Desc)
Next
```

This code declares two object variables to hold references to the user object and a list of values for the otherTelephone property of the specified user.

You use the now familiar Set statement to return the user object to our variable so that we can access its properties. Once we retrieve the object, we assign its values for the otherTelephone property to an object list variable called objList. The objList object will hold the array of values returned.

The last step is to run a loop, which in this case is a For Each/Next loop, to pick out each value and display it in a message box window using the Echo method of the WScript object.

You may notice the use of For Each Desc in the previous code sample. The Desc argument is actually the name of the value type in the object and is used to determine which value we want to look at, which in this case is the Description value.

9

ACCESSING DATA
WITH ADSI

NOTE

For those of you interested in the specific data type that is returned, you may note that the array will contain Variant data types. This means that the array is capable of holding any data type that may be returned.

Keep one other point in mind as well when you are using the `GetEx` method. You can retrieve single or multiple values with `GetEx`. You don't always have to use it just for multiple values.

GetInfo Method

You have already seen a discussion in earlier chapters about how ADSI objects are stored in a local cache when you request a property from one of the objects. This local cache is responsible for providing performance improvements when you are querying the values of the properties by placing those values closer to the requesting user or computer.

You have seen some of the reasons for using the cache. Impacting the network bandwidth less by not requiring the values to be transferred across the network each time a request is made is one prime reason for using the local cache. This is especially important in WAN environments where you may have domain controllers spanning multiple geographic locations over slower leased lines such as 56K or even ISDN.

Once the cache is populated with the requested values for an object, you only need to use the `Get` or `GetEx` methods as mentioned in the previous sections. By using either one of these methods, you realize the network performance improvements we just discussed. However, what happens if you need a value that is not in the cache or if the value you requested doesn't exist in the cache?

When you want to get a value or property that is not in the local cache, you can call the `GetInfo` method to refresh the cache or to add the necessary object property or properties into the cache.

If you are querying an object that is in the cache using the `Get` or `GetEx` methods, but the property that you want does not exist, ADSI will perform an implicit call to the `GetInfo` method to refresh the cache and load the properties needed. This will prevent any further necessary calls across the network and speed up your access to the properties.

Once you have called `GetInfo` implicitly, it will not be called again unless you are looking for an object or property that doesn't exist in the cache again. An example of using the `GetInfo` method is listed in Listing 9.3.

LISTING 9.3 An Example of Using the `GetInfo` Method to Refresh the Cache and Return Information for a Second Object

```
' ***********************************************************
' GetInfoSample.vbs
' This script file is used to demonstrate how the GetInfo
' method of the ADSI object will refresh the local cache.
'
```

LISTING 9.3 Continued

```
' Author: Gerry O'Brien
' Date: June 20, 2001
' Platform: Windows 2000/XP
' Language: VBScript
' ***********************************************************
Dim objUser
Dim objSecondUser
set objUser = GetObject("LDAP://Celeron500/CN=Gerry O'Brien,
➥ CN=Users,DC=gkcomput,DC=COM")
set objSecondUser = GetObject("LDAP://Celeron500/CN=Dianne O'Brien,
➥ CN=Users,DC=gkcomput,DC=COM")
WScript.Echo "The objUser's name is " & objUser.Get("CN")
WScript.Echo "The objUser's description is " &
➥ objUser.Get("Description")
objSecondUser.GetInfo
WScript.Echo "The description for the objSecondUser is "&
➥ objSecondUser.Get("Description")
```

This sample code is used to demonstrate the use of the GetInfo method to refresh the local cache. We will take it one step at a time to see how the code works.

First of all, we need to create the familiar object variables to hold references to the objects that we are working with. In this instance, we are going to use two user objects and have called them objUser for the first and objSecondUser for the second.

Once we have the variables declared, we assign the two user accounts to them with the GetObject function. In this case, I am using my user account and my wife's user account on our server at the office. You will need to substitute the user names and the domain name to reflect your own settings.

The next task demonstrates the use of the Get method again, but it is used to show how you will call the first user object and get two properties that are loaded into the local cache. The reason that there are two Get methods executed is to show how fast the second Get executes as a result of the properties already being in the local cache.

The second to last statement that calls the GetInfo method for the second user will show a slight delay. This will of course vary based on your network and server speed. It is used to demonstrate that the Description property for the second user is not in the cache and must be loaded by using the GetInfo method, which causes the cache to be refreshed.

9

ACCESSING DATA WITH ADSI

> **TIP**
>
> One thing that is not quite clear when you are executing your scripts sometimes are the error messages that WSH displays. One that you may find from time to time when executing these script samples here is the error that specifies that the object does not exist. This is somewhat misleading in that it can mean that the object indeed does not exist, but if you are sure it is there, check the spelling of the object name. A simple misspelling will generate this error as well.

Now that you have seen how to work with the `Get`, `GetEx`, and `GetInfo` methods, it is time to take a look at some further optimization techniques that can be performed using the `GetInfoEx` method. The next section will cover this topic.

`GetInfoEx` for Optimization

Optimizations always seem to be a hot topic when it comes to network and application performance. Everybody wants to squeeze that last bit of performance from whatever they are using. Sometimes, performance gains can be realized from some small or obscure concept. As an example, anyone who is familiar with the operation of an automobile engine will understand this next analogy.

A former co-worker of mine was involved in drag racing and for the first year didn't fare too well. Over the winter months, he sought out one of the best engine builders in the city and asked him to build a new engine for him for his drag car. The gentleman obliged, of course, because my co-worker agreed to pay the fee. However, we don't want to discuss money, but rather one of the optimizations that normally go unnoticed by those not *in tune* with the concepts.

This co-worker thought it a little strange when the engine builder sent him to the local auto parts store for 25 sets of spark plugs. That equals 50 spark plugs altogether. Of course, the reason didn't become apparent until later.

The engine builder proceeded to open a package of spark plugs and make a mark on the white ceramic insulator in line with the gap opening of the spark plug. He would then install the spark plug into the engine and tighten it up. If the mark he made did not line up with the intake valve of the engine, he would remove the spark plug and try it in each remaining cylinder until he found eight spark plugs that did indeed line up.

Why did he do this? Was he wasting my co-worker's money? Not really. You see, by aligning the opening in the gap on the electrode with the intake valve, he ensured that the spark was directly inline with the air and fuel mixture when it entered the cylinder. This resulted in a fraction of a second difference in the speed at which the fuel in the cylinder would ignite. Not much for one, but each of the eight cylinders added up to a little more.

Now, that little trick didn't send him down the track 30 or 40 miles an hour faster, but it was only one in a string of many small performance improvements that all added up to a better and faster-working car.

Now, we're not interested in going down drag strips, at least not with our company's servers powering that trip, but we can benefit from a bunch of small improvements like the drag car did.

ADSI offers the `GetInfoEx` method as one of those small improvements. The reason is quite simple. If you need to make a round trip to the server to update your local cache of object properties, you may return a large amount of data if you refresh the entire property set. For this reason, the `GetInfoEx` method allows you to specify specific properties to refresh. This results in less data transfer across the network as well as a slightly smaller load on the server's resources as well.

It's best to look at a working example to see how this works, which is what Listing 9.4 presents.

LISTING 9.4 An Example of Using the `GetInfoEx` Method to Return Only Specific Properties

```
'*************************************************************
' GetInfoExSample.vbs
' This script file is used to demonstrate how the GetInfoEx
' method of the ADSI object will load only the specific
' properties requested into the cache.
'
' Author: Gerry O'Brien
' Date: June 20, 2001
' Platform: Windows 2000/XP
' Language: VBScript
'*************************************************************
Dim arrProperty
Dim varProperty
Dim varDescriptionList
Dim objUser
Set objUser = GetObject("LDAP://Celeron500/
➥ CN=Users,DC=gkcomput,DC=com")
arrProperty = Array("name", "description")
```

9

ACCESSING DATA
WITH ADSI

LISTING 9.4   Continued

```
varProperty = arrProperty
objUser.GetInfoEx varProperty, 0
varDescriptionList = objUser.Get("description")
WScript.Echo varDescriptionList
```

What is happening with this piece of code is that we are setting up an array that will contain the properties that we want to refresh. We get the properties from the User object on the domain controller with the GetObject function.

The next thing we do is to create an array that for this purpose holds only two values. The object's property names are name and description. What this does is to simply allow us to request these properties specifically.

We then assign the array into the variable varProperty so that we have one piece of information to pass into the GetInfoEx method. Once we have that completed, we call the GetInfoEx method of the objUser object and pass it the varProperty as an argument and specifying that we want the first array item with the 0.

Once we have executed the GetInfoEx method, the only properties that are refreshed to the local cache are the Name and the Description property. We prove that by calling the Get method on the objUser object and Echo the description to the screen. You could change the property in the Get method to the name and it would Echo that instead of the description.

If you attempt to Echo a property that wasn't called with the GetInfoEx method, you will generate an error that states that the property is not in the cache.

This little performance improvement may not break any land speed records, but, when you combine it with the other performance improvements we have been talking about, it will help to add up to better performance all around.

CAUTION

You have to be careful when dealing with the GetInfoEx method and the SetInfo methods together in the same scripts. The situation that will cause you problems is if you have made some changes to the properties of an object and call the GetInfoEx method before you call the SetInfo (covered in the next section), you face the possibility of losing data as the cache will be refreshed with those properties specified as you have seen here, but, they will come from the directory store and will overwrite the values in the cache resulting in the changes not being written to the directory store.

Modifying Attributes

It only makes sense that if you can read the attributes that you should also be able to modify or write them. Now this assumption goes along with another assumption that you will have the permission to do so. You may be allowed to read an attribute but not modify it, in which case, it is a read-only attribute. This section will look at the methods used to modify the attributes in the ADSI objects.

There are three methods used to modify the attributes and each acts a little differently as you will see in their respective sections. These three methods are Put, PutEx, and SetInfo.

The Put and PutEx methods are used to write changes to the attributes in the local cache only. When you want to write the changes to the permanent store you must call the SetInfo method. This is another small performance improvement when it comes to writing the properties or attributes. Keep in mind the earlier caution though about calling the GetInfoEx method before calling SetInfo so that you don't lose any information.

Put Method

As was mentioned in the introduction to this section, the Put method is responsible for saving the value of a property for an ADSI object into the local cache. It is used to save a single value to the cache.

Once the Put method has been executed, the data value is still not permanent, as it hasn't been saved to the directory storage. You must call the SetInfo method to copy the contents to persistent storage in the directory store. Listing 9.5 shows an example code listing that will save the property value to the local cache.

LISTING 9.5 Using Put to Save a Value to the Local Cache

```
' ************************************************************
' PutExample.vbs
' This script file is used to demonstrate how the Put method
' of the
' ADSI object will set the specified properties to the
' supplied values
'
' Author: Gerry O'Brien
' Date: June 20, 2001
' Platform: Windows 2000/XP
' Language: VBScript
' ************************************************************
Dim objUser
```

9

ACCESSING DATA
WITH ADSI

LISTING 9.5   Continued

```
Set objUser = GetObject("LDAP://Celeron500/CN=Gerry O'Brien,
➥ CN=Users,DC=gkcomput,DC=Com")
objUser.Put "givenName", "Fred"
'Commit to the persistent directory store
objUser.SetInfo
```

As you take a look at this script, you can see the familiar variable declaration and assignment. We are working with the `Gerry O'Brien` user account on the `gkcomput.com` domain.

The first thing that is accomplished after the assignment statement is the `givenName` attribute is set to a value of `Fred` and then placed in the local cache with the use of the `objUser.Put` method.

Once that is completed, the `SetInfo` method is called to ensure that the value in the persistent storage is up to date with the value in the cache. It is always good practice to call `SetInfo` after making changes to the values in the local cache to avoid losing them, should a call to `GetInfo` execute and overwrite the changes in the local cache with older data values.

As you can see, there's not much to using the `Put` method. You can use `Put` for working with multiple values, but the `PutEx` method works better for that as you will see in the next section.

PutEx Method

The `PutEx` method offers some more flexibility in terms of modifying the values to be placed into the cache or storage. Like the `Put` method, `PutEx` can modify and save a single value to the local cache, but `PutEx` can also work more easily with multiple values.

The `PutEx` method makes use of what is known as control operations. These are listed and explained here:

- `ADS_PROPERTY_CLEAR`—Use this operation to clear the specified value of an attribute. When you execute `PutEx` with this operation, the attribute will have no value.

- `ADS_PROPERTY_UPDATE`—This operation will cause the present value to be replaced with the new value. This is essentially the same as using the `Put` method.

- `ADS_PROPERTY_APPEND`—Use this operation to append the specified value to the existing value already in the attribute. If the current value is `NULL`, the value will become the new value passed in.

- `ADS_PROPERTY_DELETE`—Use this operation to delete the specified values from the attributes.

Because of the way `PutEx` works with the available operations listed above, you must understand the use of each of the operations. You place the required operation from the list as the first argument to the PutEx method to indicate how you want the values to be handled in the cache when the method is called. Listing 9.6 shows various examples of using the operations listed.

LISTING 9.6   Using the Various Operations Available with the PutEx Method

```
' ************************************************************
' PutExSample.vbs
' This script file is used to demonstrate how the PutEx
' method of the
' ADSI object will set multiple values in the local cache.
'
' Author: Gerry O'Brien
' Date: June 20, 2001
' Platform: Windows 2000/XP
' Language: VBScript
' ************************************************************
Const ADS_PROPERTY_APPEND = 1
Const ADS_PROPERTY_DELETE = 2
Const ADS_PROPERTY_UPDATE = 3
Const ADS_PROPERTY_CLEAR = 4
Dim objUser
Set objUser = GetObject("LDAP://CN=Gerry O'Brien,
➥ CN=Users,DC=gkcomput,DC=com")
objUser.PutEx ADS_PROPERTY_APPEND, "otherTelephone",
➥ Array("999-3333")
objUser.SetInfo
objUser.PutEx ADS_PROPERTY_DELETE, "otherTelephone",
➥ Array("999-9999", "555-2222")
objUser.SetInfo
objUser.PutEx ADS_PROPERTY_UPDATE, "otherTelephone",
➥ Array("888-7777", "999-5555")
objUser.SetInfo
objUser.PutEx ADS_PROPERTY_CLEAR, "otherTelephone", Array()
objUser.SetInfo
```

This is kind of an interesting script for a couple of reasons. First of all, it demonstrates the use of each control property that was discussed earlier in the section on modifying values.

Secondly, you can comment out specific pieces of the code to see how it works. For example, comment the last three PutEx and SetInfo lines to leave the only executing line the PutEx method call with the ADS_PROPERTY_APPEND option enabled. You will notice that APPEND does indeed add to existing values without erasing them. (You may have to look at the user properties to see this, or you can run the previous script example called GetExSample to return all the phone numbers for that user.)

9

ACCESSING DATA
WITH ADSI

If you uncomment the DELETE option, you will see how the specified numbers are removed from the user properties. (This is of course provided that those numbers existed in the first place.)

The UPDATE option will replace the existing values with the ones passed into the method. Last, but not least, the CLEAR option will erase all entries in that property for the user.

It's important to note something new that was added to this script in comparison to other scripts you have seen so far in this book. That is, the first four lines that start with the keyword Const. This keyword stands for *constant*, which, first and foremost, means that the values cannot be changed.

CAUTION

If you are going to declare constants in your scripts as we have here, you *must* initialize them with a value as shown here. This is the only time a constant can be assigned a value.

The reason that the constants must be used here is that VBScript does not understand the names as ADS_PROPERTY_APPEND for example. You must give VBScript numeric constants to work with. This is what the Const statements do here. They provide VBScript with a reference to work with so that you can use the names rather than the numeric representations. After all, it makes your code much easier to read, doesn't it?

You will also notice that the SetInfo method was called after each PutEx method call. This is only necessary here to demonstrate how this script works. You could have left the SetInfo until the end but then you would never change the values in the persistent storage on the directory server; you would only manipulate the values in the local cache.

SetInfo Method

You have already seen the use of SetInfo in the previous sections dealing with Put and PutEx so you should understand the reasons for using it.

What you may not realize is that if you are using SetInfo with the PutEx method, any calls using one of the four operations such as ADS_PROPERTY_APPEND will cause an implicit call to the underlying operation in the directory service to perform the same function.

One other item of interest about SetInfo is that if you specify a value for an attribute that doesn't exist yet, SetInfo will create that value and place it in the attribute for the object.

Accessing the Property Cache Directly with the `IADsProperty` Interfaces

ADSI provides you with a set of interfaces for working directly with the values stored in the cache that pertain to the ADSI objects. There are actually three of these interfaces and they are described here:

- `IADsPropertyList`—deals with managing the list of properties for an ADSI object
- `IADsPropertyEntry`—manages the list of property entries for the object
- `IADsPropertyValue`—works with the values of the properties for the object

These methods work only with the local cache and do not affect the persistent store on the server. For this reason, you must still use the `GetInfo/GetInfoEx` and `SetInfo` methods to get and set the values of the properties from the store to refresh the local cache. An example of using these methods is listed in Listing 9.7.

LISTING 9.7   An Example of Using the IADs Property Interfaces

```
' ***********************************************************
' IADsInterfaceSample.vbs
' This script file is used to demonstrate how the various
' IADsProperty interface methods work on the values in the
' local cache
'
' Author: Gerry O'Brien
' Date: June 20, 2001
' Platform: Windows 2000/XP
' Language: VBScript
' ***********************************************************
Dim objPropList
Dim objPropEntry
Dim objPropVal
Dim strName
Set objPropList = GetObject("LDAP://DC=gkcomput,DC=com")
objPropList.GetInfo

Set objPropEntry = objPropList.GetPropertyItem("dc",
➥ ADSTYPE_CASE_IGNORE_STRING)
For Each v In objPropEntry.Values
    Set objPropVal = v
    WScript.Echo objPropVal.CaseIgnoreString
Next
```

9

ACCESSING DATA
WITH ADSI

As you step through this code one line at a time, you will see that we have created four variables at the onset to hold references to the objects we are using throughout the script.

The first real bit of business that we do is to set the `objPropList` equal to the root of my domain, which is `gkcomput.com`. We then call the `GetInfo` method to load that information into the local cache.

Next we set the `objPropEntry` object equal to the `dc` of the previous object. Note the use of the constant `ADSTYPE_CASE_IGNORE_STRING` in the method call. This is used to tell the method that when it searches it is doing so without care for case sensitivity.

The last thing we do is to use a `ForEach/Next` loop to access the value of the property that we returned from the object and display it in a message box. For my particular example, I returned only one value as I only have one AD server in my company.

These three interfaces can be used with scripting languages such as VBScript as shown here, or you can use them with C++ if you are creating an ADSI application with that programming language.

ADSI Attribute Syntax

In most programming topics, when a discussion turns to syntax, the concept is thought as being the proper way to use something, such as a spelled out definition of the function, topic, or other area. Most of my students come to me with a complaint that the syntax definitions for various Visual Basic procedures are extremely hard to understand. For the most part they can be until you understand how to read them.

That is a bit off topic, though, as our discussion here centers around the meaning of syntax for the ADSI attributes. Syntax in this instance deals more with the usage of certain ADSI property capabilities without specifying a laid out written definition, as in this example:

```
[Public:Private:Friend]Sub name ()
    code goes here
End Sub
```

ADSI describes eleven different syntaxes for your use with various properties. These will be listed and explained in the following sections.

BOOLEAN

This syntax is a 32-bit signed value used to indicate a `True` or `False`. Zero is equal to `FALSE` and any non-zero value is `TRUE`.

Syntax Type: ADSTYPE_BOOLEAN

CASE_EXACT_STRING and CASE_IGNORE_STRING

ADSI can make use of two possible search types when querying the directory service. You can search with or without case sensitivity. If you use the `ADSTYPE_CASE_EXACT_STRING`, the search will be performed as a case-sensitive search, which means that `Gerry` is different from `gerry`.

If your search is not returning any values, try using the `ADSTYPE_CASE_IGNORE_STRING` instead as it will return all the matching strings regardless of case.

For an idea of why this works the way it does, you need to look at how the various characters are stored internally in the computer. For the most part, you are already familiar with ASCII (American Standard Code for Information Interchange), which has been around for some time now.

ASCII uses the numbers 0 to 255 to represent the letters of the alphabet along with the numbers 0 to 9, some special characters such as punctuation characters and even some French accented characters. It mostly depends on the character set you are using as to which characters are represented as what, but for the most part, the letters are always represented by the same range of numbers.

The capital letters A–Z are represented by the numbers 65–90 and the lowercase a–z are represented by 97–122. Computers deal with binary numbers internally so, as an example, the capital letter A is represented as 1000001 in binary while the lower case a is represented as 1100001. You can see the difference when you look at the binary representation, which is what the computer sees. In this way, when the computer does a binary comparison, it checks for equality of the binary number. If it matches, you have a matching letter. When you use the case ignore type, the comparison just ensures that both are the same letter, and case doesn't matter.

ASCII has some shortcomings, however, and one of the biggest is the fact that it cannot represent all of the characters needed to display and work with foreign languages such as Russian Cyrillic, Japanese, or Chinese.

There is a newer character code that comes closer than ASCII does to providing enough space to represent the characters of the various languages, and that is Unicode. Unicode performs this feat by using twice the space that ASCII uses to represent characters. ASCII used one byte per character, which is why it could only represent 255 characters.

With Unicode and using 2 bytes per character, you can now represent 65,536 characters (still not quite enough for all the characters, but a lot closer).

Syntax Types: ADSTYPE_CASE_IGNORE_STRING, ADSTYPE_CASE_EXACT_STRING

NOTE

ADSI supports Unicode even if the directory service does not support it. ADSI will accept either ASCII or Unicode.

DN_STRING (Distinguished Name)

When dealing with your user accounts in directory services, you can specify pertinent information such as the user's manager and department. This information is a part of the user account information in the user properties.

You can use the distinguished name for linking two objects. As an example, look at the code in Listing 9.8.

LISTING 9.8   An Example Code Snippet That Shows How Two Objects Can Be Linked Using the Distinguished Name

```
Set objUser = GetObject("LDAP://Celeron500/CN=Dianne O'Brien,
➥ CN=Users,DC=gkcomput,DC=com")
objUser.put "manager", "CN=Gerry O'Brien,
➥ CN=Users,DC=gkcomput,DC=com"
objUser.SetInfo
```

What this code snippet is doing is getting the user Dianne O'Brien from the gkcomput.com domain and then setting her manager's property value equal to Gerry O'Brien, who is also a user in the domain.

Syntax Type: ADSTYPE_DN_STRING

NOTE

The user accounts must exist in the domain before you can call these methods; otherwise, you will be returned an error indicating that the objects do not exist.

INTEGER

This type is simply a 32-bit signed number. Integers on 32-bit computers are 32 bits in length. This means that single whole numbers in the range –32,765 to 32,767 are valid.

Syntax Type: ADSTYPE_INTEGER

LARGE_INTEGER

A `LARGE_INTEGER` is twice the size of an `INTEGER`, which makes it 64 bits in length. You can split the `LARGE_INTEGER` into two halves, which are known as the high and low halves, by using the `HighPart` and `LowPart` methods. An example is shown here:

```
Dim objObject
Dim objLargeInteger

Set objObject = GetObject("LDAP://DC=gkcomput,DC=com")
Set objLargeInteger = objObject.Get("UsnCreated")
WScript.Echo objLargeInteger.HighPart
WScript.Echo objLargeInteger.LowPart
```

This code creates to variables to refer to different objects. The first is set to the root of the gkcomput.com domain while the second is used to hold the `LARGE_INTEGER`.

We set the `LARGE_INTEGER` equal to the `UsnCreated` value of the root object. Once that is complete, the two parts are broken down into their respective 32-bit parts.

Syntax Type: `ADS_LARGE_INTEGER`

NUMERIC_STRING

This syntax type is used for string comparisons for matching. ADSI will not do any case checking nor does it validate the data that is entered, meaning that you can enter numeric information as well and it will be accepted. Also, any spaces are ignored when comparing the strings.

Syntax Type: `ADSTYPE_NUMERIC_STRING`

OBJECT_CLASS

This is a unique object identifier used to identify the object instance based on its `objectclass` attribute. Once you have created a class for an object, you can't change it.

Syntax Type: `ADSTYPE_CASE_IGNORE_STRING`

OCTET_STRING

This syntax will be returned as an array of bytes. The array is of type `Variant`. Octets are likely most familiar to those of you who work with IP addresses. Each octet is an 8-bit byte value. A series of these octets will produce a string of binary data.

Syntax Type: `ADSTYPE_OCTET_STRING`

PRINTABLE_STRING

The PRINTABLE_STRING syntax is the opposite of the NUMERIC_STRING syntax in that it is used where case sensitivity is required. ADSI will still accept any data in the contents for this syntax type and does not verify that the values can be printed.

Syntax Type: ADSTYPE_PRINTABLE_STRING

SECURITY_DESCRIPTOR

The SECURITY_DESCRIPTOR is used to indicate the access control information that has been associated with ADSI objects. The access rights determine what the requesting operation can perform on the ADSI object.

The SECURITY_DESCRIPTOR is stored in the *ntSecurityDescriptor* property of the ADSI objects. The access rights are determined by checking the ACLs against the currently logged on user that is executing the script or accessing the object's properties. An example follows:

```
Dim objObject
Dim objSecDesc

Set objObject = GetObject("LDAP://Celeron500
➥ /DC=gkcomput,DC=com")
Set objSecDesc = objObject.Get("ntSecurityDescriptor")
WScript.Echo objSecDesc.Group
WScript.Echo objSecDesc.Owner
```

This code uses two object variables to hold references to a root object on the Celeron500 server and the SECURITY_DESCRIPTORs for that object. The last two lines will output the SECURITY_DESCRIPTOR for the group and owner objects in the root of the server.

Syntax Type: ADS_NT_SECURITY_DESCRIPTOR

UTC_TIME

The value in this syntax is a single string that is formed from three separate parts. The first part contains the date data in the form YYMMDD. Note that the first two digits of the year are not stored in the string.

The second part contains the time value which can be either hhmm or hhmmss, while the third part consists of the letter Z used to indicate that the time is given in universal time, which is a value + or – GMT (Greenwich Mean Time).

Some examples are shown here:

- 0101312145Z—indicates the 31st of January 2001, 9:45 p.m. local time
- 751225050035—indicates Christmas day 1975, 5:00:35 a.m. local time (about the time I was sneaking out to see what Santa had left under the tree for me; I was 11 at the time)

The MSDN help files include a table that provide a side-by-side comparison of the AD syntax types and the ADSI syntax types if you are interested in seeing the comparisons.

Syntax Type: ADSTYPE_UTC_TIME

Collections and Groups

The term *collection* is normally associated with a multitude of some object, item, or concept bound into one coherent grouping with a mechanism for accessing the contents. In terms of programming and with ADSI, a collection is a combined set of objects or attributes that are specified or exist in a directory service.

You may be familiar with arrays of items, a set of like items that are contained within one grouping and access using an index value. Consider the following example.

You have a set of items such as titles of movies in your DVD library collection. You can place these titles into an array, which will list them like this sample:

ArrMovie(10)

This line is used to indicate that we are going to create an array called ArrMovie that will contain 10 titles. We specify the title's place in the array by giving it an index value. Thus if we had ten movie titles specified, they would be organized in the array like this:

```
The Patriot
Home Alone
Bicentennial Man
Dr. Dolittle
Star Wars
Monty Python and the Holy Grail
What Women Want
Miss Congeniality
War and Peace
The Matrix
```

Now, starting with the top movie, we set the index value at 0 (arrays start counting at 0), and then number each subsequent movie as 1 higher than the last, so that The Matrix will have an index value of 9. The array indexes are 0 through 9.

Now as far as storage requirements go in terms of how a computer organizes the information internally, an array can be an efficient method of storing more than one item as it allows you to gain access to the items using the same name, which translates to the same physical memory address, and all you have to do is simply specify the index value to retrieve the item you want. For example, in our array earlier, if we wanted to extract the `Star Wars` movie, we would use `ArrMovies(4)`. This refers to the `Star Wars` movie item in the array.

This is a fairly simple means of accessing the underlying items in the array but it presents one inherent problem. How can you possibly know the index value of the item you want? This is especially true if your array is large. The answer is quite simply that you can't. Arrays are hard to work with for this reason. Also, you can't easily sort an array. They can be sorted, but you have to perform some wonderful logic math routines to sort them. Another issue is when you want to add an item to an array. There is no easy method to place the item in the location with the index you want. By default, new items are added at the end of the array.

How do we solve this problem? By using a collection. Collections are lists of items as well, similar to an array in that they have an index to differentiate the items in the list. The biggest difference is realized in that collections allow you to also use a name or key to access an item.

The key in a collection is a `Named` value that is used to represent the item in the list and is much easier to work with and remember than a numbered index is.

Another advantage of collections in programming is that you can insert items into the collection and the collection can look after the sorting for you if you have specified a sort order. These features of collections make them more desirable to work with than arrays.

ADSI makes use of collections to store the objects within ADSI. ADSI will use a collection to represent an arbitrary set of objects or object properties that exist in the directory service. There is one stipulation though; the data types must be the same for the items to exist in the same collection.

A collection of objects will use the `Variant` data type, and as we discussed earlier in the book relating to data types, a `Variant` is a data type that can accept any object and will handle data type conversion as needed.

Collection objects in ADSI can be used to represent many different pieces of information. They can represent persistent storage items such as ADSI user objects, ACLs, or computers and they can also be used to represent information that is not persistent such as print jobs.

For the most part, when you need to work with the collections, you can use the methods discussed previously in this chapter such as `GetEx` and `PutEx` for dealing with multiple values. You can also use enumeration, which you will see in Chapter 10, "Enumerating ADSI Objects."

Groups

A quick and dirty explanation of a *group* is simply that it is a collection of objects that support the IADsMembers interface. This interface is used to manage lists of ADSI object references.

Because of the fact that your networks, and all networks for that matter, are large enough to contain multiple objects and properties for those objects, you will run across collections and groups as you work with ADSI and create scripts to read and manipulate the various objects and properties.

Summary

ADSI offers you the ability to manipulate the underlying objects and their properties by using methods provided with ADSI. For our discussion in this book we look at using those methods with the VBScript language and the Windows Script Host. You can also use programming languages such as Java and C++ to create applications that make use of the interfaces exposed by ADSI, but scripting does the job quite nicely.

You looked at some examples on using the local cache as well to speed the retrieval and setting of the values for various properties within ADSI. The Put and Get methods allow you to set and get the values from the local cache one at a time while the GetEx and PutEx methods are better suited at working with multiple values.

You also saw how ADSI uses collections and how they compare to arrays of items in terms of ease of use. Collections are used by many programming languages, allowing the developer to create lists of items that can be manipulated easily.

The information in this chapter has shown you how to make use of the available methods in ADSI to manipulate any available object and its properties in ADSI using WSH and VBScript. You can take this knowledge and further it on by adding more objects to the samples given to increase the use and functionality of these scripts. Like all good scripting or programming tool kits, you start with a functioning script and enhance and add to it as needed to create a set of tools that over time will save you many hours of manual administration tasks.

9

ACCESSING DATA WITH ADSI

Enumerating ADSI Objects

Most of the time, you are not aware of every object that exists in your Active Directory. As was mentioned in an earlier chapter, ADSI contains many objects that are containers, or leaf objects. How do you know what is available for objects within AD? The simple answer is to *enumerate* those objects. Enumeration is simply running through the list of objects and outputting the list either to the screen or to the printer for hard copy. Any object that is exposed (visible to a programming language) in ADSI can be enumerated, or listed as an object that exists within your Active Directory.

You are already aware of the fact that users and groups are considered objects in ADSI, but what else might be considered an object? You could safely say that printers are ADSI objects as well. But how do you really know every object that is available for you to work with in your directory services? You can find out by enumerating the ADSI objects to produce a list.

You will find the ability to enumerate ADSI objects essential when you have heterogeneous networks that consist of different providers, such as Microsoft and Novell. You will see examples of enumerating these objects in the sections that follow.

Enumeration

As an example of enumeration, using your editor, create this script and execute it on your Windows 2000 computer. Replace the //Workgroup/gobrien entry in the binding string with the workgroup or domain and computer name that exists on your computer.

LISTING **10.1**   Enumerating ADSI Objects in the WinNT Provider

```
' enumerate.vbs
'
' Demonstrates enumerating the users, groups and services that are
' a part of the ADSI WinNT provider on a local Windows 2000
' Professional computer.
'
' Author:    Gerry O'Brien
' Date:      May 3, 2001
' Language: VBScript
'


Dim objADSIObject
Dim objChild
Dim objContainer

On Error Resume Next    ' Turn off error handling
Set objADSIObject = GetObject("WinNT://WorkGroup/gobrien")
Set objContainer = objADSIObject
```

LISTING 10.1 Continued

```
If Err = 0 Then
    For Each objChild in objContainer
        wscript.echo objChild.Name
    Next
End If
```

This script can take a long time to run and you may get a little tired of closing message boxes depending on how many objects you have on your system, so I recommend that you execute it at the command line using CScript.exe. What will be returned is a listing of all the users and groups on your computer as well as a listing of the currently running services.

By using this one simple example, you can see how easy it is to determine what objects are available for you to work with on your system. Once you know what objects are available, you can determine which ones you need to work with and then go about determining what properties are available for those objects.

Once you have enumerated the ADSI objects in this way, what can you do with them? You have either a listing that is displayed at the command prompt or a bunch of message boxes that you are closing for each object enumerated. This obviously doesn't give you the ability to look at what was enumerated in a list that you can work with. How can you get this information output to a more usable format? By creating a text file.

Once again using the code that is shown in Listing 10.1, execute the script file at the command prompt using CScript.exe. This time, you will use the redirection command to create a text file and output the results into that text file. Enter the command as shown here:

```
cscript enumerate.vbs > C:\enum.txt
```

This results in the script engine running the script that you specified at the command prompt and taking the output and redirecting it to an ASCII text file. You will not see the output at the command prompt using this method as it is sent to the text file instead. Figure 10.1 shows the results of running the script and sending the output to a text file on my computer.

As you can see from this screen shot, I have opened the enum.txt file within Notepad. You can see that the same output is produced, but that a text file has been created instead. You can now use this text file as a reference when looking at what you want to work with in your ADSI scripts.

What you have just enumerated with the script in Listing 10.1 are all of the objects that pertain to the root of the computer that you ran the script on. You can actually enumerate child objects further down the tree by specifying the parent object within the binding string.

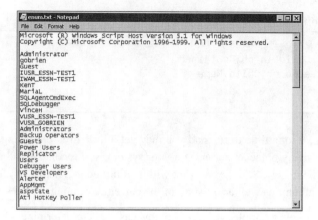

FIGURE **10.1**
The results of redirecting the output of the enumerate.vbs *script to a text file.*

Enumerating to Determine Object Properties

Another good use for enumeration is to determine what properties are available for the various objects in ADSI. This is especially useful when it comes to user accounts. It would be nice to know what properties exist for you to manipulate by reading or writing those properties. These properties can and likely will be different depending on the provider you are working with.

There are normally mandatory and optional properties for user accounts, and you can specify this as a filter when you enumerate these properties. The code in Listing 10.2 will enumerate the properties available for a specific user account on the computer.

LISTING 10.2   Enumerating the Mandatory and Optional Parameters for a User Account

```
' enumuserprops.vbs
'
' Demonstrates enumerating the users' properties both mandatory and
' optional.
'
' Author:   Gerry O'Brien
' Date:     May 3, 2001
' Language: VBScript
'



Dim objUser
Dim objUserClass
Dim objProperty
```

LISTING 10.2   Continued

```
Set objUser = GetObject("WinNT://gobrien/gobrien,user")
Set objUserClass = GetObject(objUser.Schema)

On Error Resume Next

WScript.Echo "Mandatory properties for " & objUser.Name & ":"
For Each objProperty In objUserClass.MandatoryProperties
    WScript.Echo "     " & objProperty
    WScript.Echo "          " & objUser.Get(objProperty)
Next
WScript.Echo

WScript.Echo "Optional properties for " & objUser.Name & ":"
For Each objProperty In objUserClass.OptionalProperties
    WScript.Echo "     " & objProperty
    WScript.Echo "          " & objUser.Get(objProperty)
Next
```

By executing this script, you will enumerate all of the available properties for the specified user account. The following code gives an example of the results returned on my computer when I executed Listing 10.2:

```
Mandatory properties for gobrien:

Optional properties for gobrien:
    Description
      User of Computer
    FullName
      Gerry O'Brien

    AccountExpirationDate

    BadPasswordAttempts
      0
    HomeDirDrive

    HomeDirectory

    LastLogin
      14/05/2001 11:36:04 AM
    LastLogoff

    LoginHours
```

```
LoginScript

LoginWorkstations

MaxLogins

MaxPasswordAge
  3710851
MaxStorage
  -1
MinPasswordAge
  0
MinPasswordLength
  0
objectSid

Parameters

PasswordAge
  3295118
PasswordExpired
  0
PasswordHistoryLength
  0
PrimaryGroupID
  513
Profile

UserFlags
  66049
RasPermissions
```

Any line that is blank (that is, any line that does not contain a value) indicates that this property is available, but no value has been assigned to it. As you can see here, there are quite a few properties associated with a user account under a Windows 2000/XP computer's ADSI schema.

User accounts are just one type of object that exists in ADSI. You can enumerate other objects as well, such as groups. Within the code in Listing 10.2, change the line

```
Set objUser = GetObject("WinNT://gobrien/gobrien,user")
```

to this line:

```
Set objUser = GetObject("WinNT://gobrien/Administrators")
```

When you execute the code again at the command prompt, you will receive an output similar to that shown in the following code:

```
Mandatory properties for Administrators:
    groupType
     4

Optional properties for Administrators:
    Description
Administrators have complete and unrestricted access to the computer/domain
    objectSid
```

As you can see, there are quite a number of user account properties that are not present in a group account. Once again, the available properties will differ based on the provider that you are using or querying.

Each ADSI object has its own set of properties and by enumerating them, you get to see what is available per object for manipulation. You may not need to work with every property that is exposed by an ADSI object, but at least having the complete list available to you makes picking the property much easier.

Enumeration Help Functions

ADSI includes three enumerator helper functions. These three functions are designed to be used with C or C++, and are intended as an aid in navigating Active Directory objects. Because they are meant for use with C/C++, you will not be required to program anything dealing with them in this book. They are mentioned here for the sake of completeness in documenting the programming abilities within ADSI.

ADsBuildEnumerator

This helper function is used to encapsulate the code that a programmer would write when creating an enumerator object. This function is used to create an object that is used to enumerate the ADSI objects and provide the programmer with access to these objects from within a standalone application.

ADsEnumerateNext

This function is used to loop through the elements in an enumerator object and fill an array with the data. The programmer can make use of this function and the array that is created to fill a list box or drop-down combo box providing the user of the application with a listing of the available objects to work with.

ADsFreeEnumerator

This function is used to free an enumerator object that was created using the `ADsBuildEnumerator` function. Like all objects in a programming environment, computer resources are tied up when they are created and used within a program. If you do not release the resources that the object is using, the operating system cannot reclaim those for reuse by other applications. This can result in a memory leak in the application and require you to reboot your computer to free up the memory used by that object.

This function will cause the object to be destroyed, which means that the object no longer exists and the program informs the operating system that it no longer needs the memory that the object was using. The OS will return the memory to the pool of available resources and other applications can now use that memory.

Summary

This chapter is a little on the short side, but most of the information covered here is also covered to some degree in other chapters. You can use what you have learned here to help you enumerate the various properties that exist or are exposed by a particular ADSI object.

You learned how to enumerate the root objects available on a computer so that you could see what objects were available to work with. Not all computers will have the same objects available, nor will the objects be the same from one provider to the next.

Finally, you learned how you can use enumeration to discover the properties that you can manipulate using WSH. These properties are what you will read and write when working with user and group accounts on the AD computers within your domain.

Searching Active Directory

IN THIS CHAPTER

When you work with ADSI, for the most part you are either getting or setting objects and their properties. Essentially you are searching Active Directory when you do this as you are setting up queries.

In order for you to realize the maximum benefit with your queries or searches, you should be aware of some of the key areas that affect your queries. This will help you better understand the query and search process. This will, in turn, help you to write better queries and optimize your use of ADSI and the Active Directory. That is what this chapter will provide to you.

> **NOTE**
>
> This chapter will be providing information that will give you an understanding of the concepts behind enhancing performance when searching AD. Most of the information can best be realized when developing client applications rather than scripts, but it is still pertinent.

Query Scope

What is meant by the *scope* of the query? Scope refers to how far you need to search in order to find the object you are looking for. You may have to locate an object in an organizational unit, a domain, or a forest. This determines the scope, or the magnitude, of the search.

The larger the scope, the longer the search will take to complete. You actually don't control the scope of the query. The location of the object is what determines the scope. For example, you can query the global catalog if you wish to query for objects in your entire domain. Or, maybe the object exists in an organizational unit. Your search will then be narrowed in comparison to an object that resides in another forest.

Searching the Global Catalog

In order to search your entire domain via the global catalog, you have to ensure that it is running on the computer or computers you will be searching. To verify this, follow the steps outlined here:

1. Open Active Directory Sites and Services in the Administrative Tools start menu.
2. Expand the Sites folder and the site you wish to search.
3. Select the server name in the left pane.
4. Right-click the NTDS Settings icon in the details pane and choose Properties.
5. Ensure that the Global Catalog option is selected, as shown in Figure 11.1.

FIGURE 11.1
The NTDS Settings Property sheet showing that the Global Catalog option has been enabled.

This will ensure that the computer will be running the global catalog so that you can search it.

Query Depth

When it comes to searching Active Directory, you can specify the depth of your search. The depth determines how deep into the object hierarchy your search will go. There are three levels of depth that you can use. These are explained here.

Base Query

Sometimes when you are searching Active Directory for an object, you don't always know for sure that it exists. You have to determine if the object does exist before you can manipulate it by setting properties. One way to do this is to use the *Base Query*.

A Base Query is used to search only the base object itself, and not any child objects. You provide the object's distinguished name, and only that one object will be returned if it exists.

If you do a search on an object in this manner and you want to be able to read it or use it again, it is recommended that you store its GUID rather than its distinguished name. By doing this, you will still be able to access the object should it be moved or renamed. The GUID will maintain the link to the object. *GUIDs* are 128-bit Globally Unique Identifiers that are used for object identification in programming. All objects will have their GUIDs registered in the registry, mostly under the HKEY_CLASSES_ROOT hive. An example GUID is shown here:

{85BBD920-42A0-1069-A2E4-08002B30309D}

One-Level

Using a *One-level* search will return the object's immediate children but not the object itself. One particular use of a One-level search is to enumerate the immediate children of an object.

Subtree

A *Subtree* search is used to search all objects under a particular object and return them. As with the One-level search, the root object is not returned.

Because of the way this type of search works, a fairly large amount of data can be returned. You may also find that the search may include multiple servers. Microsoft recommends that the search be performed asynchronously. This will help reduce the effect on network bandwidth or server performance. For more information on searching asynchronously, see the section titled "Asynchronous Searches" later in this chapter.

As an example of where you might use this type of search, consider a search on user accounts or computer accounts with similar settings such as expiry dates.

Working with Large Resultsets

When you perform a search on Active Directory that includes a large amount of data, such as a Subtree search mentioned earlier, you may need to look at ways to make the search more efficient and faster. Some of the bottlenecks or issues you need to be concerned with are the network bandwidth and server resources. Most networks are experiencing some sort of bottleneck anyway, and it makes sense not to add to that if you can help it. This section will look at working with the large resultsets that may be returned and how you can tweak the searches to obtain the best result.

Creating Fast Queries

So, how can you make a query speedy? There are a few areas that we can look at that you can use to tweak your searches and speed up the operation, along with minimizing the impact of network and server resources.

Some of the areas that will be covered are included in the following sections. You will look at using indexes in your searches as well as using the object categories.

You will also look at reasons why you should avoid using referrals whenever possible and how to create search strings that are efficient. Then you will look at paging operations, searching on attributes, and setting size and time limits. Finally, you will look at asynchronous searches.

Indexing

Any DBA will tell you that one of the best additions to a database in terms of speeding up queries is the use of indexes. Indexes make searching through the records faster because the index is numerically based and presents a smaller chunk of data to search through.

When you are querying Active Directory objects, searching on indexed attributes results in a faster query. How do you ensure that you search on indexed attributes? The first item to take care of is to ensure that the least significant bit of the `searchFlags` property in the schema for the objects is set to 1. For more information on setting the flags, see the Active Directory documentation for your server.

ObjectCategory

You can use either `ObjectCategory` or `ObjectClass` when searching Active Directory. These are attributes used to refer a schema class of a given directory object.

`ObjectClass` can take multiple values and refers to directory objects in any class. `ObjectCategory` refers to a specific class rather than all the classes.

`ObjectCategory` uses a single value only. For this reason, it is better for searching AD by matching object types with the single parameter used. It is also the default matching criterion used by ADSI.

An example might be to set the `ObjectCategory` to one item as shown here:

```
ObjectCategory = user
```

This way, the search will look only at user objects and not all of the other objects that aren't required.

Referrals

Unless you are searching the global catalog, you may need to enable *referrals* on the Active Directory servers. This is not necessarily good for performance. If your search does not turn up the object on the server you are searching, then that server, if enabled, will return a referral to your script or application indicating the name of another server that may have the object you want. This can continue for a while if you have a large AD domain. Obviously, this is going to take some time to complete. For this reason, it is recommended that in large installations, you search using the global catalog if you are not sure the object exists on the server you are searching.

Within Active Directory, you can use one of four possible referral services. These are listed here:

- *Never*—This setting tells the server not to send referral information to the client application or script.

- *External*—This setting is used to indicate that a server should set a referral to another server, perhaps on another directory tree, if that server can resolve the query.

- *Subordinate*—This setting tells the server that it should perform referrals if the server that can solve the query is a part of a contiguous path from the originating server. For example, say that the originating server has the context `main.sales.gkcomput.com`. This context doesn't contain the object required, but the `regionB` server does contain the object and resides in `main.sales.gkcomput.com`. The `regionB` server is part of a contiguous path for the AD tree.

- *Always*—This setting causes the server to generate referrals when the search can be resolved on either the external or subordinate types.

Remember, if your server has the global catalog option enabled, you should perform the search on the GC as it contains the objects for the entire domain and can be searched faster, thereby increasing performance.

Assembling the Query Strings

When you are setting up your searches, another small but beneficial performance enhancement is found within the query string itself. The more specific your query is, the faster the search can be completed.

The reason is in how AD performs the search. AD first evaluates all of the predicates. The *predicates* are the criteria for the search, such as a username or computer name. Once this is completed, the indices are identified, and then AD will attempt to pick the index that will produce the smallest resultset to be returned.

For this reason, it is recommended that you be as specific as possible in query strings and stay away from using wildcard characters as much as possible. An example of a poor query string is shown here:

```
"cn=*brien"
```

This portion of a query string is looking for all common names that end in `brien`. This could potentially lead to a longer-than-necessary search. Be more specific. Use the following query string instead:

```
"cn=O'Brien"
```

This will cause AD to search for a common name of `O'Brien` and nothing else. This will result in a smaller set of return values—hence, a faster search.

Paging

In the context of searching AD, *paging* refers to way in which the objects are handled on the server and returned to the script or client application.

If you are familiar with paging operations, in terms of memory and swapping to a hard disk, you will have a good grasp of this concept already. When the required memory in the computer becomes full, the operating system must swap some of this memory out to the hard drive to make room for the data that needs to reside in memory. This swapping is done using paging which specifies a certain size to use when performing this swapping.

Paging for searches in AD operates in a similar way. The only real difference is that the data is being returned to an application or script rather than swapped to a hard drive.

Let's imagine for a second that you are querying on a large amount of objects. The server must store all of the objects that you require in memory while the search is in progress. Only when the search has completed will the data be sent back to the caller.

This can have two detrimental effects on your system's performance. The first is, of course, on the server where the objects will reside in memory and consume this server's resources. Thus, this will prevent other running applications from gaining access to the memory. The second effect is when all of the data is sent back to the caller, the network bandwidth can be affected if there is a lot of information to transfer.

For these reasons, it is recommended that you break your queries into pages. This sets up a maximum size to be held on the server before sending to the caller. In this way, the server memory resources are not unnecessarily filled up with objects and smaller chunks of data are sent across the network. ADSI will not allow you to use pages larger than 1000 records anyway, so you don't have to worry about setting this limit yourself. ADSI will do this for you transparently.

This also has another added benefit if you are creating client applications that perform the searching. This benefit is seen when the client application has data returned sooner and the user can view this data while the remaining data is continuously being paged and sent in the background.

> **NOTE**
>
> Check the documentation for the directory service that you will be using as not all services support paging.

When you are using paged services on AD, your client application can abandon the search before it has completed. This is not possible if paging is not being used, as the client must wait until the entire search has completed. You also don't have to worry about setting the size of the paging on the client side, as AD will handle this automatically for you. This saves the need for you to code this into your scripts or applications.

Searches

You can also tweak the performance of your searches by using search attributes and limits on the objects you are searching. These are discussed in the following sections.

Search Attributes

You can speed up your searches when you are only interested in what type of information is available for the objects in your directory. In this case, you don't want to return the information in the attributes of the object, just the attributes themselves.

To perform this type of search, you need to set the *search attributes only* option. This will cause only the attribute names to be returned, not the values in the attributes. An example follows:

```
First Name
Last Name
Department
Phone
```

> **NOTE**
>
> If an attribute contains no value then it will not be returned. For example, in the list of attributes above, if the Phone attribute did not contain any data, it would not be returned in the list.

Search Limits

You can set limits on your searches as well to help speed the execution and return of results. You can limit the size of the search results, the time, and time out values as well. These will be discussed in the following sections.

Size

Limiting the size of the search will result in a faster execution because the amount of memory used and network bandwidth required are reduced. Limiting the objects that will be returned does this.

To limit the size of the search, the client can request only a subset of the objects in the resultset by specifying a number limit. If the search specified a size limit of 20 and an order of descending, then only the first 20 items will be returned regardless of how many objects actually exist.

Time

Setting the time limit on a search is another method to help performance. The reason for this is seen as beneficial on servers that are already under a heavy load. If your search takes too long, you will add an unnecessary load to the server and slow down all processes running on the server.

> **NOTE**
>
> The server may already have time limits imposed through administrative time limits. In this case, if the time limit you set is greater than this administrative time value, the latter will override your limit setting.

Time Out

The time out setting is different from the time limit setting because the time out runs on the client rather than on the server. You can use the *search time out* property to specify a time out value that the client will wait for a return from the server. This time out is set in the script on the client side. If there is no data returned in the specified time out limit, the client may wait and request another search later.

This setting is especially important to use when you are performing searches asynchronously. When you are searching this way, your client will make the request to the server and then continue to process other tasks while the search is running on the server.

Should the server become unavailable or disconnected, the client could potentially wait for an indeterminate amount of time for the search to complete. In this case, the time out will prevent the client from waiting for something that may never return.

Asynchronous Searches

One of the reasons that asynchronous searches are considered to be a speed improvement is due to the way the information is handled and returned.

Normally when an asynchronous search is implemented, a call to either `GetFirstRow` or `GetNextRow` is executed. Either one of these searches can take time to perform. If this is the case, you do not want to have to wait until the entire search ends before returning any results, especially if the search will be based on a large forest or domain.

By specifying an asynchronous search, you will get some results returned while the remainder of the search is carried out. This can help to give the perception of a fast search.

There is one other important point to note about using asynchronous searches and that is if you have paging enabled as well. In this case, the search will return results only in full pages. That is to say that a page of the size specified in the paging setup will be filled first before any results are returned from the search. As long as your pages are not too large, this shouldn't present too much of an issue.

Search Filter Syntax

You can specify filters on your searches, which serve as criteria for returning only required information. If you are familiar with database searching, you will understand the concept of *filters*. Essentially they are responsible for allowing only specified criteria to be returned from a search.

The filters that you require may be something as simple as wanting only information returned on user accounts that are in the same groups or perhaps share the same last name. Whatever the reason for your search filter, it will make the returned results more closely matched to what you were looking for and reduce the amount of data needed to be returned. This can be a benefit for data transfer across slow networks.

There are certain search filters that you can use, and ADSI makes use of the LDAP search filters. These search filters use Unicode strings for their representation. Unicode is a replacement for ASCII and provides enough characters in its character set for almost all of the languages in the world to use. The complete set of search filters for LDAP can be found on the Internet in RFC 2254.

The syntax for using a filtered search can take one of two possible formats. These are shown here:

```
filter = <attribute><operator><value>
```

or

```
<operator><filter1><filter2>
```

Your filters are specified as `objectClass` and `objectCategory` for two examples.

The attribute is optional and can be `ADsPath`, `Domain`, or `Name`.

The operator can be any of the ones found in Table 11.1.

TABLE 11.1 Operators Used for Comparison in Filters

Operator	Description
=	Equal to
~=	Approximately equal to
<=	Less than or equal to
>=	Greater than or equal to
&	AND (logical AND comparison)
!	NOT (logical negation)
|	OR (logical OR comparison)

An example of the syntax might be as follows. More examples will be given in the following sections on SQL dialect and LDAP dialect.

```
(objectClass = *)
```

This example will return all objects in the search.

Dialects Used for Searching Active Directory

There are two dialects used for searching AD. They are SQL, which stands for *Structured Query Language* and is the language used to query and manipulate data found in databases or OLE DB compliant data sources, and LDAP. LDAP, as you know, is the *Lightweight Directory Access Protocol* and ADSI makes use of the LDAP protocol, hence the inclusion of it in the search dialects.

SQL Dialect

As mentioned in the introduction to this section, SQL is the language used to query data sources. These can be database applications or OLE DB data sources. As it turns out, ADSI is an OLE DB data source.

ADSI exposes two interfaces for searching using SQL, ActiveX Data Objects, or ADO interfaces, and, for use with the C/C++ language, OLE DB interfaces.

The SQL dialect uses the following syntax:

```
SELECT [ALL] * | list FROM 'ADsPath' [WHERE criteria] [ORDER BY criteria]
```

When you examine this statement you will see capitalized words. These are SQL keywords and are listed and described in Table 11.2.

TABLE 11.2   Keywords Used in SQL Statements

Keyword	Description
SELECT	This is the first and most used keyword that starts the SQL string. It indicates that you will be choosing information from a data source based on the remaining information in the SQL string.
	Most of this information in the SQL string will be comma-separated values for the attributes of the objects or the * symbol which will return the ADsPath of every object.
FROM	Used to indicate the ADsPath start point or base where the search will start. The path is enclosed in single quotes as shown here:
	`'LDAP://CN=Users,DC=Sales,DC=gkcomput,DC=com'`
WHERE	This is an optional parameter and is used to specify criteria to base the search on.
ORDER BY	This is another optional parameter that is used to specify an order to sort the results in based on a particular object.
	This will cause the sort to take place on the server if it supports sorting. AD supports sorting but caution should be used as it may affect server performance.
	You can also specify a sort order by appending the ASC for ascending or DESC for descending order. The ASC keyword is not really required as ascending is the default sort order.

The following examples show some possible SQL strings that can be used to search ADSI with the SQL Dialect.

```
SELECT ADsPath, cn FROM 'LDAP://DC=gkcomput,DC=com'
➥ WHERE objectCategory = 'group'
```

This search string will return the ADsPath and common name for all the group objects from the gkcomput.com domain.

```
SELECT ADsPath, cn FROM 'LDAP://OU=Sales,DC=gkcomput,DC=COM'
➥WHERE objectCategory='person' AND objectClass='user'
➥AND sn = 'O*' ORDER BY sn
```

This is a more complex SQL string that will search in the person category under users for all users who have a last name that starts with O and contains any number of characters afterward.

> **NOTE**
>
> If you are used to SQL as a database query language, you may already be familiar with the fact that the keywords are normally typed in uppercase as a way of differentiating the keywords from the other text in the SQL string. The case is not sensitive.
>
> That is not the case with the SQL dialect used here. The keywords are case sensitive so ensure that you use the correct case when typing in the keywords.

LDAP Dialect

The second dialect used in ADSI searches is the LDAP dialect. This dialect uses the LDAP search filter syntax for creating search statements. LDAP queries can use the following interfaces:

- ADO
- OLE DB
- IDirectory Search

Both the OLE DB and the IDirectory Search are C/C++ interfaces with the former used for databases and the latter used for Active Directory. As we are not using C/C++ for our language of choice, we will not cover those aspects.

The LDAP string consists of four parts, separated by semicolons, that make up the entire search string.

The first part is known as the base distinguished name and looks like this:

```
LDAP://DC=gkcomput,DC=com
```

By now you have seen this many times and it needs no further explanation.

The second part of the LDAP string is the portion that contains the search filters. An example follows:

```
(&(objectCategory=person)(objectClass=contact)(sn=gobrien))
```

You can see here that the search criterion is based on an object category of person, a class of contact, and surname of gobrien. This search is actually based on a search that would take place in Microsoft Exchange using a contact entry in the Exchange store.

The third part of the LDAP dialect string is the Attribute section. This part would include attributes such as ADsPath, department, and manager.

The fourth part specifies the search scope. You will recall from earlier in the chapter that the search scope can be Base, One-level, or Subtree.

> **NOTE**
>
> If you were creating an application and you were using the ADO command object and had specified a search scope in that command object, this setting would override that specified in the ADO command object.

An example of an LDAP dialect search string is shown here:

```
"<LDAP://DC=gkcomput,DC=com>;(objectClass=*);ADsPath, cn; subtree"
```

This is a rather generic string in that it searches for all of the objects in a `subtree`.

You have some flexibility in the search filters section of the string as well. You can make use of wildcard characters as well as some of the more common operators. A few examples are shown here:

```
(cn>='Gerry')
```

This filter will search for entries that have a common name greater than `Gerry` in alphabetical order. It is not especially useful, but it provides an example of using operators.

```
(&(sn=obrien)(objectClass=user)(email=*))
```

This filter will search for all users with a surname of `obrien` who have an `email` attribute.

```
(!(email=*))
```

This will return all entries that exist but do *not* have an `email` attribute.

You can see that we have used some comparison operators as well as a logical negation operator in the string to filter the results.

Processing Resultsets

You have seen some reference to resultsets in this chapter when we talk about returning information from a search. A *resultset* is a group of rows that are used to represent the data that has been returned from a search. The method used to traverse this resultset differs depending on the interface used to query ADSI.

If you are using an OLE DB interface to search, the results will be returned in a SQL-like resultset. This means that the results will reside in a detached file that is no longer connected to the data source but exist as a snapshot in a file on the local computer. You can move forward and backward through this resultset with what is known as a cursor. A *cursor* is a pointer or locator to a record in a resultset. This would be utilized in an `ADODB.Recordset` object. You can create this recordset object in your scripts by making reference to the ADODB library. See the MSDN help files for more information on ADODB recordsets online at `http://msdn.microsoft.com` or `http://www.microsoft.com/data`.

The other interface is the IDirectory interface and is used when you are querying the ADSI structure from a language such as C++. This interface contains its own access mechanisms for navigating through the recordset and is beyond the scope of this book.

Client-Side Caching

As with most applications, caching is a way of enhancing performance. ADSI allows you to utilize client-side caching for your results.

Client-side caching stores the returned resultset in the memory of the client computer. This has the following effects. First, it allows for faster access to the returned data as it resides in fast computer RAM and on the client. It doesn't have to be sent across the network again.

Second, it allows the client to move freely within the resultset using what is known as a cursor. You can search forward and backward or go through the results as many times as you want.

As with most things performance related, there is a tradeoff. The tradeoff here is that depending on the size of the returned results, you can take up a considerable amount of memory on the client computer. This may be an issue if you are using thin clients or scaled down workstations that don't have a lot of memory on board.

If this is the case, you may need to turn off client-side caching. By turning off caching, the results will not reside in the client's memory therefore not allowing the use of a cursor to scroll through the results.

This means that the user can only scroll forward through the results and must load each row as it is needed. The connection is not maintained to the result. You will have to balance the effect of caching based on the available RAM in the computer and the speed at which you need to be able to scroll through the results.

Sorting

As was mentioned earlier in the chapter, you can specify that the server sort the data before returning it. Sorting is done using two possible orders, ascending and descending. Ascending is the default and need not be specified but you can do so to ensure that the results are indeed sorted in ascending order. You specify either ASC or DESC after the sort attributes following the ORDER BY clause in the SQL string.

You can also specify sorting attributes in the sort string. The server will sort the results on the attribute that you specify, such as Last Name or Department.

You can also specify multiple sort attributes by separating each by a comma in the list. This will cause the server to sort on each of the attributes in the order that they are entered. For example, if you specified sort attributes of Last Name, First Name and Department in this order, the results will be sorted based on last name first. Where there are common last names, the first name will be used next to sort the results. If there are identical last and first names, then the department will be the final deciding sort key.

> **NOTE**
>
> When performing sorts, it is recommended that whenever possible, you should sort on indexed attributes to speed the sorting.

> **NOTE**
>
> Check your directory provider's documentation to determine whether it supports multiple sort attributes. Not all do.

Query Interfaces

By now you have read that there are interfaces used for querying ADSI. There are three interfaces that you can use for searching ADSI and they are listed here:

- *IDirectory Search*—This interface is used by applications written in C/C++. It is a COM interface but it is not available to Visual Basic or VBScript so it will not be covered here.

- *ADO*—ActiveX Data Objects is an interface for OLE automation for languages that support OLE DB. You should use ADO in VBScript, Visual Basic applications, and Active Server Pages.

- *OLE DB*—This is another interface that is used by C/C++ programmers. It provides advanced functionality in ADSI providers for things such as distributed queries.

All three of these interfaces allow the use of the search parameters and settings that have been discussed in this chapter, including the following:

- Asynchronous searches
- Search Scope (Base, One-level, and Subtree)
- Size limits
- Paging
- Time limits
- Timeouts
- Sorting, including sort orders
- Referrals

Searching with ADO

ADO is Microsoft's newest data access method for accessing databases such as Microsoft Access and SQL Server but also supports OLE DB and ODBC, which allows it to be used for accessing any compliant data source that is not a database.

This means that you can access non-database data sources with it such as Exchange Server stores and of course, ADSI.

In order to use ADO you need to be aware of what is required in ADO to make the connection. The following list shows the components of ADO that you should be familiar with:

- *Connection*—A connection to a data source.
- *Command*—Used to specify commands that will be executed against the data source.
- *Parameters*—Optional collection of arguments that will be provided to the command object if needed.
- *Recordset*—The returned records, or resultset, that will be used to navigate through. Previous data access methods did not allow you to create recordset objects without first creating the objects higher up in the object model first. ADO allows you to create a recordset object directly with first creating a parent command or connection object.
- *Field*—Represents a single column in the recordset.
- *Property*—This is a collection of values that are normally supplied by the provider of the ADO interface.
- *Error*—This object contains error information that is returned from the connection object.

In order for you to connect to ADSI using ADO, you must, at the very least, create a connection and a recordset. The connection is used to authenticate you with the ADSI service and the recordset is used to hold the returned data for you to navigate through.

If you wish to use any parameters in the query such as the search scope or page size for paging, then you need to create a command object as well to handle this information.

From within your VBScript code, you can create a connection to the ADSI provider with the following code:

```
Dim cnnConnection
Set cnnConnection = CreateObject("ADODB.Connection")
CnnConnection.Provider = "ADsDSOObject"
```

ADO needs to know what provider it must use for the connection so that it can understand the access mechanisms.

If you need to provide user credentials for authentication on the server, you can do so by setting properties on the connection. The following list shows the available properties and their meanings:

- User ID—Use this setting to specify a username to be supplied to the connection string for authentication on the server.
- Password—If the username supplied requires a password, provide that password here in this property.
- Encrypt Password—a Boolean value that indicates whether the password should be encrypted. The default is False. If in doubt, leave the default.
- ADSI Flag—This property is used to specify a flag to be used from the collection of available flags. You can find these flags in the reference section for the ADSI enumerations in the ADSI Reference. The default is zero (0). This setting is used to indicate binding authentication options.

You specify the properties by using the Properties option of the connection object. An example is shown here:

```
cnnConnection.Properties("User ID")="gobrien"
cnnConnection.Properties("Password")="password"
cnnConnection.Properties("Encrypt Password")=True
```

The various properties here are hard-coded but you could have declared variables and used them to pass the necessary information to the ADO connection object. As a matter of fact, this is the recommended approach as it allows you to reuse your scripts for different users without having to change the code of the script to accommodate different users.

In order for you to issue a search on ADSI, you need to create a command object and provide it with some arguments as well. The syntax for this is shown here:

```
Dim cmdCommand
Set cmdCommand = CreateObject("ADODB.Command")
```

Once you have created the command object, you need to associate it with a connection before you can issue any commands. This is shown here:

```
Set cmdCommand.ActiveConnection = cnnConnection
```

This associates your command object with the connection object that has been used to open a connection to the ADSI data source. The next step is to create a command to send to the data source for execution. You do this by setting the command object's CommandText property as shown here:

```
cmdCommand.CommandText = "SELECT ADsPath, cn FROM
➥ 'LDAP://DC=Microsoft,DC=com' WHERE
➥ objectClass = '*'"
```

As you can see here, this command text string is the same search string that you saw built earlier in the section "Search Filter Syntax."

At this point you may be asking how you go about setting the other properties for searching that we have been talking about, such as Referrals, Paging, and caching. The answer is simply to set some more properties on the command object. You do this by setting the properties as shown here:

```
cmdCommand.Properties("Timeout")=30   ' 30 seconds
cmdCommand.Properties("searchscope")=ADS_SCOPE_SUBTREE
cmdCommand.Properties("Cache Results")=False
```

Although this is not all of the properties that have been discussed in this chapter on searches, you can substitute your search parameter into the parentheses to set that property.

As was mentioned earlier in this section, you will be returned a set of results and you need to have some place to store those results. You create and populate a recordset for this purpose. The following code does just that:

```
Dim rsRecords
Set rsRecords = cmdCommand.Execute
```

This small piece of code declares a recordset variable called rsRecords and then populates that recordset with the data returned as a result of executing the command object's CommandText.

Once you have the data returned in a recordset, you can then set about moving through the records and displaying them as needed.

If you want to move through the records that are returned, you use the navigation methods listed here:

- MoveFirst—This method is used to navigate to the first record in the recordset.
- MovePrevious—Use this method to navigate to the previous record in the recordset. If you don't include error handling in your code and you execute this method while you are at the first record, you will receive an error.
- MoveNext—This method will navigate forward one record in the recordset. Like the MovePrevious method, an error will be generated if you are at the last record in the recordset.
- MoveLast—This method is used to move to the last record in the recordset.

If you wish, you can use a loop to navigate through the recordset and display the records. It is recommended that you utilize a method to output the results to a text file or run the code using CScript to avoid creating a large amount of message boxes with the Echo command. The following code will echo the results to the command prompt window:

```
rsRecords.MoveFirst
Dim intCounter
Do While Not rsRecords.EOF

For intCounter = 0 To rsRecords.Fields.Count - 1
    Cscript.echo rsRecords.Fields(intCounter).Value
Next

rsRecords.MoveNext
Loop
```

This little code snippet first of all navigates to the first record using the MoveFirst method. This is done to ensure that we start at the beginning of the recordset and then declares a counter variable, intCounter, that will be used to increment or step through the available fields in the recordset.

Then, it sets up a Do While loop, which is responsible for checking a property of the recordset known as EOF. This stands for End Of File and is used by all ADO recordsets. These recordsets use this to indicate that there are no more records and you are at the end. Remember when I mentioned about doing error checking when using the MovePrevious and MoveNext methods? The EOF and BOF properties are ideal to check for in your code when either of these methods is used.

The next step is to set up another loop, which in this case is a For loop. We initialize the counter variable to 0 and set its upper boundary to the amount of records in recordset. The -1 is used to bring the upper boundary down by one because we are using a zero-based approach rather than starting at 1.

This loop will cause the system to navigate through the fields and echo the name of the field to the command prompt window. The MoveNext method is executed to move to the next record in the recordset and the final Loop statement causes the recordset's EOF property to be verified.

As you can see, ADO is not really a complicated search method to use and it can be used in Visual Basic applications, VBScript code running on the client computer, or as VBScript code running in an ASP page on a server.

Modifying ADSI Objects from ADO

SQL includes a statement that is used to make changes to the underlying data in a recordset or data source known as UPDATE. Using this statement would be a simple method to change the ADSI object ;however, at this time, the UPDATE method is not implemented in AD, because the OLE DB provider that is included is read-only. To get around this limitation, you can use the following code in Listing 11.1 to update or modify ADSI objects.

LISTING 11.1   Example Code Used to Modify an ADSI Object

```
'This example will update the department number for all users
'in the sales division of the gkcomput.com

Dim cnnConnection
Dim cmdCommand
Dim rsRecords
Dim objUser

Set cnnConnection = Server.CreateObject("ADODB.Connection")
cnnConnection.Provider = "ADsDSOObject"

Set cmdCommand = CreateObject("ADODB.Command")
Set cmdCommand.ActiveConnection = cnnConnection

cmdCommand.CommandText =
➥ "SELECT ADsPath, cn FROM 'LDAP://OU=Sales,
➥ DC=gkcomput,DC=com' WHERE objectClass = 'user'"

cmdCommand.Properties("searchscope") = ADS_SCOPE_ONELEVEL
Set rsRecords = cmdCommand.Execute
Do While Not rsRecords.EOF
    Set objUser = GetObject(rsRecords.Fields("ADsPath").Value)
    objUser.Put "department", "1001"
    objUser.SetInfo
    rsRecords.MoveNext
Loop
```

As the comments in the code indicate, this sample will update the department number for all users that are in the sales division of gkcomput.com. This is the recommended approach to updating fields in ADSI using ADO.

Summary

This chapter has provided information to help you enhance the performance of your ADSI searches. You saw how to define the depth and scope of your queries by specifying the properties in the search parameters. By setting the proper scope and depth, you prevent the search from looking into areas where it is not necessary, thereby reducing the length of time it takes to perform the search.

You saw other enhancement options as well, such as Paging which creates sizable chunks of data to be transferred more efficiently across network connections. You also looked at referrals, indexing, and object categories which all contribute to improving the performance of your searches.

You also saw the two search dialects that you can use with ADSI, SQL and LDAP and looked at examples of each dialect.

The chapter also discussed caching data on the client and how it gives you the ability to navigate through the data without needing to make round trips to the server. It also indicated that caching involves tradeoffs in terms of memory usage on the client computer.

Finally, you saw an example of using ADO to query ADSI and how the various parts of ADO, the connection, command, and recordset objects allow you to access and manipulate the data returned from the search.

The information presented here will allow you to make the best use of available resources on the server and client when performing your searches for objects and attributes in AD.

ADSI Security

IN THIS CHAPTER

Any interface to your user, group, or computer accounts will obviously create security concerns. ADSI is no different, and perhaps has a greater need of a security model than most interfaces due to its close ties with the Active Directory objects. It's not a good idea to open these objects up to any interface without requiring proper authorization.

You have already seen the power that scripting brings to you in your administrative tasks on the computer and AD domains. Leaving your AD open to unauthorized scripts is an invitation for disaster.

This chapter will take a look at what is involved in ADSI security and how you can implement it into your administrative scripting tasks. You will look at security aspects that are related to user authentication and access control on your directory service objects.

Taking ADSI security seriously is not something new to you as an administrator. This chapter will provide you with the information necessary to make effective use of the security model in ADSI in order to secure your scripts and ensure only authorized execution of those scripts.

Authentication

Authentication in ADSI uses essentially the same information as authentication when logging on to a network. A username and password are required. This allows ADSI to authenticate the user who is making the request.

With DCOM, security concerns are normal, but you need not worry about passing credentials across the network. DCOM uses what is known as SSPI authentication and encryption. This means that the information is sent in encrypted format. SSPI stands for Security Service Provider Interface and is supplied by the providers, such as Microsoft, for using the security features in DCOM.

Authentication with the `ADsOpenObject` Function

You can deal with authentication in two ways. One way you can authenticate is by using the `ADsOpenObject` helper function, which is used to establish the user's credentials for the directory service and operation being carried out. This requires that you provide the credentials as arguments to the function so that it can pass those credentials on to the Directory Service provider's security mechanisms for user authentication.

Using the `ADsOpenObject` function has both good and bad points. First of all, if you are providing the credentials as hard-coded values, anybody who has access to the script file also has access to the user's credentials. This is a potential security hole that should not be left open. This is why you have seen the use of variables in the scripts to hold the username and password. In this way, the credentials can be supplied at the time the script is executed and are not included in the script file itself. This requires an extra step on the user's part but is a much better choice in terms of security.

> **TIP**
>
> Remember from previous chapters when we talked about hard-coding? The security issues mentioned here are an excellent example of why you should not hard-code information into your scripts. It is easy to do, but you will be glad you didn't in the long run.

Authentication via User Logon Credentials

The other authentication option is to do nothing at all in terms of authentication. By taking this course of action, you will cause the directory service to rely on the user's logon credentials for the operating system. This means that the directory service will compare the user account that is requesting the operation with the ACLs (Access Control Lists) for the user account as dictated by the logon authentication server. Also, this will determine whether the user has access to the requests that are being made.

> **CAUTION**
>
> You likely don't need reminders about security with user and group accounts, but authentication using the logon credentials requires you to ensure that your user and group account restrictions are adequately set to reduce the possibility of scripts being executed inadvertently by users who should not have permission to do so. Remember, users are curious and will execute scripts just to see what they will do.

This method can provide the best of security, in a sense, because no credentials are passed during the process. The system will check the currently logged on user's credentials before allowing the operation. In this way, there is no need to provide any credentials up-front, and the administrator has much better control over who is allowed to access and execute certain processes.

Another advantage of using the latter method is that you can create blanket rights. This simply means that you assign rights that give more than one user permission to access the resources by assigning permissions to groups and then placing only those users who should have access to the resources within these groups. This is a more natural way for network administrators to work, as you are already familiar with creating groups and placing users in these groups for ease of administrative tasking.

Once users have been authenticated, they are given access to the resources that they have privileges for and can access files and shares and execute scripts. An example of providing user credentials with the OpenDSObject function is provided here:

```
Dim objNamespace
Dim objReturn

Set objNamespace = GetObject("LDAP:")
Set objReturn = objNamespace.OpenDSObject(gkcomput,
➥ gobrien, password)
```

This example shows declaring an object variable to hold an instance of the IADsOpenDSObject object. This variable is then set to the LDAP namespace by using the GetObject function. Finally, we set the returned data equal to the objReturn variable after opening the resultset with the OpenDSObject function and passing it a username and password as credentials for the gkcomput.com domain.

Access Control

Most of you are already familiar with the acronym ACL, which stands for *Access Control List*. ACLs are used in ADSI, as well as in NT and Win2K SAM objects. ACLs in ADSI are used to store and manage ACEs. ACEs are *Access Control Entries*, and are used by ADSI to grant or deny access to ADSI objects and their properties.

An ACE in ADSI is used to define access permission for objects based on user or group account information. As all network administrators know, it is best to create a group that will receive the access permission and then assign the individual user accounts into that group to make for easier administration. ACLs in ADSI are lists of ACEs for objects.

In order to manipulate security descriptors for the ADSI objects, you work with properties and methods. There are three interfaces that provide this functionality for you and they are listed here.

- *IADsAccessControlEntry*—This interface is used to read and write the Access Control Entry (ACE) properties.
- *IADsAccessControlList*—Use this interface to manage/enumerate all of the available ACEs on a directory object.
- *IADsSecurityDescriptor*—This interface allows you to read and write the security properties of an ADSI object.

The code listing in the following section shows these interfaces in action.

Creating a Security Descriptor Object

The security mechanisms in ADSI wouldn't be complete if they didn't allow you to modify or create security descriptors in addition to reading them. To that end, WSH, coupled with the ADSI interfaces, allows you to do just that.

You can create ACEs and ACLs using ADSI and WSH. Listing 12.1 shows how to create both an ACE and an ACL that will serve as a security descriptor for an ADSI object.

LISTING 12.1 An Example Script Used to Create a Security Descriptor on an ADSI Object

```
' ********************************************************************
' SecurityDescriptor.vbs
' This script file is used to demonstrate how to create
' a security descriptor for an ADSI object.
'
' Author: Gerry O'Brien
' Date: June 20, 2001
' Platform: Windows 2000/XP
' Language: VBScript
' ********************************************************************
Dim objIADs
Dim objIADsSecDes        'IADsSecurityDescriptor interface
Dim objSecDes
Dim objDacl           'IADsAccessControlList interface
Dim objACE           'IADsAccessControlEntry interface
' Here we are creating an ACE for group objects on the gkcomput.com domain
With objACE
    .AccessMask = 0
    .AceType = 1
    .AceFlags = 1
    .Trustee = "cn=Groups,o=gkcomput"
End With
' Here we add our newly created ACE object as the lone ACE
' in a new ACL.
With objDacl
    .AceCount = 1
    .AclRevision = 4
    .AddAce Ace
End With
' Here we use the ACL as a discretionary ACL for
' our security descriptor object and use
' the discretionary ACL instead of the defaultACL.
With objSecDes
    .Revision = 1
```

LISTING 12.1   Continued

```
    .OwnerDefaulted = True
    .GroupDefaulted = True
    .DaclDefaulted = False
    .SaclDefaulted = True
    .DiscretionaryAcl = Dacl
End With
' Now we have to attach the security descriptor
' to our ADSI object.
' We have called it ntSecurityDescriptor
objIADs.Put "ntSecurityDescriptor", SecDes
' Remember, the Put method will only place the value into the local cache
' We must call the SetInfo method to save the value to persistent storage
objIADs.SetInfo
' Now that we have create the entries and saved them to
' persistent storage, we need to refresh the local cache so
' that it contains an up-to-date copy of the data
objIADs.GetInfo
' Once we have the information in the local cache, we can
' request the information and display the value
Set objIADsSecDes = objIADs.Get("ntSecurityDescriptor")
WScript.Echo objSecDes
```

> **NOTE**
>
> You might have noticed that, unlike most of the code listings in this book, Listing 12.1 contains comments. The reason is that this listing is a little longer than most and it would be more difficult to explain it line by line if you had to switch back and forth between the code and the description.

In short, the code here creates a security descriptor for an ADSI object and first stores it in the local cache. The script then calls the SetInfo method to save the descriptor properties to the persistent storage.

Enumerating ACLs on an ADSI Object

If you can set the ACEs and ACLs on the ADSI objects, it only makes sense that you can also enumerate those values. In order for you to enumerate the various ACLs on the directory server, you must have the appropriate access permissions. If you are not logged in as an Administrator or other user account with the correct privileges, you must ensure that you pass in a username and password that has the appropriate rights.

The various ACLs may differ based on the objects that you have in your Active Directory. Your network differs from others in terms of how you have your accounts set up, how many groups you have, what network resources (for example, printers, fax modems, shared drives) you have in the network, and so on. The script code shown in Listing 12.2 demonstrates how to enumerate the ACLs on the ntSecurityDescriptor object for the Celeron500 server in my network.

LISTING 12.2   An Example Script That Enumerates the ntSecurityDescriptor ACLs for the Celeron500 Server

```
' ************************************************************************
' EnumSecObjects.vbs
' This script file is used to demonstrate how to enumerate
' the security descriptors for your ADSI objects.
'
' Author: Gerry O'Brien
' Date: June 20, 2001
' Platform: Windows 2000/XP
' Language: VBScript
' ************************************************************************
Dim objDSObject
Dim objNamespace
Dim objSecurityDescriptor
Dim objDacl

' We need to return the LDAP directory service to work with

Set objNamespace = GetObject("LDAP:")

' Login with credentials that have the appropriate access permissions

Set objDSObject = objNamespace.OpenDSObject("LDAP://Celeron500", _
    ➥ "cn=administrator", "password", 1)

' Return the values of the ntSecurityDescriptor field.
' This field is an interface pointer to the security descriptor object
' for the objDSObject object.

Set objSecurityDescriptor = objDSObject.Get("ntSecurityDescriptor")

' Echo the owner and group of the object to the screen in a dialog box.

WScript.Echo objSecurityDescriptor.Owner
WScript.Echo objSecurityDescriptor.Group
'
```

LISTING 12.2 Continued

```
Set objDacl = objSecurityDescriptor.DiscretionaryAcl

' Enumerate the ACEs in the objDacl object,
' and display the number of ACEs in the object.

WScript.Echo objDacl.AceCount

' Echo the listed attributes of the objDacl object

For Each Obj In objDacl
    WScript.Echo Obj.Trustee
    WScript.Echo Obj.AccessMask
    WScript.Echo Obj.AceFlags
    WScript.Echo Obj.AceType
Next
```

If you wish, you can execute this script from the command prompt using CScript instead of WScript. You might consider doing this if you have a large number of ACLs on your server; if you use WScript, you may get a little tired of closing out the message boxes that the Echo method creates.

Summary

This chapter has presented some information related to the security aspects of ADSI objects. If you are a network administrator, you understand the use of ACLs and the need for them. It is not always necessary to set ACLs and ACEs for more than one object at a time, but you can do so with WSH and ADSI.

Enumerating the ACLs is a good way to determine what you have assigned to specific objects in your directory. This way, you can run a quick check on them when things don't seem to be right.

Keep in mind that you really need to keep a close tab on scripts that manipulate and read the ACLs on your objects. When you are using these scripts, the username and password credentials are hard-coded into the script and if the script is not protected from prying eyes, that information can be used against your network.

WSH and the .NET Framework

IN THIS CHAPTER

As most of you know by now, Microsoft has a new initiative in terms of development languages, tools, and their operating systems known as .NET. For those not familiar with .NET, a brief introduction will be included here.

The .NET framework is the next generation set of tools and interfaces that software developers will use to develop applications on the Windows platform. The framework is more than just a new set of tools, though. The underlying structures of some tools and technologies have changed. The 3 million plus Visual Basic developers all over the world will notice the biggest changes.

Microsoft has made changes to the underlying class structures of Visual Basic. Everything in VB .NET is a class now and developers need to deal with namespaces, something they didn't have to know about before.

VB .NET also uses what are known as preprocessor directives. These are instructions to the compiler to insert files or perform actions prior to compiling the application's source code. C and C++ programmers are probably more familiar with these than VB programmers.

VB .NET maintains a lot of its language syntax, such as that for declaring variables, but it looks more like C++ now. Or is it that VB .NET and C++ .NET look more like C#? The reason I pose that question is that Microsoft is really pushing C# as the "preferred" language for .NET.

The .NET framework includes enhancements and changes to the visual interfaces that developers use in their applications. For instance, forms, which provide the most common means of interacting with the user, are now a base set of classes. VB developers are used to having a form available to drop controls on and set properties on without the need to worry about the underlying architecture of the form. They will need to deal with forms in a different way now, with .NET based on the class structure and object-oriented features built into the forms.

The .NET Common Language Runtime

All of the languages that are a part of the .NET framework will operate on what is known as a *Common Language Runtime (CLR)*. This CLR is responsible for the changes to the VB language itself. The idea behind the CLR is that all languages will work with one runtime. The *runtime* is a component that is responsible for managing the execution of code on the computer. In every version of Visual Basic, VB developers have had to include the runtime engine as a part of the installation of their application. Each time the VB application was executed, the runtime had to be loaded into memory. This runtime itself can consume a lot of resources on the computer. The CLR allows all three languages that exist in the .NET framework at present to communicate with one runtime.

Each language will compile its source code to what is known as an Intermediate Language (IL) format. The common language runtime acts as sort of an interpreter for the IL code.

Another major advantage of the CLR is that all of the languages that support it can share information contained in their data types with each other. This means that an organization can have developers who know VB, C#, or C++ and each can program in their own language. The applications they are designing can make use of all three languages, and each language can call functions and receive returned values from each of the others with no requirements for conversion.

This also means that development tool vendors, such as Borland with Delphi and Power Builder, can write their tools to the CLR specification and have them integrated into the .NET framework. This can help a company avoid the costs of retraining their base of developers.

Another potential use of the CLR, although nobody at Microsoft is indicating this, could be the ability to create a cross-platform framework for applications developed using the .NET framework. This would be similar to the Java programming language's Java Virtual Machine (JVM), which prevents the developer from having to write an application more than once: As long as a computer platform has the correctly installed JVM, the application will run. This allows the developer to create one application and have it execute successfully on the Windows platform, Unix/Linux platforms, and Mac platforms without the need to compile the application separately for each platform.

Where the .NET Components Will Be Found

The .NET framework components are built into Microsoft's newest client and server operating systems, Windows XP and Windows .NET Server. More .NET functionality will be in the next Windows OS release, code named Blackcomb. For Windows 2000, when you install Visual Studio .NET, or any part of it, there is a need to run a Windows Components Update that will install the necessary .NET components.

The changes that are present in .NET have a slight impact on scripting languages (only Microsoft knows for sure how much). The following sections will look at the various languages in terms of how they fit into the .NET framework, both from the administrative scripting standpoint and the application development standpoint.

Languages in .NET

As far as languages for development or scripting go, we can safely classify them into two categories: scripting languages and development languages. These are not "set in stone" categories, but these categories are what I like to use to separate the two styles of programming. There are enough differences between the two programming styles to warrant the separate categories. Let's begin with the two scripting languages you have used throughout the book, VBScript and JScript. After discussing these, you will cover the development languages found in .NET: Visual Basic, C++, and C#.

VBScript

At present, there is no mention of the VBScript scripting language in the .NET framework. This may be due in part to the changes to the Visual Basic language itself. Because VBScript is a subset of Visual Basic, any changes to Visual Basic will also have an impact on VBScript.

The changes made to Visual Basic will be discussed in the upcoming "Visual Basic" section, and those changes will help you understand why the two subsets will need to differ.

For the most part, the .NET framework and the components that update Windows 2000 or are present in Windows XP/.NET Server do not affect your VBScript code in any way at present. As I write this text, Visual Studio .NET is still only in Beta 1, with Beta 2 due out before this book's publication, so there may be changes. It has been indicated in some industry publications that all applications written in Beta 1 will break in Beta 2 due to the changes made. This remains to be seen.

The computer systems that I used for the examples in this text are a Windows 2000 Professional computer with the .NET framework installed and a Beta 2 version of Windows .NET Server with Active Directory installed running a domain within my network. I created and executed every code sample included in this book using VBScript, and duplicated many of them in JScript. The .NET framework has not affected the operation or successful completion of any script.

The main reason behind this is the fact that the scripting engine used, WSH 5.6, still understands and works with VBScript. This indicates that any script you create today will still run and execute for years to come on your Windows 2000/XP/.NET Server systems with no modifications required. WSH 5.6, which is still in beta form, has been integrated into Windows XP/.NET Server, and in its final form will be included within the final release of those operating systems.

Because WSH is the interpreter of the VBScript engine, .NET does not need to be concerned with the execution of the code. Given the fact that WSH is a part of the next release of Windows, Microsoft has basically indicated that they are continuing to support the VBScript language.

NOTE

I won't be too surprised if VBScript and Visual Basic go their separate ways, with VBScript maintaining its current code base and language syntax. Microsoft may, of course, change this at a later time, but this only means that VBScript will become a more powerful and flexible scripting language.

In the long run, it would be much better for all concerned if VBScript were to make changes to reflect those in VB .NET. My reasoning behind this statement is based on the fact that the world of software development is all about object-oriented concepts and programming. As mentioned in the chapters about ADSI, the interfaces for ADSI are COM components, which are based on object-oriented concepts and programming. It only makes sense to develop languages that can take full advantage of this programming paradigm. Visual Basic itself has slowly been migrating to the object-oriented abilities of other languages, such as Java and C++, but hasn't fully implemented it until VB .NET. Although VB developers have to relearn portions of the language using new methods, they now have a fully object-oriented language.

Why does this indicate that VBScript would be a better language by following suit? For the same reasons that object-oriented programming is so widely adopted and used now. The ability to create software components that closely model real-world objects and that can be reused is a compelling reason to migrate toward an object-oriented paradigm. Remember back in earlier chapters where you saw examples of using include files to reuse functionality that already existed in other scripts. This is the same concept used in OO programming: Create a generic component or process that can be reused and enhanced, saving the developer considerable time by eliminating the need to rebuild something that already exists.

JScript

JScript is mentioned throughout the .NET framework documentation in the early release of Beta 1, which indicates that the language is supported within the framework. This is not really surprising given the fact that JScript follows the ECMA script standard. Since ECMA script is a widely accepted standard, it only makes sense to include support for that standard.

Java is an object-oriented language and Microsoft had a Java equivalent in J++. Due to legal issues between Microsoft and Sun Microsystems, Microsoft no longer produces the J++ development language. The same foundation that J++ used is still somewhat prevalent in the .NET languages, or at least the syntax is identical in nature. As a result, support for Java-based languages still exists in .NET.

In much the same way as VBScript, JScript is still an integral part of the WSH engine, and is therefore included along with any installation of the WSH engine in the supported operating systems.

Because of JScript's ties with the Java programming language and its ability to work with COM objects and the technology behind them, it is only natural that it should be a part of the .NET initiative.

There are no guarantees that JScript will continue to be around in future releases of .NET, or whatever other technology Microsoft comes up with, but you can be assured that you will be using JScript for years to come as well. Any time invested in learning it will not be wasted.

13

WSH AND THE
.NET FRAMEWORK

C++

The C++ language has been a mainstay in software development for quite some time. It is actually an enhancement of the C language that was created by Dennis Ritchie and Brian Kernigan at AT&T.

Bjarne Stroustrup is credited with the extensions and additions to C++. Most of these enhancements were meant to give C the ability to function in an object-oriented development world.

C++ introduced developers to *classes*, which are ways to build software components that can model real-world objects. This enabled developers to create more robust applications and to save considerable development time by creating reusable components that could be plugged into an application quite easily.

Due to the popularity of C, C++ became an almost instant hit because the learning curve for existing C developers was low. The language syntax is the same, which means that C developers didn't have to change the way they wrote code.

There is actually a bit of controversy that still exists in the public newsgroups on the Internet concerning these two languages. The question asked is whether one should learn C first and then migrate to C++. This is, of course, an indication that some see the C language as easier to learn than C++.

For the most part, C++ developers will tell you that it is not necessary to learn C first. In fact, most will tell you that you should not learn C first, but concentrate on C++ from the start. There are two very good reasons for this thought. Reason number one actually asks a question in turn. "Why learn two languages when one will do the work of both?" Second, there are some differences between the two languages that could cause problems when you are switching from C to C++. These differences can cause new programmers some grief, as they have to unlearn the C way of doing things to embrace the C++ way of doing the same thing.

Also, the switch from a procedural type programming language to an OOP-based one also requires a rethinking in terms of application design. When you design an OO application, you need to take into consideration code reuse issues for the objects that you create. This is mostly due to the fact that other programmers may use your objects in their own applications later and you need to ensure that the interfaces to those objects are designed to allow ease of use without allowing the user to "break" the objects or change their functionality.

An example of this is the way the two languages differ in output to the console, or command prompt. The C language uses the syntax

```
printf("String to output to the screen\n");
```

whereas C++ has changed the output string to this:

```
cout << "String to output to the string\n";
```

This is actually a trivial difference, but there are quite a few other differences between the two languages, some of which are more significant. This makes for a fair bit of unlearning or relearning when you could save yourself the trouble and learn C++ from the start. This is, of course, if you want to do object-oriented programming or you intend to write applications for the Windows environment. You can safely learn and stay with C if you want to write applications for the Linux or Unix environments, as a fair bit of code is still written in C for those operating systems. This is, of course, far removed from our main topic of scripting for administrative tasks, but this chapter is designed to give you some information as to what will be available to work with in the .NET framework of operating systems and development tools.

Visual Basic

As you have already learned in the text of this book, VBScript is a subset of this language. Visual Basic has been around for quite some time now, even in the "Visual" version.

Taking its roots from BASIC, which was actually the language used by a lot of early personal computers such as Commodore's VIC-20 and C-64, it has enjoyed widespread usage by novice and professional programmers over the years.

Because of its popularity (there are somewhere in the vicinity of 3 million Visual Basic programmers worldwide), it will be around for some time to come.

Over the years, the language has, like anything else in the computer industry, evolved to keep up with technology. The Visual Basic that you will see in Visual Studio .NET looks somewhat different from the current version, 6.0. Most of the additions are long overdue for Visual Basic and developers have been asking for them for quite some time.

One of the biggest changes in the Visual Basic language for the .NET framework is the fact that it is now considered to be a full object-oriented programming language. What this means is that VB programmers can now enjoy the programming abilities that Java and C++ programmers have enjoyed for so long.

One of the advantages that make the change welcome to some is the fact that VB .NET can now do *inheritance*. Inheritance is the ability of a language to take the existing functionality of an object and use it while enhancing it as needed to meet an application's needs. Until now, Visual Basic could not do inheritance without fancy workarounds.

There is some dissatisfaction among members of the VB development community in terms of the new learning curve for existing VB developers. Most realize that with each new version, they have had to learn new features and capabilities. This version, however, adds so much more and makes so many changes to the existing language syntax that the learning curve is steeper than ever before.

Most of the reasons behind this are due to changes necessary for VB to interact with the other .NET languages, C++ and C#. The .NET framework development languages are being built on a common language runtime, mentioned earlier in the chapter. Because of this, VB's underlying data types have changed to match those of the other languages.

Of course I mentioned that VB is now fully object-oriented in the upcoming release, which means that VB developers need to grasp these new concepts as well and how to implement them in the new programs that they will develop.

How these changes to VB will affect future versions of VBScript is not yet quite clear. I have been assured by some of the Microsoft scripting staff that VBScript is not going away any time soon, but that the direction of future versions of the language has not yet been decided.

C#

The newest language in Microsoft's developer's suite of tools is C# (pronounced C sharp). C# is a musical note, but I doubt Microsoft intended you to write sheet music with the language.

The rumor mill has been in full swing since the announcement of C# and the exclusion of J++. It is no secret that Microsoft and Sun Microsystems went to court over Microsoft's use of Java in the J++ product. Microsoft lost that court battle, and was not allowed to use the core of Java outside of the guidelines set forth by Sun in the licensing agreements. Apparently, Sun felt that Microsoft was trying to make J++ incapable of creating non-Windows applications or something to that effect.

As a result, the rumors are indicating that C# is J++ with a different name and a slightly different twist to make it legal. Whatever the particulars, there is now another programming language available to developers. Is this bad? Not really—the more quality tools developers have to work with, the better the quality of the applications that they will turn out. (At least, we hope that's how it works.)

At any rate, Microsoft is really pushing the use of C# in all of their documentation, in the beta releases anyway, and in the advertisements for .NET. Is it a Java killer? It might be seen as that, but as of the current releases it cannot displace Java's hold on multiplatform capabilities.

The Common Language Runtime may be the key to solving this issue, and, if that is the case, it would empower all of Microsoft's languages (with the exception of FoxPro) with the ability to create "write-once run anywhere" code. This could be seen as a potential Java killer.

I don't foresee C# displacing Java because there are so many developers using Java now and enough anti-Microsoft camps out there that the possibility of this is far-fetched.

A look at the syntax and functionality of C# reveals the similarities to Java. *Garbage collection*, a term that describes the process of cleaning up memory resources after an application has ended or an object has been destroyed, has been used in Java for some time now and exists in C# as well. This is an added advantage to developers in either language because it frees them from having to worry about memory management tasks.

Will we see a C# scripting language? Likely not, as the existing scripting languages more than adequately cover the needs of script writers and administrators.

Summary

What the .NET framework will mean to script languages and those who write scripts is not completely clear at the moment. For the most part, the scripts that you are writing now will serve you for years to come, as a good portion of you are likely still using the Windows NT 4.0 platform. Microsoft has not committed to eliminating or renewing the script languages VBScript and JScript, but the fact that they are not going away in the near future is reassurance in itself.

The time you invest in your scripts using either language will be well spent. The .NET framework will change the landscape mostly for software developers. The changes all seem to be for the better, although there will be those who don't want to learn what is needed to change along with new methods of programming.

It is also extremely important to note that what has been mentioned in this chapter is only current as of the time of this book's writing. The .NET strategy is a dynamic concept and it continues to evolve based on industry and developer feedback along with Microsoft's own in-house changes and ideas. Look for a lot of changes to the way the languages work before the final release is on the shelves.

Scripting languages are a powerful and useful tool for administrators and will be here for the foreseeable future to provide you with the same capabilities you enjoy with them today. The .NET framework can only serve to enhance those capabilities and make creating scripts easier for you.

13

WSH AND THE .NET FRAMEWORK

WSH Reference

IN THIS APPENDIX

This appendix will provide a reference for the various objects, properties, methods, and events available in Windows Script Host 5.6. You will also find coverage of the XML elements used in WSH.

Objects

This section lists the objects that are used with your scripts. Here you will find information on each of the objects that you can gain access to in Windows Script Host and how to use them to perform the various functions required by your scripting needs.

WScript

This is the root object for the WSH object model. This object provides access to most of the objects' methods and properties in the WSH object model.

Because it is the root object, you do not have to instantiate it to gain access to its properties or methods. It is always available from any script file.

Use the WScript object to gain access to arguments that will be passed in to the script, script file names, and version information for the host environment.

Example:

```
Wscript.Echo ("Hello World!")
```

This example will output the string Hello World! in a message box.

```
var objController =
➥ Wscript.CreateObject("Wscript.Controller")
```

The WScript object contains the following properties and methods. Each of the properties and methods will be discussed further in the appropriate section in this appendix.

Properties:

- Arguments
- FullName
- Name
- Path
- ScriptFullName
- ScriptName
- StdErr

- `StdIn`
- `StdOut`
- `Version`

Methods:

- `CreateObject`
- `ConnectObject`
- `DisconnectObject`
- `Echo`
- `GetObject`
- `Quit`
- `Sleep`

WshArguments

This object is a collection that contains all of the command-line parameters that were given when the script was executed. It will contain the arguments in the order in which they were entered at the command line.

You can access both named and unnamed arguments with the `WshNamed` and `WshUnnamed` objects respectively. These objects will be covered shortly.

Example:

```
Set objArgs = WScript.Arguments
For I = 0 to objArgs.Count - 1
   WScript.Echo objArgs(I)
Next
```

This example will enumerate the arguments passed at the command line and for a script and will display them, in the order they were entered, one at a time in a message box.

Properties:

- `Item`
- `Length`
- `Count`
- `Named`
- `UnNamed`

Methods:

- Count
- ShowUsage

WshController

This object is used to create remote scripts. It is a child object of the WScript object; therefore, you must use the CreateObject method of the WScript object to instantiate an object of type WshController before you can use it.

Example:

```
// Create a WshController object (with which you can create
// instances of local or remote scripts).
var WshController = WScript.CreateObject("WScript.Controller");
// Using the WshController object, create a WshRemote object.
➡var remoteScript = WshController.CreateScript("d:\scripts\myScript.js"
➡   \\Engineering\Test1\);
// Start the script.
remoteScript.Execute();
if (remoteScript.Status != 2) {
    remoteScript.Terminate();
}
```

Methods:

This object has only one method, called CreateScript.

WshEnvironment

This object is a collection of Windows Environment Variables that are returned by the WshShell's Environment property. When you want to retrieve a specific variable from the collection, you use its name as the index.

Example:

```
var objShell = WScript.CreateObject("WScript.Shell");
var objWshEnv = objShell.Environment("Process");
WScript.Echo (objWshEnv("Os2LibPath"));
WScript.Echo (objWshEnv("include"));
WScript.Echo (objWshEnv("windir"));
WScript.Echo (objWshEnv("path"));
WScript.Echo (objWshEnv("lib"));
```

This script example will display the variables related to the specified names in a message box for each one.

Properties:

- Item
- Length

Methods:

- Count
- Remove

WshNamed

This object provides access to the collection of named arguments that is returned in the named property of the WshArguments object. The name is used as the index for the returned value.

Example:

```
' This is the command typed at the prompt.
➥cscript TestScript.vbs /c:named1 /d:named2
' TestScript contains this code.
WScript.Echo WScript.Arguments.Named.Item("c")
WScript.Echo WScript.Arguments.Named.Item("d")
```

This is the output:

```
named1
named2
```

Properties:

- Item
- Length

Methods:

- Count
- Exists

WshNetwork

The WshNetwork object is used to gain access to the network resources that are shared on your network. It is a child object of the WScript object; therefore, it must be instantiated using the WScript.CreateObject method before you can use it.

A

Example:

```
Set objNetwork = WScript.CreateObject("WScript.Network")
Set objDrives = objNetwork.EnumNetworkDrives

WScript.Echo "Domain Name = " & objNetwork.UserDomain
WScript.Echo "Computer Name = " & objNetwork.ComputerName
WScript.Echo "User Name = " & objNetwork.UserName
WScript.Echo "Network Drives:"

For i = 0 to objDrives.Count - 1 Step 2
WScript.Echo "Drive " & objDrives.Item(i) & " = " & objDrives.Item(i+1)
Next
```

The various network resources will be enumerated and returned. The `WScript.Echo` commands will display them in message boxes.

Properties:

- ComputerName
- UserDomain
- UserName

Methods:

- AddPrinterConnection
- EnumNetworkDrives
- EnumPrinterConnection
- MapNetworkDrive
- RemoveNetworkDrive
- RemovePrinterConnection
- SetDefaultPrinter

WshRemote

This object provides access to remote scripts for execution on remote computers. It is used to represent a remote script file with the extension .wsf, .wsh, .vbs, or .js.

Example:

```
// Create a WshController object (with which you can create
➥ instances of local or remote scripts).
var WshController = WScript.CreateObject("WScript.Controller");
// Using the WshController object, create a WshRemote object.
```

```
var remoteScript = WshController.CreateScript("d:\scripts\myScript.js"
➡ \\Engineering\Test1\);
// Start the script.
remoteScript.Execute();
if (remoteScript.Status != 2) {
    remoteScript.Terminate();
}
```

Properties:

- Status
- Error

Methods:

- Execute
- Terminate

Events:

- Start
- End
- Error

WshRemoteError

This object is used to hold the error information that is returned from the Error object of a remote script that was created using the WSHRemote object. This object will hold a description of the error as well as an indication as to where the error occurred.

Example:

```
Dim  objError
objError = RemoteScript.Error()
➡WScript.Echo("Error at Line " + objError.Line + ", Char " +
➡theError.Character + ": " + theError.Description)
➡ WScript.Quit(-1)
```

This example will indicate the line and character that the error occurred on as well as a description of the error.

Properties:

- Description
- Line

A

WSH REFERENCE

- Character
- SourceText
- Source
- Number

WshScriptExec

This object is returned by the Exec method of a WshShell object. It will be returned either before the script executes or after it has completed executing.

This object also provides access to the StdIn, StdOut, and StdErr objects.

Example:

```
Dim objState
Set objState = WshShell.Exec "%comspec% /c scriptName.vbs"
```

Properties:

- Status
- StdIn
- StdOut
- StdErr

Method:

- Terminate

WshShell

This object provides access to the Windows Shell. The main use for this object is to run local programs, create shortcuts, manipulate the registry, and to gain access to the local environment variables. This object is a child of the WScript object and must be created before it can be used.

Example:

```
Dim WshShell
Dim objShortcut

set WshShell = WScript.CreateObject("WScript.Shell")
strLocation = WshShell.SpecialFolders("Desktop")
set objShortcut = WshShell.CreateShortcut(strLocation &
➥ "\Shortcut Script.lnk")
```

```
objShortcut.TargetPath = WScript.ScriptFullName
objShortcut.WindowStyle = 1
objShortcut.Hotkey = "CTRL+SHIFT+F"
objShortcut.IconLocation = "notepad.exe, 0"
objShortcut.Description = "Shortcut Script"
objShortcut.WorkingDirectory = strLocation
objShortcut.Save
```

This example uses the WshShell object to create a shortcut to the Notepad application on the desktop.

Properties:

- CurrentDirectory
- Environment
- SpecialFolders

Methods:

- AppActivate
- CreateShortcut
- ExpandEnvironmentStrings
- LogEvent
- Popup
- RegDelete
- RegRead
- RegWrite
- Run
- SendKeys
- Exec

WshShortcut

This object provides you with access to the Windows Special Folders such as Desktop, Personal Documents, and the Start Menu. The information is returned in a collection and includes the path to the Special Folders. This object is used mostly for creating shortcuts.

Example:

See the previous example under the WshShell reference.

Properties:

- Item
- WshSpecialFolders

Method:

- Count

WshSpecialFolders

This object is used to provide access to the Windows Special Folders collection. The Special Folders are the Personal Documents, Desktop folders, and Start Menu folders. The collection will return the path to the Special Folders.

Example:

```
var WshShell = WScript.CreateObject("WScript.Shell");
strLocation = WshShell.SpecialFolders("Desktop");
var objLink = WshShell.CreateShortcut(strLocation +
➥ "\\Shortcut Script.lnk");

objLink.TargetPath = WScript.ScriptFullName;
objLink.WindowStyle = 1;
objLink.Hotkey = "CTRL+SHIFT+F";
objLink.IconLocation = "notepad.exe, 0";
objLink.Description = "Shortcut Script";
objLink.WorkingDirectory = strLocation;
objLink.Save();
```

This example shows a JScript file used to access the Desktop Special Folder to create a shortcut to the Notepad application.

Properties:

- Item
- Length

Method:

- Count

WshUnnamed

This object is a read-only collection of unnamed arguments returned from the Unnamed property of the WshArguments object. This collection uses a zero-based index. Script files can make use of named and unnamed arguments when executed from the command line.

Example:

```
WScript.Echo WScript.Arguments.unnamed.Item(0)
WScript.Echo WScript.Arguments.unnamed.Item(1)
```

These two lines of code will echo to the screen the two unnamed arguments that were used when the script was executed using the following command at the command prompt.

```
cscript scriptName.vbs arg1 arg2
```

Properties:

- Item
- Length

Method:

- Count

WshUrlShortcut

This object is a child of the WshShell object. The purpose of this object is to create a URL shortcut to an Internet resource on the user's desktop or computer. You must use the WshShell's CreateShortcut method to create a URL shortcut.

Example:

```
Dim objUrlLink
Dim strLocation

set WshShell = WScript.CreateObject("WScript.Shell")
strLocation = WshShell.SpecialFolders("Desktop")
set objUrlLink = WshShell.CreateShortcut(strLocation &
➥ "\Sams Publishing.url")

objUrlLink.TargetPath = "http://www.samspublishing.com"
objUrlLink.Save
```

This example creates a shortcut on the desktop to the Sams Publishing site.

Properties:

- FullName
- TargetPath

Method:

- Save

Properties

This section presents the properties that you can use to get or set the various attributes of the objects that you deal with in WSH.

Arguments

There are two objects that contain an `Arguments` Property: `WScript` and `WshShortcut`.

WScript

The `Arguments` property for the `WScript` object returns a collection of `WshArguments` that is a zero-based collection of arguments, named or unnamed.

Example:

```
Set objArgs = WScript.Arguments
For I = 0 to objArgs.Count - 1
   WScript.Echo objArgs(I)
Next
```

This example will loop through the arguments that are associated with a script at the command line.

WshShortcut

This property returns or sets a string that represents the arguments to a shortcut.

Example:

```
var WshShell = WScript.CreateObject("WScript.Shell");
var strLocation = WshShell.SpecialFolders("Desktop");
var objLink = WshShell.CreateShortcut(strLocation +
➥ "\\Shortcut Script.lnk");

objLink .TargetPath = WScript.ScriptFullName;
objLink .WindowStyle= 1;
objLink .Hotkey= "Ctrl+Alt+f";
objLink .IconLocation= "notepad.exe, 0";
objLink .Description= "Shortcut Script";
objLink .WorkingDirectory= strLocation ;
objLink .Arguments = "C:\\txtFileName.txt";
objLink .Save();
```

This example creates a shortcut on the desktop to the notepad application and provides a file-name to associate with the application when it is started from this shortcut.

AtEndOfLine

This property is a Boolean value used to indicate the end of a line in a text file as used by the StdIn object.

Example:

```
var TextFile = fso.OpenTextFile(fileName, ForReading,
➥ false, FormatASCII);
while (!TextFile.AtEndOfLine)
{
    var strInput = set + TextFile.Read(1);
}
TextFile.Close();
```

This example opens a text file and continues to read the file until it reaches the end of a line in the file. At this time, the AtEndOfLine property becomes True.

AtEndOfStream

A Boolean value used to indicate that the StdIn property has reached the end of the stream. Do not confuse this with the AtEndOfLine property that only shows True if the end of a line in the file is reached. This indicates the end of the file being input.

Example:

```
var TextFile = fso.OpenTextFile(fileName, ForReading,
➥ false, FormatASCII);
while (!TextFile.AtEndOfStream)
{
    var strInput = set + TextFile.Read(1);
}
TextFile.Close();
```

This example will continue to read the file until it detects the end of file indicator.

Character

This is a property of the WshRemoteError object. It is used to return the character in the line that caused an error in the execution of a remote script. It will return a long integer data type.

Example:

```
WScript.Echo("An Error Occurred at Line " + theError.Line +
➥ ", Char " + theError.Character + ": " + theError.Description);
```

This line of code will display in a message box, the line and character at which the error occurred along with a description of the error.

A

Column

A property of the StdIn input stream. It determines the column number of the current position in the input stream. It is a read-only integer.

The column property will be equal to 1 after a newline character is written. For example, the carriage return and line feed will generate a newline.

Example:

```
Dim fso, tsStream, strResult
Dim fileName
filename = "C:\Test.txt"
Set fso = WScript.CreateObject
➥("Scripting.FileSystemObject")

Set tsStream = fso.OpenTextFile(fileName,, false,
➥ FormatASCII)

if Not tsStream.AtEndOfStream Then
    strResult = Cstr(tsStream.Read(12))
End If

WScript.Echo strResult
WScript.Echo strResult & "Ends at column " & tsStream.Column
tsStream.Close()
```

ComputerName

This is a property of the WshNetwork object and returns a string value indicating the computer name. You can use this property in an enumeration that returns network objects.

Example:

```
Set WshNetwork = WScript.CreateObject("WScript.Network")
WScript.Echo "Computer Name = " &
➥ WshNetwork.ComputerName
```

This example creates a WshNetwork object and then displays the name of the computer that is returned when the script is executed.

CurrentDirectory

This is a property of the WshShell object and is used to retrieve or change the current directory. This directory is the fully qualified path name of the working directory. This is not necessarily the same directory that contains the script file but is the working directory at the time the script is executed.

Example:

```
var WshShell = WScript.CreateObject ("WScript.Shell");
WScript.Echo (WshShell.CurrentDirectory);
```

This JScript file shows an example of creating a WshShell object and using that object to return the current directory.

Description

This property applies to the WshShortcut object and is used to return the description of the shortcut in a string value. It also applies to the WshRemoteError object and is used to return a description of the error that caused your remote script to unexpectedly terminate. This is also a string value. If there is no error, the string will be empty.

Example:

```
set WshShell = WScript.CreateObject("WScript.Shell")
strLocation = WshShell.SpecialFolders("Desktop")
set objLink = WshShell.CreateShortcut(strLocation  &
➥"\Shortcut Script.lnk")

objLink.TargetPath = WScript.ScriptFullName
objLink.WindowStyle = 1
objLink.Hotkey = "Ctrl+Alt+e"
objLink.IconLocation = "notepad.exe, 0"
objLink.Description = "Shortcut Description"
```

This example creates a shortcut using the WshShortcut object and then, using the Description property, sets the description of the shortcut to Shortcut Description.

Example:

```
var objError = RemoteScript.Error;
WScript.Echo("An Error Occurred at Line " +
➥ objError.Line + ", Char " + objError.Character +
➥ ": " + objError.Description);
```

Environment

The Environment property is a property of the WshShell object and returns a collection of environment variables in the WshEnvironment object. This property takes an optional string argument (strType) that is used to indicate the location of the variable as shown in the example.

Example:

```
Set WshShell = WScript.CreateObject("WScript.Shell")
Set WshSysEnv = WshShell.Environment("SYSTEM")
WScript.Echo WshSysEnv("NUMBER_OF_PROCESSORS")
```

This example demonstrates returning environment variables from the System class and displaying the number of microprocessors in the computer.

Error

This is a property of the WshRemoteError object and is used to return the error information when a remote script terminates unexpectedly.

Example:

```
var colError = RemoteScript.Error;
WScript.Echo("An Error Occurred at Line " + theError.Line +
➥", Char " + theError.Character + ": " + theError.Description);
```

This example shows the use of the Error property to return the error information where it can be accessed and displayed using the line, character, and description properties.

ExitCode

This is a property of the WshScriptExec object and is returned from a script executed using the Exec method. The return code is used to indicate success or failure of a script. If the script is not successful, an error code will be returned indicating the error.

Example:

```
If WshScriptExec.ExitCode = 0 Then
    Wscript.Echo "Script completed successfully!"
Else
    Wscript.Echo "Error occurred in script"
End If
```

This example will check the code returned in the ExitCode property and if the code is 0, the message will be displayed indicating a successful execution.

FullName (WScript)

This property will return the fully qualified path to the WScript object. The property is read-only.

Example:

```
WScript.Echo (WScript.Fullname);
```

This example will produce the following output if you performed a default installation on the C drive on a computer running Windows NT:

```
C:\WINNT\System32\cscript.exe
```

FullName (WshShortcut)

This property will return a read-only value indicating the full path to the WshShortcut object.

Example:

```
Dim WshShell
Dim strLocation

Set WshShell = CreateObject ("WScript.Shell")
strLocation = WshShell.SpecialFolders("Desktop")

Dim objLink
➡Set objLink = WshShell.CreateShortcut(strLocation &
➡ "\\Shortcut Script.lnk")

objLink.TargetPath = WScript.ScriptFullName
objLink.WindowStyle = 1
objLink.IconLocation = "notepad.exe, 0"
objLink.Description = "Shortcut Script"
objLink.WorkingDirectory = strLocation
objLink.Save
WScript.Echo objLink.FullName
```

This example creates a shortcut on the desktop and then displays the fully qualified path name in a message box.

FullName (WshUrlShortcut)

This property returns the fully qualified path name of the WshUrlShortcut object. It is a read-only string value.

Example:

```
Dim objUrlLink
➡Set objUrlLink = WshShell.CreateShortcut(strLocation &
➡ "\\Sams Publishing.url")

objUrlLink.TargetPath = "http://www.samspublishing.com"
objUrlLink.Save

WScript.Echo objUrlLink.FullName
```

A

WSH REFERENCE

This example will display the fully qualified path name to the URL shortcut that was created on the desktop.

HotKey

This property is used to assign a key combination to a shortcut or URL shortcut.

Syntax:

```
Object.Hotkey = strHotKey
```

- `Object` is a `WshShortcut` object.
- `Hotkey` is the property.
- `strHotKey` is the key combination.

For the most part, these are normally a combination of the Ctrl, Alt, and/or Shift keys along with a letter key.

Example:

```
objLink.Hotkey = "Ctrl+Alt+L"
```

This example will allow the user to execute the shortcut by holding down the Ctrl, Alt, and L keys simultaneously.

IconLocation

This property is used to assign or locate an icon that will be used for the shortcut that is created.

Syntax:

```
object.IconLocation = strLocation
```

- `object` is a `WshShortcut` object.
- `IconLocation` is the property.
- `strLocation` is the fully qualified path to the file that holds the collection of icons to be used.

You can also specify an index value, starting at `0`, that is used to indicate the icon within the collection that you wish to use.

Example:

```
objLink.IconLocation = " C:\Program Files\Microsoft
➥ Office\Office\winword.exe, 0"
```

This example will use the first icon in the collection contained within the winword.exe file.

Interactive

This property sets or identifies the script mode. There are two modes that script files can run in, Batch or Interactive. When the script mode is set to Interactive, the script can output or echo information to the screen and can receive input from the user.

In Batch mode, input and output is disabled for the script file. You can set either mode by using command-line switches. //I sets Interactive mode and //B sets Batch mode.

Item

The Item property is used to access specific items from a collection.

Example:

```
Set WshNetwork = WScript.CreateObject("WScript.Network")
Set objDrives = WshNetwork.EnumNetworkDrives

For i = 0 to oDrives.Count - 1
        WScript.Echo "Drive " & oDrives.Item(i)
Next
```

This example sets up a WshNetwork object and enumerates the network drives. A For...Next loop is used to display each of the drive items in the drives collection.

Item (WshNamed)

This property is similar to the generic Item property listed above only it applies specifically to the WshNamed object.

Syntax:

```
object.Item(key)
```

- object is a WshNamed object.
- key is the name of the item to retrieve.

This property will return a string value indicating the item in the collection specified by the key value.

Example:

```
' Execute the script with this command
myScript.vbs /c: namedArg

' Use this code in a script file
WScript.Echo WScript.Arguments.Named.Item("c")

' The result will be
namedArg
```

Item (WshUnnamed)

This property is the same as the `Item` property for the `WshNamed` object except that it deals with the unnamed arguments passed to a script file.

Syntax:

```
object.item(key)
```

Example:

```
' Execute the script with this command
myScript.vbs  UnnamedArg

' Use this code in a script file
WScript.Echo WScript.Arguments.Unnamed.Item(0)

' The result will be
UnnamedArg
```

Length

The `Length` property is used only in JScript but is similar to VBScript's `Count` property. It is a read-only integer value that is used to indicate different concepts depending on the object used with it. These are listed here:

- `WshArguments`—returns the number of items in the `arguments` collection
- `WshEnvironment`—returns the number of environment variables in the `Environment` collection
- `WshSpecialFolders`—returns the number of Special Folders on the local computer system that are part of the `SpecialFolders` collection

Line (WScript)

The `Line` property is used with an input stream for the current `WScript` object and returns the number of lines in the input stream as taken from the `StdIn` property.

This is a read-only integer value. When a stream is first opened but before any writing has taken place, the line value will equal 1.

Line (WshRemoteError)

This property is used for returning the line number that an error occurred on in a remote script. The data type returned is an unsigned long integer. You can use this information in custom error handling routines that you can create or use them as a means to debugging your scripts.

Example:

```
WScript.Echo("An Error Occurred at Line " +
➡ theError.Line );
```

Name

This property will return the name of the WScript object, which is the host environment.

Syntax:

```
object.name
```

object is a WScript object.

Example:

```
Wscript.Echo Wscript.Name
```

Named

This property is used to return a collection of named arguments for the WshArguments object. The named arguments are used at the command line when executing a script.

Syntax:

```
object.named
```

object is a WshArguments object.

Example:

```
Set objArguments = WScript.Arguments
Set WshNamed = objArguments.Named

For I = 0 to WshNamed.Count - 1
   WScript.Echo WshNamed (I)
Next
```

This example enumerates the collection of named arguments and then uses a For...Next loop to iterate through the collection and display each one in a message box.

Number

This property is part of the Error object and is used to represent the Error number for the error that was generated.

Syntax:

```
object.number
```

object is a WshRemoteError object

A

WSH REFERENCE

Example:

```
WScript.Echo "Error Number " & theError.Number
```

This example will cause the error number that was generated by the remote script to be displayed to the screen in a message box.

Path

This property is used to return a read-only value indicating the full path to the WScript executable that was used to execute the script (WScript.exe/CScript.exe).

Syntax:

```
object.Path
```

object is the WScript object.

Example:

```
Wscript.Echo Wscript.Path
```

ProcessID

This property holds the Process ID (PID) for a process that was started using the WshScriptExec method. It can also be used to activate an application by specifying it as an argument to the AppActivate method.

Syntax:

```
object.ProcessID
```

object is a WshScriptExec object.

Example:

```
Dim objCalculator
ObjCalculator = shell.Exec("calc");
AppActivate theCalculator.ProcessID
```

This example will start the Calculator application in Windows.

RelativePath

This is used with the WshShortcut object to specify or return the relative path for a shortcut. The data type is string.

Syntax:

```
object.RelativePath
```

Example:

```
Dim objShell = WScript.CreateObject ("WScript.Shell");
Dim objShortcut = objShell.CreateShortcut(ScriptShortcut.lnk");
objShortcut.RelativePath = "C:\Scripts\";
```

This example creates a shortcut and then sets the `Relativepath` of that shortcut to
`C:\Scripts\`.

ScriptFullName

This property is a read-only string that returns the full path for the currently running script.

Syntax:

```
object.ScriptFullName
```

`object` is a `WScript` object.

Example:

```
Dim objLink
set objLink = WshShell.CreateShortcut(strDesktop & "\Shortcut.lnk")
objLink.TargetPath = WScript.ScriptFullName
```

This example sets the `TargetPath` property of the `objLInk` object to the `ScriptFullName`
property of the executing script.

ScriptName

This property is a read-only string that returns the name of the currently running script.

Syntax:

```
object.ScriptName
```

`object` is a `WScript` object.

Example:

```
Wscript.Echo Wscript.ScriptName
```

Source

This is a string value that is used to indicate the name of the COM object that caused the error
in the script.

Syntax:

```
object.Source
```

`object` is a `WshRemoteError` object.

Example:

```
Dim objError
objError  = RemoteScript.Error;
WScript.Echo "The Error was caused by " & theError.Source
```

This example demonstrates how the source of the error is returned as a string value and echoed to the screen in a message box.

SourceText

This property is a string value that is used to return the line of code that caused the error. This value may be empty at times when an error is generated and is dependent on the error and/or the state of WSH.

Syntax:

```
Object.SourceText
```

object is a WshRemoteError object.

Example:

```
Dim objError
objError  = RemoteScript.Error;
WScript.Echo "The Error was caused by the line " & theError.SourceText
```

This example will echo the line that caused the error in the source code to the screen in a message box. This can be very helpful in determining exactly where the error occurred and speeds up debugging of scripts.

SpecialFolders

This property is a collection that holds the Special Folders specified in the Windows environment. Special Folders are considered to be the Desktop, Personal Documents, and the Start menu folder.

Not all versions of Windows have all of the Special Folders. For example, Windows 95 does not contain the AllUsersDesktop Special Folder. If you request this folder in a script, the SpecialFolders property will return an empty string.

Syntax:

```
object.SpecialFolders(objWshSpecialFolders)
```

object is a WshShell object and objWshSpecialFolders is the name of the Special Folder you want to retrieve.

Example:

```
Dim objShell
Dim objLink
Dim strDesktop
set objShell = WScript.CreateObject("WScript.Shell")
strDesktop = WshShell.SpecialFolders("Desktop")
set objLink = WshShell.CreateShortcut strDesktop & "\Shortcut.lnk"
```

This example creates a string variable to hold the name of the Special Folder, in this case `Desktop`. It then uses that variable to create a shortcut link on the desktop.

Status (WshRemote)

This property is used to return a read-only value that indicates the status of a remote script.

Syntax:

```
object.Status
```

`object` is a `WshRemote` object.

Values:

- NoTask—The remote script was created but not executed.
- Running—The remote script is still running.
- Finished—The remote script has completed execution.

Example:

```
Dim objController
Dim objRemoteScript
Set objController = WScript.CreateObject(WScript.Controller");

Set objRemoteScript = Controller.CreateScript
➥ ("d:\scripts\remotescript.vbs" \\Celeron500\Test\

objremoteScript.Execute();

Wscript.Echo objremoteScript.Status
```

Status (WshScriptExec)

This property is used to indicate the status of a script that was executed asynchronously with the `WshScriptExec`'s `Exec` method.

Syntax:

```
object.Status
```

object is a `WshScriptExec` object.

Values:

- WshRunning—The script is still executing. Returns 0.
- WshFinished—The script has completed. Returns 1.

Example:

```
Dim objExec
objExec= WScript.Exec("Script.vbs");

Select Case (ExecObj.Status)
    case 0
        WScript.Echo("The script is still executing.")

    case 1
        WScript.Echo("The script has completed execution.")
End Select
```

This script will start the execution of a script and will then display its status using a Select Case statement to determine the status of the script.

StdErr (WScript)

This is a right-only property that is used to specify an error that has occurred in a script file. It uses the output stream for the current script.

StdErr can only be used with the CScript.exe command-line script engine. Attempting to use it with WScript.exe will generate an error.

Syntax:

```
object.StdErr
```

object is a `WScript` object.

StdErr (WshScriptExec)

This property is used to access the StdErr output stream for the Exec object for a remote script when an error occurs. The Exec object does not require a script to be running for access to the StdErr stream.

Syntax:

```
object.StdErr
```

object is a WshScriptExec object.

StdIn (WScript)

This object exposes the StdIn input stream for a running script. The return value is a string data type. You must access this object only with CScript.exe. Using WScript.exe will cause an error.

Syntax:

```
object.StdIn
```

object is a WScript object.

StdIn (WshScriptExec)

This is used to expose the StdIn input stream for the script that was executed using the Exec method of the WshScriptExec object. It is used to pass information between running processes.

Syntax:

```
object.StdIn
```

object is a WshScriptExec object.

StdOut (WScript)

This is used to expose the StdOut output stream for the current script that is executing. The value returned is a string value. You can only access the StdOut stream using CScript.exe. Using WScript.exe will cause an error.

Syntax:

```
object.StdOut
```

object is a WScript object.

StdOut (WshScriptExec)

This contains a read-only value returned from the StdOut output stream of a script that was executed using the Exec method of the WshScriptExec object.

Syntax:

`object.StdOut`

object is a `WshScriptExec` object.

TargetPath

This is used to assign the path to an executable file represented by a shortcut or the executable file itself. It is a string value.

Syntax:

`object.TargetPath`

object is a `WshShortcut` or `WshUrlShortcut` property.

Example:

```
Dim objShell
Dim objLink
Dim strDesktop
set objShell = WScript.CreateObject("WScript.Shell")
strDesktop = WshShell.SpecialFolders("Desktop")
set objLink = WshShell.CreateShortcut strDesktop & "\Shortcut.lnk"
objLink.TargetPath = Wscript.ScriptFullName
```

This example will create a shortcut on the desktop and will assign the full script name to the target path property.

UserDomain

This is a string value that is used to return the name of the user's domain.

Syntax:

`object.UserDomain`

object represents a `WshNetwork` object.

Example:

```
Set objNetwork = WScript.CreateObject("WScript.Network")
WScript.Echo "The user's domain is: "
➥& objNetwork.UserDomain
```

UserName

This is a string value that is used to return the name of the user requested.

Syntax:

```
object.UserName
```

`object` represents a `WshNetwork` object.

Example:

```
Set objNetwork = WScript.CreateObject("WScript.Network")
WScript.Echo "The user's domain is: " &
➥ objNetwork.UserName
```

Version

Used to return a string value that represents the version of Windows Script Host.

Syntax:

```
object.Version
```

`object` is a `WScript` object.

Example:

```
Wscript.Echo Wscript.Version
```

WindowStyle

This property is used to assign or retrieve a window style for a shortcut. The value is an integer value.

Syntax:

```
object.WindowStyle = intWindowStyle
```

- `object` is a `WshShortcut` object.
- `intWindowStyle` is one of the constants listed in Table A.1.

TABLE A.1 Window Style Constants

Constant	Description
1	Activates and displays a window using its original size and position
3	Activates the window and maximizes it
7	Minimizes the current window and activates the next window that is a top-level window

Example:

```
Dim objShell
Dim objLink
Dim strDesktop

set objShell = WScript.CreateObject("WScript.Shell")
strDesktop = WshShell.SpecialFolders("Desktop")
set objLink = WshShell.CreateShortcut strDesktop & "\Shortcut.lnk"
objLink.TargetPath = Wscript.ScriptFullName
objLink.WindowStyle = 1
```

This example will cause the window to restore to its original size and position even if it is minimized or maximized.

WorkingDirectory

Used with a WshShortcut object to specify the working directory for the shortcut or to retrieve the working directory for a shortcut. It is a string value.

Syntax:

```
object.WorkingDirectory = strDirectory
```

- object is a WshShortcut object.
- strDirectory is a string value representing the directory name for the shortcut.

Example:

```
Dim objShell
Dim objLink
Dim strDesktop

set objShell = WScript.CreateObject("WScript.Shell")
strDesktop = WshShell.SpecialFolders("Desktop")
set objLink = WshShell.CreateShortcut strDesktop & "\Shortcut.lnk"
objLink.TargetPath = Wscript.ScriptFullName
objLink.WorkingDirectory = strDesktop
```

This example sets the working directory equal to the value specified in the strDesktop variable earlier in the script.

Methods

This section lists the methods that you can use with WSH to perform the actions needed when working with WSH and ADSI.

AddPrinterConnection

This method is used to add a remote MS-DOS-based printer connection to the computer. This method will only work with DOS-based printers. You must use the `AddWindowsPrinterConnection` method to add a Windows-based printer to the computer.

Syntax:

```
object.AddPrinterConnection(LocalName, RemoteName,
➥[updateprofile], [username], [password])
```

- `object` is a `WshNetwork` object.
- `LocalName` is what will be assigned to the printer on the local computer.
- `RemoteName` is the name of the printer on the remote computer.
- `updateprofile` is an optional parameter that is a Boolean value and is used to indicate whether or not to store the printer mapping into the user's profile.
- `username` and `password` are optional parameters that may be required to install the printer.

Example:

```
Set objNetwork = WScript.CreateObject("WScript.Network")
objNetwork.AddPrinterConnection "LPT1", "\\Celeron500\HPOfficeJet"
```

This example adds a printer connection to the local computer on the LPT1 port from the Celeron500 server that has a network printer called HPOfficeJet.

AddWindowsPrinterConnection

This method performs the same action as `AddPrinterConnection`, but is used to add a Windows-based printer to the local computer.

Syntax:

```
For Windows NT/2000
Object.AddWindowsPrinterConnection(printerpath)
For Windows 9x/Me
Object.AddWindowsPrinterConnection(printerpath, drivername, [port])
```

- `object` is a `WshNetwork` object.
- `printerpath` is the full path to the printer on the network.
- `drivername` is a string value used to indicate the driver name for the printer.
- `port` is an optional parameter used to specify the port for the printer.

A

WSH REFERENCE

Example:

```
Set objNetwork = WScript.CreateObject("WScript.Network")
Set PrinterPath = "\\Celeron500\DefaultPrinter"
objNetwork.AddWindowsPrinterConnection(PrinterPath)
```

AppActivate

This method is used to activate or start an application on the computer and returns a Boolean value indicating if the method was successful. The focus will be set to the application that was started, but the application will not be minimized or maximized by this method.

Syntax:

```
object.AppActivate title
```

- object is a WshShell object.
- title is the title of the application to activate. Title can be a string value or it can be the application's TaskID.

Example:

```
set objShell = WScript.CreateObject("WScript.Shell")
objShell.Run "calc"
WScript.Sleep 100
objShell.AppActivate "Calculator"
```

This example will run the Calculator application and then wait for 100 milliseconds before activating it.

Close

This method is used to close a text stream as used with the StdIn, StdErr, or StdOut properties. You can only use this with scripts executed using CScript.exe. Using WScript.exe will cause an error.

Syntax:

```
object.Close
```

object is one of StdIn, StdOut, or StdErr.

Example:

```
var objStdOut = WScript.StdOut;
var strOutput = "Hello World";
objStdOut.Write(strOutput);
objStdOut.Close();
```

ConnectObject

This method is used to connect an object's events to the script file after you have created the object. Events are something that happens as a result of a user or program action.

Syntax:

```
object.ConnectObject(strObject, prefix)
```

- object is a WScript object.
- strObject is a string value used to indicate the object that you will connect.
- prefix is a string value that is used to indicate the function prefix in the object.

Example:

```
Dim objMyObject
Set objMyObject = WScript.CreateObject("SomeObject")
WScript.ConnectObject(objMyObject, "MyObject_")

MyObject.SomeMethod()

Public Sub MyObject_OnBegin(strName)
    WScript.Echo strName
➥WScript.DisconnectObject(MyObject)
```

This example creates an object and then connects it to your script file. It then calls a method in the object called SomeMethod. If an object fires an event as a result of something happening as discussed previously, then the event that was fired will be called using the prefix MyObject_ that was given.

Count

This method is used to count the number of switches used in the WshNamed or WshUnnamed objects. It will return an integer data type for a value.

Syntax:

```
object.Count
```

object is the Arguments object.

Example:

```
Wscript.Echo Wscript.Arguments.Count
```

A

CreateObject

This method is used to create a COM object. All objects must be created using the CreateObject method before you can use them in your scripts.

Syntax:

```
object.CreateObject(progID, [prefix])
```

- object is a WScript object.
- progID is a string value used to specify the programmatic identifier for the object that you will create.
- prefix is an optional string value used to specify a function prefix for the object.

Example:

```
Set objNetwork = WScript.CreateObject("WScript.Network")
```

CreateScript

This method is used to create a remote script object known as a WshRemote object and returns a handle to the instance of that object.

Syntax:

```
object.CreateScript(commandline,[machinename])
```

- object is a WshController object.
- commandline is a string value that specifies the path to the script and any command-line switches that are needed. This command line is the same string that would be typed at the command line to run the script locally.
- machinename is an optional string argument that is used to specify the name of the computer to create and run the script on.

Example:

```
Dim objController
Set objController= WScript.CreateObject
➥("WScript.WshController")

Dim objRemoteScript
Set objRemoteScript = Controller.CreateScript
➥("d:\scripts\scriptname.vbs")

objRemoteScript.Execute()
```

This example creates a controller object and then a remote script object and executes it.

CreateShortcut

This method is used to create or open shortcuts. It can be used with WshShortcut or WshURLShortcut objects. You must use the Save method before the shortcut is actually created.

Syntax:

```
object.CreateShortcut(pathname)
```

- object is a WshShell object.
- pathname is a string value indicating the full path for the location of the shortcut.

Example:

```
Dim objShell
Dim strPath
Dim objLink
set objShell = WScript.CreateObject("WScript.Shell")

strPath = WshShell.SpecialFolders("Desktop")

set objLink = WshShell.CreateShortcut(strPath &
➡ "\Shortcut Script.lnk")

objLink.TargetPath = WScript.ScriptFullName
```

This example demonstrates creating a shell object, setting its path equal to the Desktop Special Folder and then creating a shortcut there.

DisconnectObject

This method disconnects an object from the event source for that object. WSH will no longer respond to the events for the object once it has been disconnected.

Syntax:

```
object.DisconnectObject(object)
```

- object is a WScript object.
- Object is the name of the object that will be disconnected in a string value.

Example:

```
Dim objMyObject
Set objMyObject = WScript.CreateObject("SomeObject")
WScript.ConnectObject(objMyObject, "MyObject_")

MyObject.SomeMethod()
```

A

WSH REFERENCE

```
Public Sub MyObject_OnBegin(strName)
    WScript.Echo strName
➥WScript.DisconnectObject(MyObject)
```

Echo

This is used to output text to the command-line window when using CScript.exe or in a message box for WScript.exe.

Syntax:

```
object.Echo [argument1], [argument2]
```

- `object` is a `WScript` object.
- The optional arguments are string values used to specify what will be displayed.

Example:

```
Wscript.Echo Wscript.Version
```

This example will display the version of the scripting engine in a message box window.

EnumNetworkDrives

This is a collection that returns the current mapped network drives. The collection will hold the drive name and its UNC specifying the complete path to the drive. The collection is zero-based.

Syntax:

```
objDrives = object.EnumNetworkDrives
```

- `objDrives` is a variable used to hold the collection returned.
- `object` is a `WshNetwork` object.

Example:

```
Dim objNetwork
Dim objDrives
Set objNetwork = WScript.CreateObject("WScript.Network")
Set objDrives = WshNetwork.EnumNetworkDrives
```

This example enumerates the network drives on the local computer.

EnumPrinterConnections

This method is used to return a collection of printer connections that are mapped on the local computer. The collection contains local printer names as well as their UNC names.

Syntax:

```
objPrinter = object.EnumPrinterConnections
```

- `objPrinter` is a variable used to hold the collection of printers.
- `object` is a `WshNetwork` object.

```
Dim wshNetwork
Dim objPrinters
Set WshNetwork = WScript.CreateObject("WScript.Network")
Set objPrinters = WshNetwork.EnumPrinterConnections
```

Exec

This method is used to run an application in a command shell and also provides access to the standard streams, `StdIn`, `StdOut`, and `StdErr`.

Syntax:

```
object.Exec(command)
```

- `object` is a `WshShell` object.
- `command` is a string value used to indicate the command line to execute. This is the same command line that you would type at the command prompt if you were running the script from the command prompt. This method can only execute command-line applications.

Example:

```
Dim objJob
Set objJob = WshShell.Exec("%comspec% /c Script.vbs")
```

This script demonstrates using the `Exec` method to execute the `Script.vbs` script file with the `/c` switch.

Execute

Used with a `WshRemote` object for executing a remote script on another computer on the network.

Syntax:

```
object.Execute
```

`object` is a `WshRemote` object.

Example:

```
Dim objController
Set objController = WScript.CreateObject
➥("WScript.WSHController")
```

```
Dim objremoteScript
ObjRemoteScript = Controller.CreateScript
➡("d:\scripts\myScript.js")

remoteScript.Execute()
```

This example creates a remote script and calls the `Execute` method to start the execution of the script.

Exists

This is a Boolean value used to indicate if a specific key value exists in a `WshNamed` object.

Syntax:

```
object.Exists(key)
```

- `object` is a `WshNamed` object.
- `key` is the value to check for in the arguments to the `WshNamed` object.

Example:

```
WScript.Echo WScript.Arguments.Named.Exists("C")
```

This example will echo `True` to the screen if the `WScript` object contains the `"C"` argument.

ExpandEnvironmentString

This method returns the expanded environment variable's value in a string value. It works with environment variables in the PROCESS space only and the variable names must be enclosed in `%` signs.

Syntax:

```
object.ExpandEnvironmentStrings(string)
```

- `object` is a `WshShell` object.
- `string` is the value of the variable that you want to expand.

Example:

```
set WshShell = WScript.CreateObject("WScript.Shell")
WScript.Echo "WinDir is " &
➡ WshShell.ExpandEnvironmentStrings("%WinDir%")
```

GetObject

This method is used to retrieve an existing object. It will create a new object from a file if the specified object does not exist. It uses `ProgID` as a reference.

Syntax:

```
object.GetObject(Pathname, [ProgID], [Prefix])
```

- object is a WScript object.
- Pathname is the full path to the object.
- ProgID is an optional argument that specifies the program ID for the object.
- Prefix is optional and is used if you want to work with and sink the object's events.

Example:

```
Dim objObject
Dim objApp
Set objObject = GetObject("C:\test.txt\Schema.txt")
objApp = objObject.Application
```

GetResource

This method is used with the <resource> element of a script file and returns the value of the resource defined. The value returned is a string value.

Syntax:

```
GetResource(resourceID)
```

resourceID is the <resource> required from the script file.

Example:

```
<resource id="strSampleID">
    Sample string to be returned.
</resource>

Dim strValue
strValue = getResource("strSampleID ")
```

LogEvent

This method is used to add an entry event to a log file for logging of information. It returns a Boolean value used to indicate if the log was successful. The information will be stored in the Windows NT/2000 Event Log.

Syntax:

```
object.LogEvent(intType, strMessage, [strTarget])
```

- object is a WshShell object.
- intType is an integer that is used to represent the type of event.

- strMessage is the string value that is used to represent the text to be entered in the log.
- strTarget is an optional argument that indicates the computer to log the event onto.

Values:

- 0—Success
- 1—Error
- 2—Warning
- 4—Information
- 8—Audit_Success
- 16—Audit_Failure

Example:

```
WshShell.LogEvent 0, "Logon Script Completed Successfully"
```

MapNetworkDrive

This method is used to add a shared drive on the network to the computer. If you try to map to a drive that is not shared, you will receive an error.

Syntax:

```
object.MapNetworkDrive(strLocalName, strRemoteName,
➥[bUpdateProfile], [strUser], [strPassword])
```

- object is a WshNetwork object.
- strLocalName is a string value used to indicate the name of the drive on the local computer.
- strRemoteName is a string value used to represent the name of the remote shared drive.
- bUpdateProfile is a Boolean value and optional. It is used to indicate whether the value should be reflected in the current users entry in the registry.
- strUser is an optional parameter used to specify a username if required.
- strPassword is an optional parameter used to specify a password if required.

Example:

```
Dim WshNetwork
Set WshNetwork = WScript.CreateObject("WScript.Network")
WshNetwork.MapNetworkDrive ("E:", "\Server\Public")
WshNetwork.RemoveNetworkDrive ("E:")
```

PopUp

Use this method to display a message in a pop-up window style message box.

Syntax:

```
intButton = object.Popup(strText,
➥[nSecondsToWait],[strTitle],[nType])
```

- `intButton` is a variable that will hold an integer value returned from the pop-up telling you which button was used to close the pop-up.
- `object` is a `WshShell` object.
- `strText` is the text that will be displayed in the pop-up box.
- `nSecondsToWait` is an optional value that is used to specify a maximum time the pop-up will be displayed.
- `strTitle` is the text that will appear in the title bar of the pop-up box.
- `nType` is a numeric value used to indicate the type of buttons and icons to display on the pop-up. The values are given below.

Button values:

- O—Ok Button
- 1—Ok and Cancel
- 2—Abort, Retry, and Ignore
- 3—Yes, No, and Cancel
- 4—Yes and No
- 5—Retry and Cancel

Icon values:

- 16—Stop icon
- 32—Question icon
- 48—Exclamation icon
- 64—Information icon

Return values:

- 1—Ok button was clicked
- 2—Cancel button was clicked
- 3—Abort button was clicked

A

WSH REFERENCE

- 4—Retry button was clicked
- 5—Ignore button was clicked
- 6—Yes button was clicked
- 7—No button was clicked

Example:

```
Dim WshShell
Dim intButton
Set WshShell = WScript.CreateObject("WScript.Shell")
intButton = WshShell.Popup("Errors have occurred,
➡ do you want to continue?", 7, "Error!", 3 + 32)
Select Case intButton
    case 6
        WScript.echo("Are you sure you want to continue?")

    case 7
        WScript.Echo("Probably a wise decision")

    case 2
        WScript.echo("Canceling can be good too")

End Select
```

Quit

Use this method to stop the execution of a script. The method can optionally return an error code as well.

Syntax:

```
object.Quit ([errorcode])
```

- object is a WScript object.
- errorcode is an optional error code that can be returned indicating the code when the script exits. If you want to return the error code, include it in the function call.

Example:

```
WScript.Quit (1)
```

Any line of code after this line will not execute.

Read

This method is used with an input stream and will return the specified number of characters from the stream. Cannot be used with WScript.exe.

Syntax:

```
object.Read(characters)
```

- `object` is an `StdIn` object.
- The `characters` parameter is an integer value indicating the number of characters to return from the stream.

Example:

```
Dim strInput
strInput = StdIn.Read(1)
```

ReadAll

Like the `Read` method, this method will read the characters in the `StdIn` stream with the exception that `ReadAll` will return all of the characters in the stream.

Syntax:

```
object.ReadAll
```

`object` is an `StdIn` stream object.

Example:

```
Const intNum = 0
Const ForReading = 1
Const FormatASCII = 0
Dim fso, ts, str
Dim fileName
filename = "C:\test.txt"
Set fso = WScript.CreateObject("Scripting.FileSystemObject")
Set ts = fso.OpenTextFile(fileName, ForReading, false, FormatASCII)
if Not ts.atEndOfStream Then
    str = ts.ReadAll
End If
ts.Close()
WScript.Echo(str)
```

ReadLine

This method is used with an `StdIn` stream and returns a complete line from the stream. The method knows where the end of the line is when it reaches a newline character. The newline character is not returned.

Syntax:

```
Object.ReadLine
```

Object is an StdIn stream object.

Example:

```
Const intNum = 0
Const ForReading = 1
Const FormatASCII = 0
Dim fso, ts, str
Dim fileName
filename = "C:\test.txt"
Set fso = WScript.CreateObject("Scripting.FileSystemObject")
Set ts = fso.OpenTextFile(fileName, ForReading, false, FormatASCII)
if Not ts.atEndOfStream Then
    str = ts.ReadLine
End If
ts.Close()
WScript.Echo(str)
```

RegDelete

Use this method to delete a key or value from the registry. You must use the following abbreviated versions of the root key.

Syntax:

```
object.RegDelete(string)
```

- object is a WshShell object.
- string is the name of the key or value you want to delete. You specify a key name by using a backslash character after the string value. Leave the backslash off for value names.

Key abbreviations:

- HKEY_CURRENT_USER—HKCU
- HKEY_LOCAL_MACHINE—HKLM
- HKEY_CLASSES_ROOT—HKCR
- HKEY_USERS—HKEY_USERS
- HKEY_CURRENT_CONFIG—HKEY_CURRENT_CONFIG

Example:

```
WshShell.RegDelete "HKCU\Software\GKComput\"
```

RegRead

This method returns a string value that represents the value of the key or a value-name pair from the registry.

Syntax:

```
object.RegRead(strName)
```

- object is a WshShell object.
- strName is the name of the key or value-name that you want to return from the registry.

Example:

```
WScript.Echo WshShell.RegRead
➥("HKCU\Software\GKComput\ColorPicker\Users")
```

RegWrite

Use this method to

- Add a new key to the registry
- Rename an existing key
- Add or rename a value-name pair

Syntax:

```
Object.RegWrite(name, value, [type])
```

- Object is a WshShell object.
- name is a string value used to indicate the key or value-name to write.
- value is the string for the value you want to add to the key or name.
- type is an optional string used to represent the value's data type.

Example:

```
WshShell.RegWrite ("HKCU\Software\GKComput
➥ \ColorPicker\", 1, "REG_BINARY")
```

A

Remove

Use this method to remove environment variables from the following types of environments: PROCESS, USER, SYSTEM, and VOLATILE.

Syntax:

```
object.Remove(name)
```

- `object` is a `WshShell` object.
- `name` is the name of the variable you want to remove.

Example:

```
WshEnv.Remove "TestVar"
```

RemoveNetworkDrive

This method is used to remove a network drive mapping from the computer.

Syntax:

```
object.RemoveNetworkDrive(strName, [bForce],
➥ [bUpdateProfile])
```

- `object` is a `WshNetwork` object.
- `strName` is the name of the drive mapping to remove.
- `bForce` is a Boolean value used to indicate whether or not to force the removal of the drive.
- `bUpdateProfile` is a Boolean value used to indicate if the mapping should be removed from the user's profile as well.

Example:

```
WshNetwork.RemoveNetworkDrive "E:"
```

RemovePrinterConnection

This method is used to remove a network printer connection from the local computer. This method will remove both the DOS- and Windows-based printers from the computer.

Syntax:

```
object.RemovePrinterConnection(strName, [bForce],
➥ [bUpdateProfile])
```

- `object` is a `WshNetwork` object.
- `strName` is used to identify the name of the printer to delete.
- `bForce` is a Boolean value used to indicate if you want to force the removal of the printer.
- `bUpdateProfile` is an optional Boolean value used to indicate if the printer should be removed from the user's profile.

Example:

```
WshNetwork.RemovePrinterConnection (PrinterPath, true, true)
```

Run

This method is used to run a program in a new process.

Syntax:

```
object.Run(strCommand, [intWindowStyle], [bWaitOnReturn])
```

- `object` is a `WshShell` object.
- `strCommand` is the name of the command to run the application, same as the command line you would use to execute the application from the command line.
- `intWindowStyle` is an optional integer value used to indicate how you want the program to run, for example maximized.
- `bWaitOnReturn` is an optional Boolean value used to indicate if the script should wait until the application has finished executing before the script code will continue to run.

Window Styles:

- 0—Hides the window and activates another window.
- 1—Activates a window. If the window is minimized or maximized, it will restore the window to its original size.
- 2—Activates and minimizes the window.
- 3—Activates and maximizes the window.
- 4—Displays the window in its most recent size and position.
- 5—Activates the window and displays it in its current position and size.
- 6—Minimizes the window and activates the window that is next in the Z-order.
- 7—Minimizes the window but keeps it active.
- 8—Displays the window in its current state but keeps the active window active.
- 9—Activates.
- 10—Will set the show state referencing the state of the application when it was started.

Example:

```
Set WshShell = WScript.CreateObject("WScript.Shell")
WshShell.Run ("%windir%\notepad" & WScript.ScriptFullName)
```

Save

This method is used to save a shortcut to disk after using `CreateShortcut` to create it.

Syntax:

```
object.Save
```

`object` is a `WshShortcut` or `WshURLShortcut` object.

Example:

```
set objUrlLink = WshShell.CreateShortcut(strDesktop & "\Microsoft Web Site.url")
objUrlLink.TargetPath = "http://www.microsoft.com"
objUrlLink.Save
```

SendKeys

Use this method to send keystrokes to the active window. It is mostly used to send keystrokes to applications that contain no visual interface but may still require keystrokes such as key combinations or accelerator keys.

Syntax:

```
object.SendKeys (string)
```

- `object` is a `WshShell` object.
- `string` is a key or keys you want to send.

Some keystrokes do not have character representations; therefore, you must send arguments to represent the keys. These arguments are shown in Table A.2.

TABLE A.2   Arguments Used with `SendKeys` for Various Keystrokes

Key	Argument
Backspace	{BACKSPACE}, {BS}, or {BKSP}
Break	{BREAK}
Caps Lock	{CAPSLOCK}
Delete	{DELETE} or {DEL}
Down Arrow	{DOWN}
End	{END}
Enter	{ENTER} or ~
Esc	{ESC}
Help	{HELP}

TABLE A.2   Continued

Key	Argument
Home	{HOME}
Ins or Insert	{INSERT} or {INS}
Left Arrow	{LEFT}
Num Lock	{NUMLOCK}
Page Down	{PGDN}
Page Up	{PGUP}
Print Screen	{PRTSC}
Right Arrow	{RIGHT}
Scroll Lock	{SCROLLLOCK}
Tab	{TAB}
Up Arrow	{UP}
F1–F16	{F1}–{F16}

If you need to send a combination of keystrokes such as Shift + key or Ctrl + key, use the special characters listed here to represent the keys.

- Shift   +
- Ctrl   ^
- Alt   %

For example, to send a combination of Ctrl and F2 you would use the following example:

```
WshShell.SendKeys "^{F2}"
```

SetDefaultPrinter

Use this method to set the default printer. This method can only be used with Windows-based printers. If you try to use it with a DOS-based printer you will generate an error.

Syntax:

```
object.SetDefaultPrinter (strPrinterName)
```

- `object` is a `WshNetwork` object.
- `strPrinterName` is the name of the remote printer specified using a UNC name.

Example:

```
Dim WshNetwork
Dim objRemotePrinter
Dim strPrintPath
Set WshNetwork = WScript.CreateObject("WScript.Network")
Set strPrintPath = "\\Celeron500\HPOfficeJet"
Set objRemotePrinter = WshNetwork.AddWindowsPrinterConnection
➡ (strPrintPath)
WshNetwork.SetDefaultPrinter strPrintPath
```

This example creates a connection to a remote printer in the Celeron500 server and then assigns it to be the default printer.

ShowUsage

This method makes use of the description and helpstring fields used in a script file to present usage information to the user. This information can be found in the `<runtime>` section of the .wsf file.

Syntax:

```
object.ShowUsage
```

object is a WScript object.

Example:

```
Wscript.ShowUsage
```

Sign

Use this method when working with script security to digitally sign a text string. You must have a valid, code-signing certificate to sign a script.

Syntax:

```
object.Sign (FileExtension, Text, Certificate, Store)
```

- object is a Scripting.Signer object.
- FileExtension is string value used to represent the script file's extension such as .vbs or .js.
- Text is the text to be written.
- Certificate is the name of the certificate that will be used to sign the script.
- Store is an optional argument that is used to indicate the certificate store to use if the certificate is not stored on the local computer.

Example:

```
Dim objSigner
Dim strUnsignedText
Dim strSignedText
Set objSigner = CreateObject("Scripting.Signer")
strUnsignedText = "This is unsigned text"
strSignedText = Signer.Sign(".VBS", strUnsignedText, "CertificateName")
```

SignFile

This method is used to digitally sign a script file with a digital certificate. Don't confuse this method with the previous Sign method.

Syntax:

```
object.SignFile (FileName, Certificate, [Store])
```

- object is a Scripting.Signer object.
- FileName is a string value used to indicate which script file you want to sign.
- Certificate is a string value indicating the name of the certificate to use for signing.
- Store is an optional argument used to specify a certificate store where the certificate is located if it is not local.

Example:

```
Set Signer = CreateObject("Scripting.Signer")
Signer.SignFile "C:\Script.vbs", "GK Computer", "GKComput"
```

Skip

This method is used with an input text stream to specify a number of characters to skip when reading from the stream. All restrictions apply when working with the StdIn stream.

Syntax:

```
object.Skip(characters)
```

- object is a StdIn text stream object.
- The characters parameter is an integer value indicating the number of characters to skip.

Example:

```
var objStdIn = WScript.StdIn;
objStdIn.Skip(5);
Input = objStdIn.Read(1);
```

SkipLine

This method is used with the StdIn text stream input to skip the next line when reading the stream. The next line is determined by the newline character.

Syntax:

```
object.SkipLine
```

object is an StdIn text stream object.

Example:

```
Dim objStream
Dim fso
Dim strFileName
Const ForReading = 1
Const FormatASCII = 0
StrFileName = "C:\Test.txt"
Set objStream = fso.OpenTextFile(fileName, ForReading,
➥ false, FormatASCII);
objStream. SkipLine()
```

Sleep

Use this method to cause your script to sleep or pause for a specified amount of time before continuing. This will actually suspend the thread execution, which will free the CPU resources used by that thread.

Syntax:

```
object.Sleep(intTime)
```

- object is a WScript object.
- intTime is an integer value used to represent the time value that the script will sleep. It is measured in milliseconds.

Example:

```
set WshShell = WScript.CreateObject("WScript.Shell")
WshShell.Run "calc"
WScript.Sleep 100
WshShell.AppActivate "Calculator"
```

This script creates a shell object to run the Calculator application. It will pause for 100 milliseconds before activating the Calculator window.

Terminate

Use this method to stop the execution of a script that was started using the Exec method. This method does not return a result and should only be used as a last resort due to the fact that not all of your variables will get cleaned up, which could lead to memory leaks.

Syntax:

```
object.Terminate
```

object is a WshScriptExec method.

Example:

```
Dim objRemScript
objRemScript = WScript.Exec("Script.vbs")
objRemScript.Terminate()
```

Verify

Use this method to verify a digital signature that has been returned in a string variable.

Syntax:

```
object.Verify (FileExtension, Text, ShowUI)
```

- object is a Scripting.Signer object.
- FileExtension is the extension for the script file.
- Text is the text that is to be verified.
- ShowUI is a Boolean value used to indicate whether the user should be prompted when determining whether a certificate provider is secure.

Example:

```
Dim objSigner
Dim strUnsignedText
Dim strSignedText
Set objSigner = CreateObject("Scripting.Signer")
strUnsignedText = "This is unsigned text"
strSignedText = Signer.Verify(".VBS", strUnsignedText, "CertificateName")
```

VerifyFile

Use this method to verify the digital signature that is included in a script file.

Syntax:

```
object.VerifyFile(filename, ShowUI)
```

- object is a Scripting.Signer object.
- filename is the name of the script file you want to verify.
- ShowUI is a Boolean value used to indicate if the user should be prompted to verify a trusted source.

Example:

```
Dim objSigner
Dim strFileName
Dim blnResult
Set objSigner = CreateObject("Scripting.Signer")
strFileName = "C:\test.vbs"
blnResult = objSigner.VerifyFile(strFileName, True)
If blnResult Then
    WScript.Echo File & " is trusted."
Else
    WScript.Echo File & " is NOT trusted."
End If
```

Write

This method is used with the StdOut text stream to send a string to the output stream.

Syntax:

```
object.Write(strText)
```

- object is an StdOut text stream object.
- strText is the text string to send.

Example:

```
var fso, textStream;
var i = 0;
var arrText
strfileName = "c:\\myFile.txt";
fso = WScript.CreateObject("Scripting.FileSystemObject");
arrText = new Array("Welcome to the Write example.",
➥"This is test text for the array",
➥"It is only used for demonstration.");
textStream = fso.CreateTextFile(strfileName, true);
for(i = 0; i < aText.length; i++)
   textStream.Write(aText[i]);
textStream.Close();
```

WriteBlankLines

This method is used with the output stream to send a specified number of blank lines to the output stream.

Syntax:

```
object.WriteBlankLines(intLines)
```

- object is one of either the StdOut or StdErr objects.
- intLines is an integer value used to indicate the number of blank lines to write.

Example:

```
objTextStream.WriteBlankLines(3)
```

WriteLine

This method is used with the output stream to send a string of text with the newline character. WriteLine will always append the newline character to the end of strings.

Syntax:

```
object.WriteLine(strText)
```

- object is an StdOut or StdErr object.
- strText is the text that you want to send to the output stream.

Example:

```
arrText = ("this is some sample text to send")
for(i = 0; i < arrText.length; i++)
    ts.WriteLine(arrText[i]);
ts.Close();
```

Events

This section lists the events that you can write code to take action for when the events take place. Events are a natural part of Windows programming and WSH is no exception.

End

This event is used with a WshRemote object; the End event occurs when the remote script has ceased execution.

Error

This event is a member of the `WshRemote` object and is fired when an error occurs during the execution of the remote script.

Start

This event is used with a `WshRemote` object and is the event that fires when a remote script is executed using the `Execute` method.

XML Elements

WSH 5.6 makes use of XML elements to provide certain functionality in your script files such as job separation and script file self-documenting capabilities. These elements are listed here with explanations of their use.

<?job ?>

This element is used to specify attributes for error handling.

Syntax:

```
<?job error="flag" debug="flag" ?>
```

- error is a Boolean value where `True` indicates that error messages are allowed.
- debug is a Boolean value used to enable or disable debugging.

Example:

```
<?job debug="true"?>
```

<?XML ?>

Use this to indicate whether or not a file should be parsed as XML.

Syntax:

```
<?XML version="version" [standalone="DTDflag"] ?>
```

- version is a string value that specifies the XML level in the format *n.n*.
- standalone is an optional argument of type Boolean which specifies if there is an external reference such as DTD.

Example:

```
<?XML version="1.0" standalone="yes" ?>
```

<description>

This element is used to specify the descriptive text to be displayed when the script is called with the ShowUsage method.

The description can be longer than one line and should not include quotes if you do not want them to appear in the ShowUsage display.

Syntax:

```
<description>
    This section describes the script
</description>
```

Example:

```
<runtime>
    <description>
This script will create new user accounts on the server
    </description>
</runtime>
```

<example>

This element is also used to make your scripts self documenting by providing an example to the user when the ShowUsage method is called.

Syntax:

```
<example>
    Example text
</example>
```

Example:

```
<job>
    <runtime>
<description> This script will create new user accounts on the server
    </description>
        <named
            name = "Server"
            helpstring = "Server to run the script on"
            type = "string"
            required = "true"
        />
 <example>Example: createuser.wsf /Server:scripting</example>
    </runtime>
</job>
```

`<job>`

This element is used to mark the start and end of a job in a .wsf file. Each job in a script file must be identified uniquely.

Syntax:

```
<job [id=JobID]>
    job code
</job>
```

JobID is an optional argument that is used to specify which job to run when the script is executed.

Example:

```
<package>
    <job id="firstJob">
    <?job debug="true"?>
        <script language="VBScript">
            WScript.Echo "This is the first job"
        </script>
    </job>
    <job id="SecondJob">
    <?job debug="true"?>
        <script language="JScript">
            WScript.Echo("This is the second job");
        </script>
    </job>
</package>
```

`<named>`

This element is used to mark a specific argument to the script. This element is enclosed within a set of `<runtime></runtime>` tags.

Syntax:

```
<named
    name = namedname
    helpstring = helpstring
    type = "string|boolean|simple"
    required = boolean
/>
```

- `name` is a string value used to indicate the name of the argument that is being tagged.
- `helpstring` is a string value used to indicate the descriptive text used in the helpstring when `ShowUsage` is called.

- `type` is optional and is used to describe the type of argument. The default is `simple`.
- `required` is an optional Boolean value used to indicate whether the argument is required or not.

Example:

```
<job>
    <runtime>
        <named
            name="Server"
            helpstring= "server to run the script on"
            type = "string"
            required="true"
        />
        <named
            name="User"
            helpstring= "user to run the script as"
            type = "string"
            required="false"
        />
    </runtime>
</job>
```

`<object>`

This element is used to define objects within the script file (.wsf) that can be accessed by other scripts. You can use this element to expose objects as global. If you do this, the `CreateObject` function is not required for that object.

Syntax:

```
<object id = "objID" [classid = "clsid:GUID" | progid="progID"]/>
```

- `objID` is a string value representing a name to be used for the object referenced in the script. It must begin with a letter and can contain letters, numbers, and underscores. It also must be unique throughout the script.
- `GUID` is an optional argument that is the Class ID of the object.
- `progID` is optional and is the program ID of the object. You can use this in lieu of the `GUID`.

`<package>`

If you have multiple jobs that you want contained in one .wsf file, you enclose that file in the package tags.

Syntax:

```
<package>
   code for one or more jobs
</package>
```

Example:

```
<package>
    <job id="firstJob">
    <?job debug="true"?>
        <script language="VBScript">
           WScript.Echo "This is the first job"
        </script>
    </job>
    <job id="SecondJob">
    <?job debug="true"?>
        <script language="JScript">
           WScript.Echo("This is the second job");
        </script>
    </job>
</package>
```

<reference>

This element is used to include references to external type-libraries. This allows you to use constants that are defined in your scripts.

Syntax:

```
<reference [object="progID"|guid="typelibGUID"] [version="version"] />
```

- progID is the program ID of the type library that you will reference. It can include version numbers as well.
- typelibGUID is the GUID of the type library that you will reference.
- version is the version number of the type library to use if there are multiple versions.

<resource>

This element is used to indicate any text data that should not be included in a script as hard-coded data.

Syntax:

```
<resource id="resourceID">
    text or numbers
</resource>
```

resourceID is a unique identifier for the resource within the script file.

`<runtime>`

This element is used to group a set of runtime arguments for a script. This information is used by the ShowUsage method.

Syntax:

```
<runtime>
    <named attributes />
    <unnamed attributes />
    <example>Sample Text</example>
</runtime>
```

Example:

```
<job>
    <runtime>
        <named
            name="server"
            helpstring="The server to run the script on"
            type="string"
            required="true"
        />
    </runtime>
</job>
```

`<script>`

Use this element to specify script that is used to define the behavior of a .wsf file. By specifying `<?XML?>` at the top of the file, you turn on XML parsing, which ensures that < and > symbols are not mistaken for XML tags so they can be correctly reflected in script code.

Syntax:

```
<script language="scriptlanguage" [src="strFilename"]>
    script code goes here
</script>
```

- language specifies the script language that will be used such as VBScript or JScript.
- src is an optional argument that is used to include an external script file into the block.

Example:

```
<package>
    <job id="firstJob">
    <?job debug="true"?>
        <script language="VBScript">
            WScript.Echo "This is the first job"
        </script>
    </job>
```

```
<job id="SecondJob">
<?job debug="true"?>
    <script language="JScript">
        WScript.Echo("This is the second job");
    </script>
</job>
</package>
```

<unnamed>

This element is used to mark an unnamed element to a script file. The unnamed element must be enclosed in a set of <runtime></runtime> elements.

Syntax:

```
<unnamed>
    name       = unnamedname
    helpstring = helpstring
    many       = boolean
    required   = boolean or integer
</unnamed>
```

- name is used to indicate the name of the unnamed argument.

- helpstring is used to create a string that will be displayed as a help description when the ShowUsage method is called.

- many is an optional Boolean value used to indicate if the unnamed argument is allowed to have multiple occurrences.

- required is an optional Boolean value used to indicate if the unnamed argument is required by the script.

Example:

```
<job>
    <runtime>
        <unnamed
            helpstring= "server to run on"
            type = "string"
            required="true"
        />
        <unnamed
            helpstring= "user to run the script as"
            type = "string"
            required="false"
        />
    </runtime>
</job>
```

ADSI Reference

IN THIS APPENDIX

Writing programming code or scripting code makes use of variables, intrinsic data types, and constants. Some are built into the languages and some you create yourself. ADSI includes some intrinsic data types as well as constants. These are shown in this appendix for your reference.

Data Types

Table B.1 lists the available data types that exist for ADSI and gives a description of each data type.

TABLE B.1   ADSI Data Types

Data Type	Description
ADS_BOOLEAN	DWORD[1]
PADS_BOOLEAN	Pointer to an ADS_BOOLEAN
ADS_CASE_EXACT_STRING	LPWSTR[2]
PADS_CASE_EXACT_STRING	Pointer to an ADS_CASE_EXACT_STRING
ADS_CASE_IGNORE_STRING	LPWSTR
PADS_CASE_IGNORE_STRING	Pointer to an ADS_CASE_IGNORE_STRING
ADS_DN_STRING	LPWSTR
PADS_DN_STRING	Pointer to an ADS_DN_STRING
ADS_INTEGER	DWORD
PADS_INTEGER	Pointer to an ADS_INTEGER
ADS_LARGE_INTEGER	Large_Integer[3]
PADS_LARGE_INTEGER	Pointer to an ADS_LARGE_INTEGER
ADS_NUMERIC_STRING	LPWSTR
PADS_NUMERIC_STRING	Pointer to an ADS_NUMERIC_STRING
ADS_OBJECT_CLASS	LPWSTR
PADS_OBJECT_CLASS	Pointer to an ADS_OBJECT_CLASS
ADS_PRINTABLE_STRING	LPWSTR
PADS_PRINTABLE_STRING	Pointer to an ADS_PRINTABLE_STRING
ADS_SEARCH_HANDLE	HANDLE[4]
PADS_SEARCH_HANDLE	Pointer to an ADS_SEARCH_HANDLE

TABLE B.1 Continued

Data Type	Description
ADS_UTC_TIME	SYSTEMTIME
PADS_UTC_TIME	Pointer to an ADS_UTC_TIME

[1]—*A DWORD is a 32-bit unsigned integer. It can also be used as the address of a memory segment or the offset.*
[2]—*LPWSTR is a term used to indicate a long pointer to a string that is in Unicode. The letters have the following meanings:*
    L—Long
    P—Pointer
    W—Wide (Microsoft's term for Unicode characters)
    STR—String
[3]—*Large_Integer is a term used to describe a 64-bit signed integer.*
[4]—*A HANDLE is normally a 32-bit numeric identifier used to identify windows or device contexts (DC) in the operating system for the purposes of handling messages sent to and received from the windows or DCs.*

Constants

Constants are used in programming as a means of providing a text based identifier to a data type used in your application in lieu of the number that it represents. As you will see in Table B.2, the value is a numeric representation that the computer will work with. The constant is a text string that makes it easier for people to read when looking at the source code for the application.

TABLE B.2 ADSI Constants

Constant	Value	Description
ADS_ATTR_APPEND	3	This will cause the new values to be appended to the existing attributes. The attribute and this constant are specified using an ADS_ATTR_INFO array.
ADS_ATTR_CLEAR	1	This will cause the directory service to remove the attribute values from the object. The attribute and constant will be specified in the ADS_ATTR_INFO array.
ADS_ATTR_DELETE	4	This setting will cause the directory service to delete the named attribute value or values that are specified in the ADS_ATTR_INFO array.

B

ADSI REFERENCE

TABLE B.2 Continued

Constant	Value	Description
ADS_ATTR_UPDATE	2	This causes the directory service to update the named attribute values that are specified in the ADS_ATTR_INFO array.
ADS_EXT_ INITCREDENTIALS	1	This is a control code that is used to indicate that there is custom data being supplied to the IADsExtension::Operate method, and that it contains user credentials. The IADsExtension::Operate is used in C++ applications.
ADS_EXT_INITIALIZE COMPLETE	2	This is a control code used with the IADsExtension::Operate method. It is used to indicate that extensions can perform the necessary initialization. This is dependant on the functionality supported by the parent object.
ADS_EXT_MAXEXTDISPID	16777215	This constant is used to specify the largest DISPID[5] that an extension object can use for its methods, events, and properties.
ADS_EXT_MINEXTDISPID	1	The opposite of the the ADS_EXT_MAXEXTDISPID constant. Used to specify the lowest DISPID an extension object can use for its methods, events, and properties.
DBPROPFLAGS_ ADSISEARCH	0x0000C000	Use this constant when you are accessing the ADSI services using the OLE DB interfaces.

[5]—*DISPID is short for Dispatch ID. The DISPID is a numeric value that is compiled into the type library of a component. It is used as a reference in the events, methods, or properties of the component.*

ADSI Error Codes

Most of these error codes relate to C++ and other developers creating standalone applications. They are included here for completeness of the reference as you may come across them in your scripting and will also serve as a reference should you create your own applications at a later date.

Win32 COM Error Codes

Table B.3 lists the common generic error codes that can be returned by an application on any Win32 platform.

TABLE B.3 Win32 COM Error Codes

Error	Hex Value	Description
E_ABORT	0x80004004	The operation was aborted.
E_FAIL	0x80004005	An unspecified error occurred.
E_NOINTERFACE	0x80004002	This interface is not supported.
E_NOTIMPL	0x80004001	Not implemented yet.
E_POINTER	0x80004003	An invalid pointer was used.
E_UNEXPECTED	0x8000FFFF	Catastrophic failure.

Generic ADSI Error Codes

ADSI has generic error codes that are used to describe errors during operations that are executed in code segments. These are listed in Table B.4.

TABLE B.4 ADSI Error Codes

Value	Code	Description
0x00005011L	S_ADS_ERRORSOCCURRED	During a query, one or more errors occurred.
0x00005012L	S_ADS_NOMORE_ROWS	The search operation has reached the last row.
0x00005013L	S_ADS_NOMORE_COLUMNS	The search operation has reached the last column for the current row.
0x80005000L	E_ADS_BAD_PATHNAME	An invalid ADSI pathname was passed.
0x80005001L	E_ADS_INVALID_DOMAIN_OBJECT	An unknown ADSI domain object was requested.
0x80005002L	E_ADS_INVALID_USER_OBJECT	An unknown ADSI user object was requested.
0x80005003L	E_ADS_INVALID_COMPUTER_OBJECT	An unknown ADSI computer object was requested.

B

ADSI REFERENCE

TABLE B.4 Continued

Value	Code	Description
0x80005004L	E_ADS_UNKNOWN_OBJECT	An unknown ADSI object was requested.
0x80005005L	E_ADS_PROPERTY_NOT_SET	The specified ADSI property was not set.
0x80005006L	E_ADS_PROPERTY_NOT_SUPPORTED	The specified ADSI property is not supported.
0x80005007L	E_ADS_PROPERTY_INVALID	The specified ADSI property is invalid.
0x80005008L	E_ADS_BAD_PARAMETER	One or more input parameters are invalid.
0x80005009L	E_ADS_OBJECT_UNBOUND	The specified ADSI object is not bound to a remote resource.
0x8000500AL	E_ADS_PROPERTY_NOT_MODIFIED	The specified ADSI object has not been modified.
0x8000500BL	E_ADS_PROPERTY_MODIFIED	The specified ADSI object has been modified.
0x8000500CL	E_ADS_CANT_CONVERT_DATATYPE	The data type cannot be converted to/from a native DS data type.
0x8000500DL	E_ADS_PROPERTY_NOT_FOUND	The property cannot be found in the cache.
0x8000500EL	E_ADS_OBJECT_EXISTS	The ADSI object exists.
0x8000500FL	E_ADS_SCHEMA_VIOLATION	The attempted action violates the directory service schema rules.
0x80005010L	E_ADS_COLUMN_NOT_SET	The specified column in the ADSI was not set.
0x80005014L	E_ADS_INVALID_FILTER	The specified search filter is invalid.

Win32 Error Codes for ADSI

Table B.5 shows the relationship between ADSI values, LDAP error messages, and the Win32 codes for ADSI.

TABLE B.5 ADSI Error Code Comparisons and Descriptions

ADSI Value	LDAP Message	Win32 Error Message	Description
0x8007001fL	LDAP_OTHER	ERROR_GEN_FAILURE	An unknown error has occurred.
0x800700eaL	LDAP_PARTIAL_RESULTS	ERROR_MORE_DATA	Partial results and referrals received.
0x800700eaL	LDAP_MORE_RESULTS_TO_RETURN	ERROR_MORE_DATA	There will be more results returned.
0x800704c7L	LDAP_USER_CANCELLED	ERROR_CANCELLED	The operation was cancelled by the user.
0x800704c9L	LDAP_CONNECT_ERROR	ERROR_CONNECTION_REFUSED	A connection cannot be established.
0x8007052eL	LDAP_INVALID_CREDENTIALS	ERROR_LOGON_FAILURE	The logon credentials are invalid.
0x800705b4L	LDAP_TIMEOUT	ERROR_TIMEOUT	The search timed out.
0x80071392L	LDAP_ALREADY_EXISTS	ERROR_OBJECT_ALREADY_EXISTS	A copy of the object already exists.
0x8007200aL	LDAP_NO_SUCH_ATTRIBUTE	ERROR_DS_NO_ATTRIBUTE_OR_VALUE	The requested attribute does not exist.
0x8007200bL	LDAP_INVALID_SYNTAX	ERROR_DS_INVALID_ATTRIBUTE_SYNTAX	Invalid syntax.
0x8007200cL	LDAP_UNDEFINED_TYPE	ERROR_DS_ATTRIBUTE_TYPE_UNDEFINED	An undefined type was used.
0x8007200dL	LDAP_ATTRIBUTE_OR_VALUE_EXISTS	ERROR_DS_ATTRIBUTE_OR_VALUE_EXISTS	Either the attribute already exists or the value has been assigned already.
0x8007200eL	LDAP_BUSY	ERROR_DS_BUSY	The server is busy.
0x8007200fL	LDAP_UNAVAILABLE	ERROR_DS_UNAVAILABLE	The server is unavailable.
0x80072014L	LDAP_OBJECT_CLASS_VIOLATION	ERROR_DS_OBJ_CLASS_VIOLATION	An object class violation has occurred.

B

ADSI REFERENCE

TABLE B.5 Continued

ADSI Value	LDAP Message	Win32 Error Message	Description
0x80072015L	LDAP_NOT_ALLOWED_ON_NONLEAF	ERROR_DS_CANT_ON_NON_LEAF	The requested operation is not allowed on non-leaf objects.
0x80072016L	LDAP_NOT_ALLOWED_ON_RDN	ERROR_DS_CANT_ON_RDN	Operation is not allowed on RDN.
0x80072017L	LDAP_NO_OBJECT_CLASS_MODS	ERROR_DS_CANT_MOD_OBJ_CLASS	Object class cannot be modified.
0x80072020L	LDAP_OPERATIONS_ERROR	ERROR_DS_OPERATIONS_ERROR	An operations error has occurred.
0x80072021L	LDAP_PROTOCOL_ERROR	ERROR_DS_PROTOCOL_ERROR	A protocol error has occurred.
0x80072022L	LDAP_TIMELIMIT_EXCEEDED	ERROR_DS_TIMELIMIT_EXCEEDED	The time limit has been exceeded.
0x80072023L	LDAP_SIZELIMIT_EXCEEDED	ERROR_DS_SIZELIMIT_EXCEEDED	The size limit has been exceeded.
0x80072024L	LDAP_ADMIN_LIMIT_EXCEEDED	ERROR_DS_ADMIN_LIMIT_EXCEEDED	The Administration limit on the server has been exceeded.
0x80072025L	LDAP_COMPARE_FALSE	ERROR_DS_COMPARE_FALSE	Compare returned FALSE.
0x80072026L	LDAP_COMPARE_TRUE	ERROR_DS_COMPARE_TRUE	Compare returned TRUE.
0x80072027L	LDAP_AUTH_METHOD_NOT_SUPPORTED	ERROR_DS_AUTH_METHOD_NOT_SUPPORTED	The requested authentication method is not supported.
0x80072028L	LDAP_STRONG_AUTH_REQUIRED	ERROR_DS_STRONG_AUTH_REQUIRED	Strong authentication is required.
0x80072029L	LDAP_INAPPROPRIATE_AUTH	ERROR_DS_INAPPROPRIATE_AUTH	Requested authentication is inappropriate.
0x8007202aL	LDAP_AUTH_UNKNOWN	ERROR_DS_AUTH_UNKNOWN	An unknown authentication error has occurred.
0x8007202bL	LDAP_REFERRAL	ERROR_DS_REFERRAL	A referral.

TABLE B.5 Continued

ADSI Value	LDAP Message	Win32 Error Message	Description
0x8007202cL	LDAP_UNAVAILABLE_CRIT_EXTENSION	ERROR_DS_UNAVAILABLE_CRIT_EXTENSION	A critical extension is not available.
0x8007202dL	LDAP_CONFIDENTIALITY_REQUIRED	ERROR_DS_CONFIDENTIALITY_REQUIRED	Confidentiality is required.
0x8007202eL	LDAP_INAPPROPRIATE_MATCHING	ERROR_DS_INAPPROPRIATE_MATCHING	An inappropriate matching has occurred.
0x8007202fL	LDAP_CONSTRAINT_VIOLATION	ERROR_DS_CONSTRAINT_VIOLATION	There has been a constraint violation.
0x80072030L	LDAP_NO_SUCH_OBJECT	ERROR_DS_NO_SUCH_OBJECT	The requested object does not exist.
0x80072031L	LDAP_ALIAS_PROBLEM	ERROR_DS_ALIAS_PROBLEM	An invalid alias was used.
0x80072032L	LDAP_INVALID_DN_SYNTAX	ERROR_DS_INVALID_DN_SYNTAX	The distinguished name has an invalid syntax.
0x80072033L	LDAP_IS_LEAF	ERROR_DS_IS_LEAF	The requested object is a leaf object.
0x80072034L	LDAP_ALIAS_DEREF_PROBLEM	ERROR_DS_ALIAS_DEREF_PROBLEM	The alias has been dereferenced.
0x80072035L	LDAP_UNWILLING_TO_PERFORM	ERROR_DS_UNWILLING_TO_PERFORM	The server is unwilling to perform the task.
0x80072036L	LDAP_LOOP_DETECT	ERROR_DS_LOOP_DETECT	A loop was detected.
0x80072037L	LDAP_NAMING_VIOLATION	ERROR_DS_NAMING_VIOLATION	A naming violation has occurred.
0x80072038L	LDAP_RESULTS_TOO_LARGE	ERROR_DS_OBJECT_RESULTS_TOO_LARGE	The results returned are too large.
0x80072039L	LDAP_AFFECTS_MULTIPLE_DSAS	ERROR_DS_AFFECTS_MULTIPLE_DSAS	Multiple directory service agents are affected.

B

ADSI REFERENCE

TABLE B.5   Continued

ADSI Value	LDAP Message	Win32 Error Message	Description
0x8007203aL	LDAP_SERVER_DOWN	ERROR_DS_SERVER_DOWN	The LDAP server cannot be contacted.
0x8007203bL	LDAP_LOCAL_ERROR	ERROR_DS_LOCAL_ERROR	A local error has occurred.
0x8007203cL	LDAP_ENCODING_ERROR	ERROR_DS_ENCODING_ERROR	An encoding error has occurred.
0x8007203dL	LDAP_DECODING_ERROR	ERROR_DS_DECODING_ERROR	A decoding error has occurred.
0x8007203eL	LDAP_FILTER_ERROR	ERROR_DS_FILTER_UNKNOWN	The search filter is bad.
0x8007203fL	LDAP_PARAM_ERROR	ERROR_DS_PARAM_ERROR	A bad parameter has been passed to a routine.
0x80072040L	LDAP_NOT_SUPPORTED	ERROR_DS_NOT_SUPPORTED	This feature is not currently supported.
0x80072041L	LDAP_NO_RESULTS_RETURNED	ERROR_DS_NO_RESULTS_RETURNED	No results are returned.
0x80072042L	LDAP_CONTROL_NOT_FOUND	ERROR_DS_CONTROL_NOT_FOUND	The requested control was not found.
0x80072043L	LDAP_CLIENT_LOOP	ERROR_DS_CLIENT_LOOP	A client loop was detected.
0x80072044L	LDAP_REFERRAL_LIMIT_EXCEEDED	ERROR_DS_REFERRAL_LIMIT_EXCEEDED	The referral limit has been exceeded.

INDEX

SYMBOLS

A

syntax   329

StdErr property
  WScript object, 264
  WshScriptExec object, 29,
    264
StdErr stream, accessing, 29
StdIn object, properties
  AtEndOfLine, 251
  AtEndOfStream, 251
  Column, 252
StdIn property
  WScript object, 265
  WshScriptExec object, 29,
    265
StdIn stream, accessing, 29
StdOut property
  WScript object, 265
  WshScriptExec object, 29, 265
StdOut stream, accessing, 29
streams, 33
string types, registry access
  methods, 72
strings
  binding, 143
    LDAP, 148-149
    WinNT, 143-148
  Split function, 91
strName argument,
  RegWrite method, 71
strType argument, RegWrite
  method, 71
Structured Query Language.
  See **SQL**
subprocedures, 10
SubschemaSubentry
  property, rootDSE, 150
Subtree searches, ADSI, 202
SupportedControl property,
  rootDSE, 151
SupportedLDAPVersion
  property, rootDSE, 151
switches. *See also* **argu-**
  ments
  grouping, overview, 24-25
  named, 25-26
  unnamed, 26

syntax
  <?job?> XML element, 294
  <?XML?> XML element, 294
  AddPrinterConnection
    method, 269
  AddWindowsPrinterConnecti
    on method, 269
  AppActivate method, 270
  attributes
    BOOLEAN, 182
    CASE_EXACT_STRING,
      183
    CASE_IGNORE_STRING,
      183
    DN_STRING, 184
    INTEGER, 184
    LARGE_INTEGER, 185
    NUMERIC_STRING, 185
    OBJECT_CLASS, 185
    OCTET_STRING, 185
    overview, 182
    PRINTABLE_STRING,
      186
    SECURITY_DESCRIPTOR,
      186
    UTC_TIME, 186-187
  Close method, 270
  Command object properties,
    217
  connecting to ADSI with
    VBScript, 216
  Connection object properties,
    216
  ConnectObject method, 271
  Count method, 271
  CreateObject method, 272
  CreateScript method, 272
  CreateShortcut method, 273
  creating and populating a
    recordset, 217
  CScript.exe, 96
  <description> XML element,
    295
  DisconnectObject method,
    273

  Echo method, 274
  EnumNetworkConnections,
    275
  EnumNetworkDrives, 274
  <example> XML element,
    295
  Exec method, 28, 275
  Execute method, 275
  Exists method, 276
  ExpandEnvironmentString
    method, 276
  filters, ADSI searches,
    208-209
  GetObject method, 277
  GetResource method, 277
  HotKey property, 256
  IconLocation property, 256
  Item property, 257-258
  <job> XML element, 296
  LDAP binding strings, 148
  LDAP searches, 211-212
  LogEvent method, 277
  MapNetworkDrive, 278
  Name property, 259
  Named property, 259
  <named> XML element, 296
  Number property, 259
  <object> XML element, 297
  <package> XML element,
    298
  Path property, 260
  PopUp method, 279
  ProcessID property, 260
  Quit method, 280
  Read method, 281
  ReadAll method, 281
  ReadLine method, 282
  <reference> XML element,
    298
  RegDelete method, 282
  RegRead method, 283
  RegWrite method, 283
  RelativePath property, 260
  Remove method, 283
  RemoveNetworkDrive, 284

X-Y-Z